Punished

Punished

A mother's cruelty
A daughter's survival
A secret that couldn't be told

VANESSA STEEL

with Gill Paul

L173, 496/362.7

HarperElement
An Imprint of HarperCollins*Publishers*
77–85 Fulham Palace Road,
Hammersmith, London W6 8JB

The website address is: www.thorsonselement.com

and *HarperElement* are trademarks of
HarperCollins*Publishers* Ltd

First published by HarperElement 2008

1 3 5 7 9 10 8 6 4 2

© Vanessa Steel 2008

Vanessa Steel asserts the moral right to be
identified as the author of this work

A catalogue record of this book is
available from the British Library

ISBN-13 978-0-00-725679-2 (hardback)
ISBN-10 0-00-725679-5 (hardback)
ISBN-13 978-0-00-725680-8 (paperback)
ISBN-10 0-00-725680-9 (paperback)

Printed and bound in Great Britain by
Clays Ltd, St Ives plc

Mixed Sources
Product group from well-managed
forests and other controlled sources
www.fsc.org Cert no. SW-COC-1806
FSC   © 1996 Forest Stewardship Council

Acknowledgements

My deepest thanks go to the following people:

Gill Paul – what would I have done without you? You're a true star.

Richard Steel – 'His Nibbs' – my son, who has been the source of my strength.

Bob Steel – as always.

Terry Somerfield, aka 'Mr Analytical' – thank you a million times.

Samantha Catterall and Natalie Cardwell – my love to you always.

Paul and Jeanette Smith (Blackhams Solicitors) – thank you for everything.

Katy Carrington, my editor at HarperCollins – thank you for believing in me.

And Daisy Bones – for letting me love and cuddle you in bad times!

Prologue

I turned my key in the lock of Mum's door and pushed, but it wouldn't open. Something was stuck behind it, blocking it. I pushed harder but couldn't shift the obstruction.

What's she done now? I wondered. Is she deliberately trying to keep me out?

Then I looked through the letterbox and saw a beige-stockinged leg – her leg.

'Mum!' I yelled. 'Mum, are you all right?'

Stupid question. Of course she wasn't all right. I shouted at the top of my voice – 'Help me!' – and the next-door neighbour hurried out to see what was going on.

Stuttering with shock, I called for an ambulance and told the operator we'd probably need the fire brigade as well to break the door down. While we waited for them I sat on the step calling to Mum through the crack of the door but getting no response. Was that her breathing I could hear? I wasn't sure. My heart was racing like crazy and so many thoughts flooded my head I felt dizzy.

No, she can't die. Please don't let her die!

I couldn't help feeling guilty that I hadn't been there when she needed me, even though I had been dropping in every day to do her washing and cleaning.

'Hold on in there, Mum,' I whispered through the door. 'You can make it, I know you can.'

Tears filled my eyes as I heard a distinct, low-pitched moan. She was alive.

* * *

One of the ambulance men managed to get his arm through the crack and shift her so that they could get in without breaking the door down. They gave her oxygen and she regained a groggy kind of consciousness. I stood, useless, a huge lump in my throat and sadness engulfing me.

It was at that moment I realized that it was finally time to let loose all the dark childhood memories I had suppressed for decades. The woman lying crumpled on the floor and fighting for every breath had made my childhood a living hell. Now I knew I was in no way ready for her death, because while she was still alive I might be able to force her to answer the questions that had plagued me throughout my adult life.

What had I done to make her hate me so much that she did so many cruel things to me? Did she remember all the times she almost killed me? Why did she allow me to be a victim of terrible abuse? Why didn't Dad or any other family member protect me from her? Why did I still feel a responsibility towards her and long for her to show me some affection, despite all that she had put me through?

Punished

As my mother was lifted into the ambulance, I knew that I didn't have much time left to find out.

What crime had I committed? Why had she punished me, endlessly and thoroughly and with spite and cruelty, from the day I was born?

Chapter 1

Muriel Pittam was never really cut out to be a house-wife and mother.

She was the second of Charles and Elsie Pittam's four daughters, and judging from the photographs in the family albums, she was much prettier than her sisters. From the way she looks at the camera, you can tell that she knows she is cute and is challenging you to acknowl-edge it. The Pittams were not rich – Grandpa Pittam was a watch and clock repairer – but it's obvious from the pictures of little Muriel in her pretty dresses and ballet tutus that she didn't want for anything.

By the time she was in her twenties, Muriel Pittam was an absolute stunner, and she knew it. The photographs in the family album show her as a glamorous young blonde. In one picture she is leaning against a gate in a two-piece suit with a tightly belted waist and high-heeled shoes that must have taken her well over the six-foot mark. In another, she's wearing a smart floral dress with a fitted bodice and flared skirt. There's even one of her posed on a rock like a mermaid, wearing a bikini. Bikinis were only invented in 1947, the year after the A-bomb was tested on

Bikini Atoll in the Pacific. Muriel must be wearing one of the first on the market.

All through my childhood, Mum often harked back to the glory days of her youth, when she worked as a seamstress and part-time model.

'I used to make ball gowns, you know. Suits, day dresses, coats, wedding dresses, all of them hand sewn,' she would say. 'I worked for Isabel's in Birmingham, where the fashionable ladies shopped. The wife of the head of Woolworths got her clothes there. And Arthur Askey's wife. And I modelled. I had a perfect figure,' she boasted. 'Five foot eleven with a twenty-three-inch waist. My skin was flawless and photographers used to say I had the best profile they'd ever seen. There were photos of me modelling hats in the *Daily Mirror*.'

Young and gorgeous, Muriel Pittam had no problem attracting men. Over the years she often boasted to me about all the suitors she'd had and the marriage proposals she'd received and I'm sure it was all true. I saw at firsthand how she flirted with every man she came in contact with, from the plumber to her brothers-in-law. She obviously had the knack of twisting men round her little finger, with a shimmy of her slender hips and a coy smile. So when the youthful and less experienced Derrick Casey got within her sights – well, he didn't stand a chance.

My father was engaged to a girl named Margery Wyatt when his elder sister Audrey brought home Muriel, her friend from the tennis club, for tea one day. The Caseys owned a very successful electro-plating business in Birmingham and Derrick already earned a good salary from it, so to Muriel's eyes he must have seemed a good catch. The Caseys' imposing house stood in several acres of grounds and they had a gardener and housekeeper to help run it. Thomas Casey was well connected as a prominent member of the local Conservative party and a leading figure in the Anglican Church. By contrast, the Pittams lived in a semi-detached house in a working-class area and had very little social life outside its four walls. It was obvious that Derrick was Muriel's way out of a life as a seamstress and into a respectable and comfortable upper-middle-class life, so using her intelligence, her wiles and her physical charms, she set out to win his heart.

A lot of other men Dad's age were called up to fight in the Second World War, but Derrick hadn't been because he had a shattered kneecap after a cricket ball injury which left him with a permanent limp and unable to straighten his left leg. He still loved to play sports – golf, cricket, snooker – and he was also a great reader, particularly fond of Shakespeare and poetry. He looks unbearably young in photos of that time – plump-cheeked, dark-eyed, hair not yet receding but already wearing his customary shirt and tie in every shot. He's the kind of man any young girl would have been proud to take home to their parents: upstanding and respectable, with a nice face without being conventionally handsome. Muriel's fashion-model looks must have completely turned his head. In a matter of weeks, he broke off his engagement to Margery and asked Muriel to marry him instead, and she accepted straight away.

I remember once gazing at Mum's engagement ring, a square-cut sapphire set in white gold and surrounded by little diamonds. I asked if I could try it on and she snapped, 'No, you cannot. I had to work hard enough to get this ring and no one else is having it now.'

Who knows what kind of person Muriel pretended to be to enchant young Derrick Casey? The modelling shots she kept so carefully in the back of our albums show her statuesque and proud, her long neck and sculpted face a perfect foil for little pillbox hats with feathers on top, cartwheel straw hats or classic black toques. She's slim as a gazelle but despite her beauty and elegance, she looks hard. You wouldn't mess around with her.

No doubt she was sweetness itself in the run-up to her wedding and I suspect it was now that Muriel affected her act as a well-brought-up, church-going Christian girl. The Pittams weren't religious at all, but the Caseys were staunch believers. It was important for Muriel to seem like the right sort of girl if she were going to be accepted as a member of the family and win Derrick's affections. He was very devout, and often helped out at church fêtes and charitable events. No doubt Muriel seemed just as pious, although later, once she was safely married, she would dispense with formal religion and turn her own idea of God into a particularly dreadful weapon in her well-equipped arsenal.

Muriel and Derrick got married in 1941. The wedding photos are posed studio shots showing Mum with her hair swept up into a high style while she wears a dress of shimmering floor-length satin. She doesn't smile in any of them but I can read a glint of triumph in her expression. She hadn't just married into money; the Caseys were also very well connected socially. Now she could give up work and take her place in society as Mrs Derrick Casey, enjoying the dances and functions that they were invited to as a couple. The photos show her enjoying the fruits of her marriage: she's never in the same outfit twice and the albums are full of pictures of my parents partying and socializing, relaxing on the beach, or standing in front of Dad's brand new Ford motor car. Muriel, with her modelling background, is always camera-conscious, adopting a pose of some kind, with hair flicked back and lips pouting. They look like everyone's idea of the glamour couple – young, attractive, well-off and in love.

* * *

In 1949, Muriel's success seemed complete. She was blessed with the arrival of a baby, my brother Nigel. In the family photographs, he is an angelic-looking little thing, with white-blond hair and a shy smile. Mum holds him on her knee, looking at him and smiling, her attitude relaxed.

It's a different story in the pictures that follow. In those, she holds a plump, ruddy-skinned, scowling baby. She never looks at it and there's an obvious look of disgust on her face. She resembles one of those people who secretly loathe babies and who try to hide their dismay after someone has plonked one down on their lap. She is angry, tight-lipped and bored. The baby she is holding is me.

I arrived in 1950, the year after my brother, and it seems that right from the start, my mother was displeased with me. In my baby pictures, even the earliest ones, I appear nervous and uncomfortable. I'm not smiling in any of the photos, except one where I'm being cuddled by Nan Casey, Dad's mother. I look wary and uncomfortable and often on the point of tears. What had happened to make me like that?

'You were such a cry-baby,' I remember Mum saying. 'Nothing I did was ever good enough for you.'

* * *

Any young mother who has had two babies in quick succession might feel stressed and possibly resentful. In Mum's case, she claimed she had given up her dreams of success as a top model in exchange for two wriggling, crying babies. Her previously bright and buzzing social life was abruptly stopped – no more carefree evenings dancing and drinking with friends when there were two young children needing babysitters. Her whole life was now dominated by her routine at home with us. It must suddenly have seemed as though she'd picked a very short straw.

But thousands of young mothers had the same experience as they adapted to their new lives caring for children and a home. They didn't become what my mother became, and their children didn't suffer what I was to endure at the hands of the woman who was supposed to love me best in the world. Something in my mother was so bitter and resentful that she became evil. It's a strong word, but I can't think of any other way to describe what she did.

The danger signs were there from the very earliest days, when Nigel and I were still very young.

My first serious injury occurred when I was eighteen months old. Mum had left me on a bed and I rolled off on to the floor, breaking my leg. That was the story, anyhow. But although I have no memory of what happened, I do remember our house. The bedrooms were thickly carpeted and the beds not high off the floor. I was a plump, well-padded little thing. Would a roll from a low bed on to a soft carpet have been enough to break my leg? There were no witnesses, so I'll never know.

There was a witness to another incident, though. Aunt Audrey told me that she glanced into the bedroom one night when Nigel was just one year old to see Mum holding a pillow over his face as he thrashed and writhed around.

'Muriel, what on earth are you doing?' she cried, rushing in to pull the pillow away.

Mum gave her a sharp look. 'Sometimes it's the only way to get him to stop crying,' she said. 'You know how I can't stand listening to them cry.'

'But he's just a baby! You could kill him!'

Audrey said that Nigel's breathing was very shallow and there was a blue tinge to his lips. Muriel shrugged and didn't seem to take it seriously. Needless to say, Audrey made sure she never left any of her own children alone with Mum from that point on.

These things occurred before I was old enough to have any conscious memories. Once I do begin to remember, from around the time I was two years old, then the nightmare begins.

Chapter 2

I was a very timid child, shy around strangers and prone to creeping into my favourite little hidey-holes behind the settee or round the corner of Dad's shed in the garden. I'd take Scruffy, a yellow-furred teddy bear, or Rosie, my rag doll, with me and could sit still for hours on end hugging them, out of sight of any adults.

I'm told I was very slow to talk. At two I'd hardly uttered a word and even at three I couldn't manage more than a few incoherent phrases, so that Mum and Dad were beginning to worry that I was retarded in some way. Toilet training was also very traumatic for me. The slightest upset or fear could cause me to have an accident, which always enraged Mum. I was supposed to ask her permission when I wanted to go to the bathroom but she didn't always grant it straight away, saying she was trying to train me to have more control. Several times when I asked to go, she made me squat down in the kitchen, bladder bursting and cheeks getting hotter, tiny fists clenched with the effort of trying to hold it in – and then there'd be the warm release of urine soaking my pants, that ammonia smell and a little puddle on the linoleum floor. Afterwards there was always the anger and the shouting, and my own sense of bewilderment at how I made her so cross.

The love of my life was Nigel, my big brother, much braver than me and always the ringleader in our games. He was a sweet-natured, affectionate child who had a bit of a temper when pushed. He never took it out on me, but injustice of any kind could make him see red. He wasn't scared of things I was scared of, like dogs and noisy motorbikes and tradesmen who came to the door. I'd cower behind Mum's skirt in the face of strangers, trying to avoid being noticed, while Nigel would stand his ground and ask questions like 'Who are you? What's your name?' The roots of extreme shyness lie in a feeling that you are not quite good enough and you're scared that other people will find out; I had that in spades as a toddler.

Nigel and I were solitary children, dependent on each other for company. I remember there were twins about our age living just up the road, but we were never allowed to play with them. We liked make-believe games, such as pretending that we were a king and queen going round the garden ruling over our subjects – in my case Scruffy and Rosie, and in Nigel's his collection of wooden soldiers. Indoors, we would build little villages with houses and cars out of Bayko – a system of blocks and connecting rods somewhat like Meccano.

We rarely argued or fell out about anything. I remember one time I pushed him off his tricycle because he wasn't sharing it with me, but that was exceptional. We agreed that we were going to get married when we were grown up, and then we would live together in a house of our own and be happy forever and ever.

Nigel and I rarely saw Dad during the week. I suppose he got home late from work when we were already in bed – and some nights, I know he didn't get home at all. At weekends he'd be off playing cricket or golf at least part of the time. When he was there, though, I was Daddy's little girl. He called me Lady Jane (Nigel was Little Boy Blue) and he carried me round the garden on his shoulders. We weren't allowed out the front of the house – Mum didn't like it – but while he was gardening out the back we'd follow him up and down as he mowed the lawn and persuade him to play chase or hide and seek with us.

He was a master of silly voices and we had to guess who each one was supposed to be. It might be Mickey Mouse or Little Weed from *Bill and Ben*, or any one of a number of cartoon characters. He was good at doing the animal noises in his rendition of 'Old Macdonald', and he was also very talented at whistling; the favourite tune I remember was 'Blue Danube'.

We lived at number 39 Bentley Road, a large, stone-built, semi-detached house with bay windows and a big garden in a leafy, middle-class suburb of Birmingham. While my father looked after the outside, indoors was Mum's domain, and it was kept spotless at all times. She would catch the dust as it fell, carefully lifting all her ornaments of pretty ladies in fancy hats from shelves and tables to make sure the surfaces were spick and span underneath. At the front of the house there was the immaculate dining room, whose bay windows overlooked the street. Nigel and I were only allowed in there on very rare occasions, but I remember a fold-up table in the bay with a chair by either side and a big picture of Jesus surrounded by a glowing halo on the wall. I would come to fear this room and what went on in there when Mum locked herself in it.

Upstairs there were three bedrooms and the bathroom. My bedroom was in some respects a little girl's dream, with curtains and a bedspread made from a beautiful fabric printed with tiny pink and red rosebuds, some open and some closed, surrounded by sweeps of green stalks and leaves. The detail was extraordinary; I can remember the pattern of whorls and curlicues to this day. There were pink flannelette sheets and a bedside table with a pink lamp, and the glass in the bay window was made up of little twinkling squares. Woe betide me if I ever got a fingerprint on that glass; I learned from a very early age that it was a huge mistake to touch it as I peered out to see what was going on in the road below.

An outside observer looking at the room might have mistaken it for a seldom-used guest bedroom rather than a little girl's room because there were no dolls, toys, pictures, books or teddies in sight. I was never allowed to bring Scruffy or Rosie up to bed with me. Bedrooms were for sleeping not playing, according to Mum, and upstairs was out of bounds during the day, except for permitted trips to the bathroom.

At the rear of the ground floor was a family room with large patio windows looking out on to the garden and a marble-effect tiled open fireplace. There was regency-striped wallpaper, a patterned carpet and a brown leather Chesterfield settee and matching chairs – all considered very chic in the early 1950s. You would never see any toys in evidence in that room – or anywhere else in the house for that matter. Nigel and I had very few toys and they had to be kept tidily out of sight in the family-room toy box if we wanted to avoid them being confiscated.

* * *

In my pre-school years I idolized my beautiful, glamorous mother. I thought that she was the most gorgeous woman in the world, with her perfect hair, red lips, rouged cheeks, long varnished nails and stylish outfits, always surrounded by a cloud of lily-of-the-valley scent. I liked watching her straightening the seams of her stockings, or reapplying the lipstick that she wore constantly, even in the house when there was no one else there except us kids.

'Mummy pretty' was one of my first phrases, but I was always aware that it wasn't true of me.

'You're a very ugly child,' Mum would tell me, pinching my cheeks. 'No amount of makeup would camouflage that ugly mug. There's not a lot we can do about it.'

I became obsessed with wanting to be pretty because I thought this would make Mummy love me and stop her being cross with me all the time. I'd gaze in the mirror, willing a different face to look back at me, but it never did.

One day when I was three I found Mum's pot of rouge lying out in the bathroom. I managed to prise off the lid and put a couple of spots of it on my cheeks. I looked in the mirror and liked the effect, so I ran downstairs in great excitement to show her.

'Look, Mummy, I'm pretty!'

'What do you think you're doing?' she shouted, pulling me to her and rubbing hard at my cheeks with a dishtowel. 'How dare you touch my makeup!'

I stood, horrified. I had honestly thought Mummy would laugh and would be pleased with me. How could it have gone so badly wrong?

'You're going to have to learn not to meddle with things that aren't yours.'

I shrieked as she grabbed my hair and pulled me down the hall to the cupboard under the stairs, where the vacuum cleaner and other cleaning materials were kept. It had a sloping ceiling and shelves on one wall that served as a kind of pantry with lots of jars and tins and bottles. There was a bolt on the outside of the door and no light inside.

'There's a spider's web in the corner.' Mum pointed out. 'I'm going to lock you in here for a while to keep you out of mischief, but you'd better stay very, very quiet and very still or the spiders are going to get you.'

I was shoved inside and the door slammed and bolted. I could just make out a thin outline of the light round the door through the musty darkness. I gulped back my sobs, trembling with fear, and felt that familiar trickle between my legs as I wet myself. I didn't dare sit down or reach out my hands to touch the wall or make any movement or noise. I could barely breathe. I genuinely thought the spiders were going to eat me. How could I know otherwise?

Soon I became hysterical, banging and kicking the door as hard as I could and screaming at the top of my voice. I heard Mum's footsteps come clicking down the hall. She opened the door and I reached up my arms to be lifted, hoping for a comforting hug, but instead she hit me across the head with a sharp admonition to 'shut up!' Then she slammed and bolted the door again. I was shocked into silence. My legs trembled and an occasional sob escaped me but otherwise I stood quietly, alert for the feel of a spider's creepy feet on my skin or a nibble from their fangs. More than the physical fear, though, I felt the terror of being abandoned by the person who was supposed to take care of me. I was only three and I was bereft of adult protection.

At last, after an interminable period, Mum opened the door and yanked me out again. 'How many spiders did you count? Did they bite your toes?' There was a malicious glint of pleasure in her eyes as I shivered with fear, longing in vain for a kind word.

This is the first real punishment I remember Mum inflicting on me. Far from being a one-off, confinement in the spider cupboard became an almost daily occurrence. Young children don't have much of a sense of time but I know that sometimes it was broad daylight when I was thrown in there and dark when I came out. I frequently missed meals and had to push my fists into my stomach to combat the rumblings of hunger. If he was feeling brave, Nigel would come and whisper to me through the crack of the door: 'It's all right, Nessa, I'm here – don't be scared.' But as soon as Mum heard him he would be dragged away.

It was hard to predict the crimes for which I would be locked in the cupboard. Picking flowers, scribbling in my *Noddy* book, spilling a little talcum powder on the bathroom rug, squealing, asking for a drink, not finishing my supper – any of these could result in a period in captivity.

Nigel and I had the natural liveliness you'd expect of any toddlers and we could be naughty with the best of them. One day we shook the petals off the rose bushes and laid them out all over the garden path in wavy patterns.

Mum went absolutely berserk when she saw them because, she said, we had 'stolen' Dad's flowers.

Another time a painter had left a ladder leaning against the wall at the back of the house and Nigel and I decided to climb it to see how high we could get. He went first and had almost reached the bedroom window when he fell to the ground below and his screams brought Mum rushing out. I remember that I was the one who was punished for that escapade, despite the fact that he was older and had been the ringleader.

'I'm going to give you away to the ragamuffin man next time he comes,' she'd taunt, a prospect I found very scary, although I didn't have a clue what a ragamuffin man was.

'No, Mummy, please,' I'd beg tearfully, but she would maintain that next time he came she was definitely going to hand me over.

* * *

There were some mornings when Mum woke up in a foul mood with the world and couldn't stand the sight of me so I'd be locked in the cupboard from breakfast onwards. My only respite was at weekends when Dad was around, or on the two mornings a week when Mrs Plant, our cleaner, came over.

Mrs Plant was a lovely, dark-haired lady with a lively imagination. She would lift me up to sit beside the sink while she washed dishes or peeled potatoes and made up lots of stories to tell me. She couldn't understand why I started crying when she told me about Little Miss Muffet who sat on a tuffet. I was too young and too inarticulate to be able to put into words the chronic fear of spiders that had taken hold of me, so that even a mention of one in a nursery rhyme was distressing.

I wonder if she ever suspected what was going on in that household when she wasn't around. Once, when she was cleaning the cupboard under the stairs, I said to her, 'That's my place for when I'm naughty.'

She looked aghast and turned to Mum, who had emerged from the kitchen.

'What an imagination the child has!' Mum smirked. 'Have you ever heard the like?'

'Mummy put me there,' I protested.

She raised her eyebrows at Mrs Plant and winked. 'Was that in one of your story-books, darling?' she asked me.

Mrs Plant looked relieved and went back to work, obviously content with Mum's explanation. I was to learn that this would always happen when I tried to tell other adults the truth about what went on in our house. Mum was the mistress of keeping up appearances and from the outside, we looked like a typical, middle-class family: two happily married, prosperous parents and their well-turned-out son and daughter. Neighbours in Bentley Road undoubtedly saw us as completely normal, if a little insular.

What they didn't realize was that our father increasingly spent as much time as he could out of the house, leaving us at the mercy of a mother whose resentment of her two young children was growing, and with it, her desire to punish them.

Chapter 3

One sunny afternoon when I was outside with Nigel in the garden, something terrifying happened. One moment we were playing happily, and the next he fell down and started rolling around on the patio. At first I thought it was a silly game and giggled, but then I saw that his face looked twisted and he was jerking and throwing his arms about in a very odd way.

'Nigel?' I tried to get his attention by pushing his shoulder but his writhing knocked me over on to my bottom. He was making an odd moaning sound as well and I got scared and called Mum. 'Mummy, Nigel's hurt!'

She came running out of the kitchen and when she saw Nigel, she exclaimed, 'Oh my God, not again!' She picked him up and carried him indoors to the sitting room.

I followed, very alarmed. 'Is he all right? What's the matter?'

She ignored me, kneeling on the floor beside him and doing something funny to his mouth.

'What's wrong, Mummy?' I persisted.

'Just shut up and go back out to the garden,' she snapped. I obeyed, scared enough of her by now that I didn't take any risks when she used that sharp tone of voice.

A few hours later, Nigel seemed better again, though he was pale and tired.

When I next saw Daddy, I told him what I'd witnessed and he listened gravely, then explained to me: 'Your brother has an illness called epilepsy. Sometimes it makes him get funny turns called fits that make him roll around on the ground like you saw. If that ever happens again, you just have to run and get Mummy or me or any other grown-up so they can look after him.'

'Will he get better?' I asked.

He looked sad. 'The doctors are trying to find some medicine that will help him. It's nothing for you to worry about.'

I was still three and Nigel was four when his diagnosis was confirmed, and the fits started happening quite frequently. It must have been a huge strain on Mum, who had to make sure his airway was clear, that he wasn't choking on his tongue, and that there was nothing nearby he could hurt himself on as he flailed around. It always made her very grumpy with me when he had a fit, and more than once she told me it was my fault, that I had made him ill. I wasn't sure what I had done wrong, but I felt guilty all the same.

* * *

On top of looking after us and keeping up with the house-work, Mum had started dress-making for private clients. She worked on a treadle-operated Singer sewing machine in the corner of the family room, sitting there for hours on end with her foot pumping up and down as she guided fabric smoothly under the needle. I would have loved to watch as she hand-sewed tiny pearls on elaborate wedding dresses or ran contrasting piping round the lapels of jackets, but it seemed to irritate her if I hung around nearby and she'd jab me with the pins or needles she was holding.

She made many of her own clothes and ours as well. I had exquisite, hand-smocked dresses and little matching coats, but I didn't feel any excitement when Mum announced she was making a new garment for me because while she did the fitting, she would tie my legs to the metal supports around the machine table, next to the treadle, and she'd jab me like a pincushion as she turned up the hem or adjusted the armpit darts.

'See what it's like when a pin goes into you?' she'd say. 'It hurts, doesn't it? That's what your life is going to be like – full of hurt and pain. It hurts me just to look at you.'

Sore as the pin-pricks were, her words were more devastating to me. I adored her and yearned desperately for her to love me and not be angry. She just seemed to get more and more irritated with me, especially after Nigel's illness was diagnosed. He couldn't be punished any more for fear of bringing on a fit, so I bore the brunt of her frustration.

* * *

One day we were having breakfast when Mum spotted a solitary cornflake on the kitchen floor. In a terrifying voice, she demanded, 'Who dropped that? Own up right now!'

Nigel and I looked at each other. We genuinely didn't know which of us was responsible. What three- and four-year-olds would?

'Tell me or it will be worse for you,' she shouted, making us gulp with fear. We said nothing, but bowed our heads. 'All right,' she snapped, grabbing me by the arm and wrenching me to my feet. 'I want you to stand right here.' She grabbed Nigel and lined him up beside me. 'Don't move a muscle.'

She reached round and got her Mrs Beeton cookery book from the shelf and placed it on the floor, lined up with our feet. 'I will be able to tell if you move because you won't be in line with the book any more. No talking, no moving, while I go and ask God who was responsible for dropping that cornflake.'

She stormed out of the room and into the dining room, slamming the door shut behind her. Nigel and I stayed where we were, staring down at the floor. What was Mum doing in the dining room all on her own? Perhaps we reached out our fingers to hold hands, or maybe we were too scared that first time. I could hear a clock ticking somewhere. My throat was dry and my heart was beating hard in my chest. What was going to happen next? I racked my brains to think if it had been me who dropped the cornflake but I really had no idea. Time seemed to stand still as we waited for the verdict.

The dining room door burst open. Mum came dashing out and back to us.

'You evil child!' She grabbed my hair and pulled my head back. 'God says it was you and that I have to teach you a lesson.' I started crying and she pushed me away in disgust. 'Snivelling brat. Just you wait.'

She went out the back door and returned a few seconds later holding one of the canes Dad used to train his runner beans around in the vegetable patch.

'Pull down your pants,' she ordered.

'N…n…n…o, please,' I sobbed.

She grabbed me and pulled my pants down herself, then pushed me so that I was bent over a kitchen chair.

'Mummy, don't! Stop!' I heard Nigel yell, but she ignored him. I felt a sharp thwack on my bottom as the cane came down and I screamed at the top of my voice and tried to wriggle away. Mum placed one hand on the small of my back to stop me escaping as she administered blow after stinging blow to my bottom.

My normal fear response set in and I wet myself, making her beat me with increased vigour.

'You dirty, disgusting child! Why should I clean up after a brat like you?'

She stopped beating me, grabbed my hair again and forced me to the floor where she rubbed my nose in the puddle of urine, backwards and forwards, as some people do when trying to house-train a dog. I was gasping and gulping, finding it hard to breathe as my nose was squashed against the floor. I could vaguely hear Nigel still calling her to stop in the background, sounding hysterical, and then I think I passed out.

When I woke up I was outside on the patio and Nigel was leaning over me whispering, 'Wake up, Nessa, wake up.'

My bottom and nose were so sore that I started to cry. Nigel tried to get me to stand up but Mum saw him out the window and came charging out, bean cane in hand.

'Go to your room!' she ordered Nigel.

'No, you have to leave Nessa alone,' he yelled. Then he picked up a small stone and threw it at her.

She was absolutely livid. 'Look what you've done, you devil child,' she told me. 'You're making your brother evil as well.'

She pushed Nigel out of the way and whacked the backs of my legs with the bean cane. Nigel started to scream and then he collapsed on the grass, jerking and writhing with an epileptic fit.

'Help Nigel,' I pleaded with Mum as she continued to hit me with the cane. 'God, please help me!'

'How dare you talk to God!' Mum screamed at me. 'God is not your friend. He won't listen to you. I'm the only one who talks to God, do you understand?'

She threw down the cane, lifted Nigel in her arms and carried him into the family room to rest on the settee. I crawled up to the French windows to look in, and she glared out at me. Once she had settled Nigel and he'd stopped fitting, she came out to where I sat whimpering with fear.

'You will never drop anything on the floor again. You will never talk to God directly again. And you will stop this disgusting habit of wetting yourself, so help me …' She shook me by the shoulders then pushed me away harshly so I banged my head on the cold stone patio.

I was sent to my room and I wet myself again with fear and distress. Dad came up to see me when he got home and found me lying snivelling in urine-soaked sheets. He sniffed the air and realized what had happened.

'Lady Jane, you have to stop wetting yourself,' he said sadly. 'You're nearly four, old enough to know better. Poor Mummy has to do lots and lots of extra washing because of you.'

I tried to explain that I wet myself because I was scared of Mummy but I don't know how much sense it made to him. I probably wasn't expressing myself very clearly at such a young age.

'Why is Mummy always cross with me?' I asked him.

He shrugged his shoulders and looked worried for a moment, then said, 'It's because you keep wetting yourself. Just try not to do it and everything will be fine. Try to be a good girl.'

* * *

Why didn't Dad see what was happening and try to protect me? I kept hoping he would step in and tell her to stop, but my parents seemed to have a classic 1950s marriage where childcare was her domain and wage-earning was his. Mum ruled the roost at home and Dad generally toed the line, trying to keep everyone happy and avoid conflict. I adored my father, but I soon learned that my mother would always be believed over me. Her stories sounded so reasonable and so plausible that I almost believed them myself. I began to think that I really was a stupidly clumsy child who kept having accidents and being naughty. I was the black sheep, the cause of all the trouble, although I couldn't work out what I was doing wrong.

Chapter 4

Every morning when we got up, Nigel and I would glance at each other nervously, sensing the atmosphere, trying to judge what kind of day it was going to be. Mondays were always bad because they were washdays when Mum had piles of laundry to do in an old twin-tub washing machine. She hated washdays and I frequently got beaten with the wooden tongs she used for lifting out the wet clothes. She seldom smacked me with her bare hands; I suppose she didn't want to risk breaking a nail.

After her first interview with the Almighty, Mum began to go regularly into the dining room whenever she felt the need to talk to God. We never heard a noise, but I imagined her sitting in front of the picture of Jesus and his golden halo, her eyes tight shut and her hands pressed together as she prayed and communed with God. Whenever she went in, Nigel and I huddled together, petrified. God was *her* friend, she told us. He didn't like little children, especially horrible, ugly ones like me.

When she found something out of place – maybe a piece of tissue on the bathroom floor, or a speck of dirt on the

carpet – she'd always demand to know who was responsible. Nigel and I would never tell on each other; we
protected each other as far as we dared.

'I'll ask God,' Mum would say. 'He'll tell me. Do you
want me to go and do that? You know what will happen
when I find out.'

God, it seemed, wanted every tiny infringement of
Mum's rules punished as severely as possible at all times
and he wanted me to take the blame for everything that
happened, whether it was my fault or not. I told myself
that God must want me to be punished instead of Nigel
because he was sick, but it was still a puzzle why God so
often told Mum something that wasn't true.

Once when she was in the dining room, I accidentally
let out a nervous giggle and it came out much louder than
it should have. Mum charged out and dragged me to the
kitchen for a beating.

'You disturbed God while I was talking to him and he's
very angry,' she said, with a quiver of self-righteousness.
'God said I have to punish you.' And she started whacking
me with the bean cane, which was now kept in the corner
of the kitchen.

I always sobbed and cried with pain, telling her how
sorry I was between gasps but nothing would make her
stop. If anything, my tears and contrition fired her up even
more, so that she sliced the cane even harder through the
air. Nothing would mollify her.

While I was being punished, Nigel would do his best to
protect me by shouting at Mum to stop, and afterwards he
would comfort me, putting his arms round me to give me
a hug if Mum wasn't looking. I loved him to pieces. His
presence obviously deterred Mum a bit – my punishments

got much worse in the year when he, aged five, had started school but I, aged four, was still at home.

The garden was slightly safer than the house, because Mum tended to be working indoors and left me to my own devices, so I spent a lot of time there, keeping out of her way. I remember one time she came out, though, and saw me collecting worms and dropping them into a jam jar I'd found.

'What are you doing, you nasty girl?' she demanded. She picked up a worm, yanked my head to one side and dangled the worm so that it was wriggling inside my ear. 'He's nibbling your ear, and he's going to get stuck right inside your head. Can you feel him wriggling?'

I was petrified of the worm getting stuck and screamed and screamed for her to stop. Where were the neighbours? I suppose they must have been out that day, and maybe Mum knew it. She hated me talking to our next-door neighbour, Edna Crisp, over the fence and would call me indoors if she was in the garden hanging out her washing.

Edna saved my life one day, though. I had refused to eat some carrot that Mum had served for tea and she grabbed a bit and forced it into my mouth, pushing it back until it got stuck in my throat. I gasped in panic and managed to inhale the carrot and soon I was choking and coughing, scarlet in the face and unable to breathe. I'm not sure what happened next because I was in such a state, but I think Nigel ran next door to get Edna. She hurried into the room and thumped me on the back repeatedly until I coughed up the carrot, then she took me on her lap and hugged me as I cried and shivered in shock. Mum turned her back on us and started washing the supper dishes.

'That could have been nasty,' Edna said to my mother's back, obviously surprised at the lack of reaction to my nearly choking to death.

'She's all right now, isn't she? You were here. It'll teach her to eat more carefully in future,' said my mother.

'Well – if you say so.' Edna was clearly taken aback by the cool response the whole event had got from my supposedly loving mother. When she left, it was with a suspicious air and I had the feeling she would be watching carefully from now on.

* * *

Mother must have guessed that she'd given away something of her callous attitude towards me. Most of my punishments took place inside the house so that the neighbours wouldn't hear anything untoward, but one sunny afternoon when I was four, Nigel and I were playing in the garden. He was pedalling his red tricycle with me standing in the trailer behind it and holding on to his shoulders. I called for him to stop when I saw a pretty butterfly fluttering around the roses. I'd loved butterflies ever since Dad had told me that my name was the name of a type of butterfly.

I found a jam jar lying in the soil and unscrewed the lid to find some bits and pieces of garden twine inside. I emptied them out. Just then, Nigel spotted a bumblebee alighting on a pink rose and we decided to try and catch it. Carefully we crept up on it, put the jar over the top then slammed the lid and twisted it shut. Neither of us had any idea that bees could hurt you. I looked at it buzzing furiously inside the jar and I remember thinking that it had a

27

friendly face, like a child. I wanted it to be my friend. We put the jar in the trailer of the tricycle and cycled off round the garden squealing with delight as we gave our new furry friend a ride.

The squeals soon brought Mum out from the kitchen, demanding to know what was going on.

'We've got a new friend,' I said nervously, suddenly unsure of myself. I picked up the jar to show her.

'You cruel, horrible child,' she hissed, and dragged me by the arm to the path along the side of the kitchen. 'I'm very angry with you for doing something so cruel. God is angry and the bee is going to be angry with you as well. Just you wait and see.'

She unscrewed the lid of the jar and pressed the opening against my thigh. 'Don't move,' she instructed. 'You'll make the bee even more angry.' She tapped the bottom of the jar until the bee fell on to my skin, where I felt it crawling around, buzzing away. Suddenly there was a sharp jab that made me scream, and a throbbing pain unlike anything I'd ever felt before.

'The bee's going to die now,' Mum told me, 'and it's all your fault. You killed him.'

She dragged me, sobbing uncontrollably, to the cupboard under the stairs and locked me in. 'I'm going to get more bees to keep stinging you until you learn not to be cruel to poor defenceless creatures,' she told me.

As I stood in the dark, scratching my sting in a futile attempt to relieve the pain, I felt desperately sad. Was it really my fault the bee had died?

That night Dad got home early and came up to tuck me into bed. I said to him 'Mummy hurt me with a bee and made me cry', but he didn't believe me.

'Your Mum says the bee stung you because you made it angry by shutting it in a jar. You have to be careful with bees, Lady Jane.'

'But she did it!' I protested.

He said, 'If Mummy was angry with you today, it must have been because you'd done something naughty.'

I remember clearly how devastated I was that he didn't believe me when I was telling the truth. I had thought I was 'Daddy's little girl' but he was taking Mum's side instead of mine. Children have an innate sense of justice and I felt strongly how unfair this was. It also meant I was powerless against my mother's rage. I was a lot more vulnerable if I couldn't get my Dad to take me seriously.

I suppose he went downstairs and told Mum about our conversation because the next morning she was livid.

'How dare you tell tales to your father! You're a devil child and I'm going to have to keep teaching you lesson after lesson until you learn to behave better.'

Straight after breakfast she went out to the garden with a jam jar and hunted around until she found another bee. I tried to run away and hide behind the sofa but she caught me and dragged me out. Knowing what was going to happen, this time I struggled like mad to get away from the bee in the jar but she held me in a grip of iron until it had delivered its sting. Once again, I was locked in the spider cupboard for the day as the poison raised another red, angry lump on my leg and the horrible, throbbing pain made me scream and cry. I clawed and clawed at the stings until the whole area was raw.

* * *

This happened a few more times, each occasion bringing me a fresh sting on my chubby thighs and a painful red lump afterwards. I knew better than to tell Dad, though. That's one lesson I had learned. Mum had told him I was an unusually clumsy child, always tripping over and bumping into things, and he never seemed to question if I had a black eye or bruises on my arms and legs. He didn't bath me so he never saw the sting marks under my dress, or the stripes from the cane on my bottom. Mum was in charge of our baths and I grew to fear hair-washing nights twice a week when she took great glee in getting soap in my eyes. If Nigel had already got out, she held my head under water as she rinsed off the shampoo until I was left gasping for breath and very scared.

She brushed my teeth roughly then it was straight to bed with the door shut. If Dad was home, he'd come up to tuck me in but more often than not I got into bed on my own. I wasn't allowed to bring Scruffy or Rosie with me – they stayed downstairs. I would say the prayers I'd been taught by rote – thank you for a good day, keep me safe in the night, bless my grandmas and grandpas – then lie in the dark with the counterpane pulled up to my nose, praying that tomorrow Mummy would be happy and love me.

Chapter 5

While Mum was punishing me, I felt very scared, and sad, and determined to try harder not to put a foot wrong.

'Please love me,' I'd plead with her. 'Why don't you love me?'

'You would have to make me love you, and you haven't. You're not a loveable girl.'

She loved Nigel, though. He was her Little Boy Blue with his white-blond hair, and she always dressed him in powder blue when he was little. He got clips round the ear and raps on the knuckles, like me, but he was never beaten with the bean cane or locked in the spider cupboard. Whenever Mum went into the dining room to ask God who had been naughty, it was always me. I could tell quite clearly as a four-year-old that God didn't love me at all and I didn't know what I could do about it.

Sometimes I wondered if Mum loved Nigel because of his illness. Did she refrain from beating him with the cane in case it brought on an epileptic fit? Would she love me if I became ill? But no. When I caught measles, I was put to bed upstairs and left there on my own with no food and just a glass of water to drink. No doctor was called. I was left to get better by myself over the coming week.

* * *

One night I was trying to sleep when my attention was caught by a movement by the window. I looked over and saw that round the top of the curtains were some white shapes. They were moving about, dancing along the top of the curtain rod. I blinked hard and as they became clearer, I realized they were little eyes, children's eyes. Petrified, I gripped the cover tightly round me but I couldn't stop looking at them. There was no sound at first but, as I watched, more appeared until there were four or five pairs of eyes, all looking at me, and then I began to hear a whispering noise like the sound of very small voices. This was too much. I screamed in terror, convinced they were God's people coming to get me because of all the naughty things I had done. What would they do to me? I had no idea. I was relieved to hear Mum's footsteps coming up the stairs.

'Mum,' I sobbed, sitting up in bed. 'There are eyes in the curtains and I can hear voices!'

I wanted her to comfort me, to give me a hug and tell me everything was fine, but instead she raised her hand and gave me a hard slap across the face. She pushed me back down on the bed.

'Moaning brat, there's nothing in the room. Go to sleep now. If I hear another word from you I'll be back. You'll be sorry if you make me climb these stairs again.'

She turned the light off and slammed the door, and a minute later there were the eyes and the whispers again. I began to whimper in fear and slid further down under the covers to try and get away from them. Mum must have heard my whimpers – maybe she was listening outside – because suddenly the door burst open and the light was switched on. She whisked the covers off me and dragged me out of bed by the hair. My legs hit the floor with a thud and, as she yanked me across the hall, I wet myself in sheer fright.

'You disgusting, ugly, repulsive child,' she screamed, totally infuriated now.

Nigel came out of his room, rubbing his eyes.

'Get back to bed,' she screamed.

He tried to grab hold of me and Mum pushed him away so roughly that he fell and cracked his head against the spindles of the banister. He started to cry and then to scream, and I suppose she was worried that he might have a fit because she shoved me away, telling me to go to bed, and went to pick him up.

I climbed into bed but my nightdress was sopping wet, which made me feel cold, and I was shaking with sobs as well. Gradually I calmed myself down, keeping my eyes tight shut, a picture of Mum's ugly expression in my head. Anger transformed her beautiful face into something quite hateful.

I must have nodded off to sleep but I was woken by a hand over my mouth.

'Now it's time to deal with you, madam.' She pulled the covers back and felt the dampness of the sheet. 'You think I haven't got enough to do without washing your disgusting sheets and pants and clothes all the time. Do you?'

She yanked me out of bed and over to the stairs, hitting me across the head all the way. She dragged me down the stairs, opened the door of the spider cupboard and shoved me hard on the back, bolting the door behind me.

'Mummy, please don't. I'll be a good girl now and I'll go straight to sleep.'

'It's too late. You had your chance,' she gloated.

And then, for once, a streak of defiance came through. 'You cow! I hate you!' I called, then bit my lip, regretting it almost immediately.

The bolt slid back but not because she was letting me go back to bed. I felt a sharp, stinging pain as she hit me hard across the body with the bean cane, again and again, in a frenzied attack. I started screaming at the top of my voice so she grabbed a yellow duster from the cupboard shelf and forced it into my mouth. It smelled sickly, of lavender furniture polish. She threw me down on to the hall floor and continued hitting and hitting me all over as I twisted and tried to escape. She was like a woman possessed, all the frustrations of her curtailed life being channelled into sheer fury with me.

At last she stopped beating me and threw me back in the cupboard, where I collapsed on the floor. She slammed the door, pulling the bolt across.

'Vanessa,' she whispered viciously through the crack. 'Be careful of the big hairy spiders. They're going to crawl all over you in the night and nibble away at you. They'll start at your toes and work their way up. You can't come out till morning now.'

I lay in a heap on the red tiled floor, every part of my body raw and stinging from the caning, the taste of furniture polish in my mouth, the smell of urine coming strongly from my cold, wet, nightdress, and I sobbed and sobbed. I hated her that night. I wanted to run away and live anywhere in the world except there with her. I shook with cold, and fear, and pain, and the sheer injustice of it all. True to her word, Mum left me there till morning.

That night was the first time I saw eyes and heard voices in my bedroom, but it was soon happening every night when I went to bed. I had learned my lesson, though, and didn't make any noise that would bring Mum up to my room. As I became accustomed to them, I felt less scared. After all, they never hurt me. And I couldn't face the terror of spending another night in the spider cupboard.

Where was Dad that night? Why didn't he come home? Was it because he hadn't come home that Mum was in such a foul temper? I had no way of knowing. If I ever asked where he was, Mum would say 'Working to keep you', or 'Out with Granddad', or 'At a meeting'.

I didn't have contact with any other children so I didn't realize it was unusual for daddies to be away all week. When he got back on Friday nights, I was so overjoyed to see him that I just threw myself into playing and jumping on top of him and begging him to do his silly voices, putting the hurts and cares of the week behind me for a short while. I could revel in his affection and forget for a while what a bad, naughty, disgusting girl I was, and how much Mummy hated me.

Chapter 6

There was one place where I learned about love as a child, and that was at my Nan and Granddad Casey's, Dad's parents. Nan Casey was a big-boned woman with dark, waved hair and smiling eyes. She had a soft gentle voice and a face that was full of compassion and humour. I was usually taken to visit her every second weekend and she'd throw open the front door and run down the path to sweep me up in a huge hug, crying 'My baby! My baby!' She didn't seem to get on very well with Mum, and Nigel and I were often left there with her while Mum and Dad went off somewhere else.

We'd have such fun those weekends. Nothing was too much trouble and a huge fuss was made of us. Nan and Granddad were very well-off and lived in a big house with large gardens in Rugeley, Staffordshire. I liked to sit in the kitchen helping Nan to bake. We made fairy cakes and decorated them with coloured sprinkles, or pastry figures with currants for eyes. She had a black Aga cooker that always seemed to have a kettle billowing steam on top, and the room was very warm and cosy. In the centre was an old table with a pretty cloth covered in hand-embroidered daisies in lots of different pastel shades. I loved that cloth.

Nan took me for walks in the afternoons and we picked wild flowers, especially our favourite cowslips. As I carried them home in my sweaty little hands, she'd say 'Careful not to hold them too tightly or they'll wilt and die.'

When we got home, we would lay them carefully in her old flower press and tighten the screws on either side of the frame. We had quite a collection of pressed wildflowers that we stuck in a scrapbook. Nan drew daisies round them and my job was to colour them in. Frequently, after our walks I would fall asleep in the rocking chair beside the Aga, having happy dreams of flowers and cakes and pretty things.

'I love playing with you two,' Nan told Nigel and me. 'It makes me feel young again.'

She had toys in her house: rag dolls, a spinning top and a jack-in-the-box that I loved with a passion. She taught me how to play hopscotch, chalking the squares on her garden path and hopping along them herself. She was a great story-teller, never needing a book to come up with exciting tales of adventures and fairies and princesses, all of them with happy endings. I sat in her comfortable lap in the rocking chair, rocking to and fro, as she told us different stories every time.

Granddad Casey was a tall man with a very deep voice. He wore glasses and when he was pretending to be serious, he would slide them down his nose and peer over the top at me. We had a lovely, jokey relationship when I was younger. He could always make me squeal with laughter and Nan would pretend to be stern and say to him, 'Stop making that child squeal!' and he would wink at me and put his finger to my lips. 'Shush, Lady Jane, we'll get into trouble with Nan,' he'd say; then he'd proceed to make me squeal with laughter all over again.

Granddad's pride and joy was his collection of forty-odd racing pigeons that he kept in a coop out in the garden. They were soft and grey and gentle and I loved the throaty cooing noise they made. Granddad used to let me help to tag them. You put the bands through a time clock that punched the time on them, then the band went round the pigeon's leg so that you could tell where it came from and what time it had set out.

The gardens at Rugeley had lots of separate lawns, paths, flower and vegetable borders, the pigeon coop, and plenty of low hedges, making it an ideal place for hide and seek. There was a fishpond in the garden – about six feet square with a concrete border – and it was full of big orange goldfish. Granddad taught me how to lean over and tap the surface of the water gently so that the fish came up for a nibble, thinking that your finger was a tasty fly.

There was a gardener to look after the grounds, and Nan had a housekeeper to help indoors, although she did all the cooking herself. Every autumn we had a special job to do when the apples and pears fell from the trees in the orchard. Nigel and I would collect them and put them carefully in huge baskets. In the kitchen we would perch on the edge of the table and remove all the stalks, while a local girl peeled, cored and chopped the fruit, and Nan would stew them on the stove before bottling them in big glass jars.

The bottled fruits were kept downstairs in the cellar, which was reached via a door that led off the kitchen. I always wanted to go down there but Nan said it wasn't a suitable place for little girls in pretty dresses. She was careful to tie an apron round my neck when we were bottling the fruit or baking so my clothes didn't get dirty. I think she was wary on my behalf because she had seen firsthand the kind of trouble I got into with Mum if I got my clothes dirty.

Once when we visited, I was wearing an exquisite outfit that Mum had made for me. It was a dress in an eggshell blue colour with white spots on it, and a matching coat that was lined in the dress fabric. It had a little velvet collar and I absolutely adored it. Granddad took me for a walk down to the farm to collect some eggs and as I picked one up it slipped from my grasp. I tried to catch it and the shell broke, splattering egg down the front of my coat.

I was nervous as we walked back to the house because I knew Mum was there.

'Don't worry,' Granddad assured me. 'We'll sponge that off good as new.'

But when she saw the mess, Mum went wild. She snatched the coat from me, grabbed a pair of sharp scissors that were hanging on a hook on the kitchen wall and proceeded to cut it into tiny pieces.

'See what I'm doing? See what you've made me do?' Mum's voice rose as she became more furious. The velvet collar fell to the floor in shreds as I watched in horror. 'You're a dirty, messy girl who doesn't deserve to have anything nice!'

Nan and Granddad tried to stop her. 'Muriel, she's only a child. Accidents happen,' they remonstrated, but she was in a frenzy, not listening to anyone. I stood and sobbed, upset that yet again Mummy was cross with me, and Nan pulled me on to her knee for a hug, whispering, 'It's all right, don't worry. You'll get another coat even nicer than that one.'

Mum didn't often lose her temper to this extent in front of Nan and Granddad but there was another occasion when Granddad saw her wrench the spinning top from me and hurl it across the room. I suspect they knew that she was volatile and it must have been hard for them to send me back home with her again, but what could they do? It was not the done thing to interfere with the way somebody brought up their children. But Nan could see how terrified I was of my mother and how much I hated my life at home. As the time to leave approached, I'd get more and more miserable. When it actually was time, I'd be filled with dread and beg my grandmother to hide me in the cellar, but of course she couldn't. I didn't tell her about all the punishments I suffered at home – the bean cane, the spider cupboard, the bee stings – because I assumed these were all normal things that happened to little girls who were naughty. Nevertheless, I'm sure she could sense that my fear was in no way normal.

I was very secure in Nan Casey's love for me, and maybe this gave me some of the resources I needed to survive the treatment I experienced in the rest of my life. She was a traditional grandmother and Nigel and I were the only grandchildren she had to fuss over, because Aunt Audrey had emigrated to Canada by this time and Dad's brother Graham and youngest sister Gilly hadn't yet had children. I felt very protected by Nan when I was at Rugeley, the way all young children should feel.

If we were staying the weekend at Nan's, she took us to Sunday school. Once I was chatting to her as we walked home together.

'Today we learnt a hymn called "Jesus Loves the Little Children",' I said.

'Did you, sweetheart? That sounds nice.'

'But Jesus doesn't love me.'

Nan looked at me, frowning. 'Why do you say that?'

'God doesn't love me, so Jesus doesn't love me either,' I said, confident of my childish logic. 'God doesn't love me because I'm ugly and fat and naughty.'

Nan looked horrified. 'Vanessa, God loves all his children equally and you are a very, very special child. Never forget that.'

'But God tells Mummy I've done horrible things and that I need to be punished,' I told her. 'He doesn't like me at all.'

'What do you mean she punishes you? What does she do?'

'I can't tell you or God will be cross with me.'

She shook her head vehemently. 'Oh my baby, that's not God. That's definitely not God. God doesn't get cross with little children. You must tell me any time if you are upset about something and I'll sort it out for you. Will you promise to do that?'

I don't remember being reassured by this conversation. If anything, I felt even more confused. Nan couldn't explain it to me properly because she didn't know the truth about what happened at home and I never told her anything like the whole story. I was too scared – of God, and of Mum.

* * *

One day I was at Nan and Granddad Casey's house – I could not have been more than about four years old –

enjoying the rare sensation of safety that I felt in their home. Mum was there but Dad must have been off playing cricket or golf. It was a sunny day and I wandered out into the garden to play. I crouched down by the fishpond to watch the fish gliding to and fro, big fish and little fish. I bent over to tickle the top of the water, as Granddad had showed me, and sure enough the fish came over to nibble my fingers, thinking they were food. I liked the nice sucking feeling.

In the background I heard a door opening and soft footsteps coming down the stairs but I was too engrossed to turn around. Next thing there was a huge shove on my back and I toppled headfirst into the water and it closed above my head. I remember the shock of the cold wetness, and struggling to get my head above the surface, but it was too deep for me to touch the bottom. Seemingly I was floating face down when Nan happened to look out the kitchen window and screamed to Granddad: 'Thomas! The baby! Get my baby out!'

Granddad came running full tilt through the garden, jumped into the pond and yanked me out by the back of my dress. He wasn't sure if I was still breathing at first, and then I began to gasp and splutter for air. He carried me into the kitchen where Nan grabbed me for a big hug. Then she said, 'We've got to get her out of these wet things or she'll catch her death of cold.' There was a fluffy towel warming by the side of the Aga and she gave my hair a rub and started to unbutton the back of my dress.

'Stop!' Mum said, hurrying into the kitchen. 'Let me do that.'

She grabbed the towel and pulled me away from Nan to the corner of the kitchen. I think she might have been worried about any marks Nan might notice on my little body if she was allowed to undress me herself. I was shivering compulsively now.

'I'll get some spare clothes,' Nan said and left the room.

Mum stripped my wet clothes off and began to rub me roughly with the towel. 'You stupid girl, you're always so clumsy. Look – you've ruined your dress. It'll never be the same again.'

'But you pushed me, Mummy,' I said.

Granddad was heating some milk on the Aga and he glanced over sharply at this.

'Don't be silly.' Mum laughed, her eyes glinting fiercely at me. 'Of course I didn't push you. I was in the house the whole time. You must just have lost your balance.'

Nan came in with a change of clothes and I was dressed in them, then Nan sat me on her lap in the rocking chair, hugging me and saying, 'My baby, my poor baby' as I drank my milk. Granddad got the spinning top and set it spinning across the red tiled floor. Mum sat at the table, bored, examining her nails and glancing at the clock to see how long it would be before Dad picked us up again.

I felt safe again, in warm dry clothes, hugged tightly by Nan Casey. But I also knew that my mother had pushed me into the pond, even if she had managed to fool Granddad with her story.

She must hate me very much, I thought. I must try and make her love me. I must be a better girl.

But it was impossible to please her, no matter how hard I tried.

Chapter 7

There could not have been more of a contrast between
Dad's loving, kind parents and Mum's parents, Charles
and Elsie Pittam. From a very young age I would seize up
with dread when we set out to visit them for the afternoon, a lump constricting my throat and a knot twisting
my stomach. They lived in Yardley Wood, a bus ride away,
and Mum would take us on our own. Dad never came
along.

'I see you've brought the brats,' Grandma Pittam would
say as she opened the front door and glared down at Nigel
and me. She had tightly curled grey hair, an unsmiling
face and wore smart, tidy clothes in shades of grey, brown
and black. I remember her as formal, upright and colour-
less.

The house was gloomy and austere, situated up a slight
embankment. As you walked in the front door there was
a musty smell, like gas. Huge pieces of dark furniture
seemed to tower over us oppressively. There was a grandfather clock in the hall that chimed every quarter of an
hour and I can't say why exactly but I was always scared
of that clock. The face seemed to have eyes that followed

you around, and I always imagined that when it chimed a hand was going to come out of the casing and grab hold of me. The walls were covered in photographs of very old people – more eyes to watch over us – and every surface seemed to be cluttered with ornaments of little old men with gnarled faces and wizened hands.

'You know where to go. Sit down and be quiet,' Grandma would tell Nigel and me, and we'd troop into the front room to sit on the big, scratchy horsehair sofa, our feet sticking outwards, careful not to let our shoes touch the seat. Here we could smell the strong scent of Grandpa's pipe tobacco and it used to catch the back of my throat and make me cough.

There were no toys in that house. Nigel and I were supposed to sit quietly, waiting while Mum chatted to her mother. I overheard snippets of conversation that referred to us sometimes. One in particular stuck in my head, although it made no sense to me at all.

'If God had wanted you to have children, he would have given them to you,' Grandma said. It was very obvious she didn't like us and didn't want us to be there, but I didn't know why.

Of course, Nigel and I were young and found it hard to sit still for long. We'd start to fidget and one of us would giggle and Grandma would come charging through to tell us off. Children should be seen and not heard in that house. At teatime, she always served salmon and cucumber sandwiches cut into triangles. The slightest infraction of table manners was punished by a sharp rap on the knuckles with a bread knife. We would be told off for running, bumping into furniture, dropping crumbs, or virtually everything that two lively young children got up to. She seemed to have eyes in the back of her head and always caught us for any minor misdemeanours, even if we'd thought she wasn't watching.

Some days when we arrived, she wouldn't even let us in the house. 'I'm in no mood for you today,' she'd say. 'You'll have to stay out in the garden.'

Other times, when we were getting on her nerves, she'd send us to wait in the garage. It was always cold there and the wind blew dead leaves under the door and into corners. There were strange, toxic smells from the old pots of paint and tins of creosote that lay around, and the shelves were stacked with tools and ladders. Ancient broken toys were scattered around the garage, presumably relics of Mum's childhood. A painted metal rocking horse stood to one side – it makes me shudder to think of it. Its tail and mane were matted and rough to the touch. When I climbed on to it to ride, it made an awful squeaking noise, like a creaky old gate, that used to grate on the nerves and make my teeth feel funny. There seemed something evil about that rocking horse, a kind of malignant look in its eyes.

If we'd been sent out to the garage for being naughty we wouldn't be allowed to have any tea, but Grandma would quite often come out and wave the plate of sandwiches and maybe even tiny cakes under our noses so we could see what we were missing.

'These are only for *good* children,' she'd say. 'You're too naughty to have any.' Then she would take the plate away again, shutting the garage door behind her as she went up the step into the kitchen. Nigel and I called her 'Nasty Nanny' and talked about how we wished we could go and see Nan Casey instead.

Grandpa Pittam was a big man with white, slightly curly hair and a rugged face. He wore a monocle and scratchy, tweedy clothes. He was a watch- and clockmaker by profession and there was always a fob watch on a chain pinned to his waistcoat. I hated the way he used to bounce me on his knee and kiss me on the lips and I hated the smell of stale tobacco that lingered in a cloud around him. He had a loud, raspy voice and he'd pretend to be jovial with us, but his smile would never reach his eyes.

Grandpa Pittam had an aviary full of blue, green and yellow budgerigars in the back garden. Sometimes he'd take Nigel and me out to look at them but unlike the visits to Granddad Casey's racing pigeons, we hated being on our own out there with him. He'd make me go inside the aviary where all the birds fluttered round my head, making me scream. I was frightened their claws would get caught in my hair, or that they'd peck me as they darted around twitching and blinking, but Grandpa just laughed at my distress.

I never felt comfortable when he lifted me on to his lap and bounced me up and down, but Mum said 'Be nice to your grandfather. He loves you very much.'

I'd say, 'But I want to sit on the floor' and she'd say, 'Do what your grandfather wants.'

She was very affectionate with him, often kissing his cheek and being flirtatious and giggly, the same way she was with Dad when he got home from work. He'd pat her bottom and tell her to behave herself, which just made her giggle more.

Grandpa's eyes were deeply set in his head and he used to look at me in a strange sort of a way, as though he was seeing someone else and not me. Was it just my imagination? I got the impression sometimes that he was quite sad and lonely, but I didn't feel sympathy. He was far too creepy for that.

On the whole, I tried to behave my very best when we visited Grandma and Grandpa Pittam but I hated going there. One day, when Mum was getting us ready to go over there, I said out loud: 'I don't want to go to Grandma Pittam's. I want to go to Nan Casey's.'

'You'll go where you're told and like it. Now hold your tongue.' She accompanied this with a hard smack round the head. A bitter little seed of rebellion was planted inside me.

As we travelled there on the bus, a voice whispered in my head that I should tell Grandma Pittam that I didn't like her. She had to know. I could ask her why she was so nasty to me. Was it because she didn't like little girls, or because I was sometimes naughty? Or was it because I wasn't pretty? I was nervous but convinced myself that it was right for me to speak my mind.

We arrived at Yardley Wood and Mum pressed the front door chime. Grandma opened the door and gave Mum a kiss on the cheek, saying, 'Hello, dear, I've just put the kettle on.' Then she looked down at us. 'I'm in no mood for children today so you two can play quietly in the garden. You're not coming in.'

The bitter seed in me burst out and I told her: 'I don't like you. You're not a nice lady. I hate coming to your house and I wish we were going to Nan Casey's because she's kind and she plays with us.' Once I'd started the words just came tumbling out.

Grandma's eyes widened and she looked at Mum in horror. Mum grabbed me by the hair and snapped, 'You ungrateful brat! Apologize to your grandmother at once. Tell her you're sorry for being unkind.'

'I won't,' I said defiantly. 'I meant it all.' In my naive, four-year-old way, I'd somehow imagined that Grandma might be nicer to me if I told her how I felt. Now I understood that it would only make everything a lot worse.

'We can't let her get away with this, Muriel,' Grandma said.

Nigel was sent to sit on the sofa; then Grandma dragged me into the hall, crying and pleading while Mum went to find something to beat me with. She came back with an old paint-covered stick from the garage and started to whip me with it. I struggled to avoid the blows that rained down on my arms, legs and body and Mum got more and more cross as the stick never seemed to land where she wanted it to. I screamed and screamed as each stroke stung my skin, begging her to stop.

'P-p-please Mummy, no. I'm sorry. Please stop.'

And then, as usual, I wet myself in sheer fright and there was a telltale puddle on the hall carpet. As soon as it happened, I started to pray silently, 'Please don't let her notice', but she soon did. She stopped beating me and yanked me up by the hair.

I looked pleadingly at the ugly expression on her face, too terrified to utter a word.

'You're a dirty, filthy child, still wetting yourself like a baby when you're four years old. You disgust me. I'm ashamed to call you my daughter.' She dropped the stick and started slapping me hard round the face – right, left, right, left – until my cheeks were on fire. 'I'm not going to stop until you apologize to your Grandma for what you said, and for wetting her carpet.'

Despite the fact that I was petrified when Mum got into a frenzied attack like this, I stuck to my guns. 'But it's true that I don't like her and I don't want to come here.'

There was an almighty whack that made me see stars and I let out a deafening scream. I tried to look up into Mum's eyes, begging for mercy, but saw only a cruel, cold glee.

A banging and crashing noise was coming from the kitchen and Mum dragged me down the hall to see what was going on. Grandma had pulled out an old corrugated tin tub that she kept under the sink and had filled it with cold water.

'We need to clean up the little *****,' she said to Mum, using a word I didn't understand but that sounded ugly. 'Get her clothes off.'

I didn't struggle as their rough fingers stripped off my dress, then my vest, pants and socks. I was gulping back sobs, partially dazed by all the blows to my head, and I had no idea what was coming next. Mum lifted me up and lowered me down into the icy water. As soon as my feet touched the surface, I struggled to get away, so Grandma joined in and they both pushed me down until I was shuddering in ice-cold water that came up to waist height.

Grandma pulled out a brittle old scrubbing brush and a bar of antiseptic-smelling pink soap from under the sink. 'This is what I use for cleaning the dirtiest laundry when it needs a really good scrub,' she said. She rubbed the soap on the bristles to raise a lather and then she started to scrub the skin of my back, chest, legs and arms, rubbing with such vigour that I was soon red-raw and sore all over. She rubbed suds into my eyes, nose and mouth, and I just sobbed and sobbed without stopping, feeling completely without hope.

When she'd finished, she yanked me out, rubbed me down roughly with a towel and then marched me across to the door that led to the garage. I was pushed headlong, still stark naked, and the door slammed behind me. The rocking horse's eyes looked at me mournfully.

I crouched down on the floor hugging myself and shivering, every inch of me stinging and sore. I started to rock back and forwards on my heels. There were whispering voices in my head but I couldn't make out what they were saying. I felt cold and scared and vulnerable and utterly, utterly alone. I now knew that I wasn't safe in Grandma's house and that I couldn't risk rebelling again because she obviously hated me as much as Mum did.

Chapter 8

I have a clear memory of my first day at St Peter's primary school in Bentley Heath, aged five. Dad dropped me off at the classroom and gave me a kiss goodbye, telling me to 'be a good girl'. I slunk inside, desperately trying to fade into the background and avoid being noticed. I had no social skills whatsoever. I didn't know how to talk to other children, or how to play with them, and I used to hide from grown-ups I didn't know. After a slow start, my speech was still less fluent than that of my contemporaries and I often had trouble expressing myself.

Nigel had already been at St Peter's for a year but he hadn't talked about it much so I had no idea what to expect. One thing worried me in particular. I'd heard that you had to put your hand up if you wanted to go to the toilet and then wait for the teacher to give you permission. What if the teacher didn't see me? Or I couldn't hold it in long enough? I was petrified that I might wet myself at school and all the children and teachers would be able to see what a baby I was.

Of course, it happened frequently in the early days because I was too frightened to put my hand up and ask.

Mum was incensed when she got a phone call from the school asking if she could drop off some spare pairs of pants for me to change into. I got a severe beating for that.

I was still quite a stocky child, with reddish chubby cheeks and light brown hair that I wore in bunches – certainly not cute or angelic-looking. I totally believed Mum when she told me that I was fat and ugly and no one would ever love me because I was unloveable. Rather than risk rejection by my peers, I kept well away; but still some cruel classmates would tease me from time to time, shouting 'Wee-wee face, smelly girl, dirty girl!'

Nigel was more confident than me and had a little crowd of friends of his own, but we would always eat lunch together, and we'd walk to and from school together along a gully that led straight up to our back garden. Breaktimes in the playground were difficult and I stood on my own near the door back into the school. It was a kind of defence mechanism. I felt safer being near a door because it meant I could escape, although I hated having my back to the door because I had no idea who might be sneaking up on me.

I found the lessons hard that first year at school. It took me a long time to understand that letters formed words that you could read, and I had especial trouble understanding that some words that sounded the same could have more than one spelling and more than one meaning – for example, to, two and too. I grew to like sums, though. There was something satisfyingly controllable about numbers that appealed to me. I understood how they worked. They didn't have different meanings and outcomes; two plus two was always four.

Probably part of my timidity at school was due to a fear of anyone finding out what a bad girl I was. Mum had impressed on me very strongly that I had to prevent teachers or other children seeing any cane marks or bruises on my skin when we got changed for PE, and if anyone commented on a cut or a bruise I was to say that I fell over playing in the garden. She drummed into me over and over again that if they found out how horrible I was at home then they would all hate me, and I really believed that was true. I was a hateful person. I tried not to be but I was. I yearned for love and friendship, to be able to join the games of skipping and the groups huddled giggling in the corner. But if I let anyone close, they might find out the secret about how evil I really was.

There was a positive side to being at school all day, though, in that I wasn't spending so many hours in Mum's company, so I didn't get on her nerves quite as much. I think she got back some of her former social life and was able to meet friends once we were out of the house during the day. At any rate, I wasn't getting punished so frequently and this made me hopeful that I could at last make her love me.

* * *

On Mother's Day, just after my sixth birthday, we were embroidering tray cloths to take home as presents for our mums. Our sewing skills were very limited but I attacked mine with a determination to make it the most beautiful cloth ever so I could show Mum how much I loved her. Sewing was her great skill and surely she would be proud of me if I was good at it as well? A nice teacher saw the effort I was making and helped me with it, and the end result was very pretty. It said Happy Mother's Day in the middle (the teacher did that bit) and there were little bows and flowers and kisses all around and curly decorative corners. I took it home that day, apprehensive but sure that Mum would be pleased with such a lovely present.

'Mum, I made you something,' I said as I handed it over.

She peered at it. 'What kind of a mess is that?' she demanded, pointing to a bit at the edge where I'd sucked the material, causing it to fray; the teacher had cut it at an angle to try to disguise it. 'These stitches are all uneven,' Mum continued, 'and I don't know why you chose those colours.' She flipped up the lid of the kitchen wastebin and threw it in. 'Absolute rubbish,' she said. 'What would I want with that?'

It was a huge blow but the little defiant core in me was not going to give up on something I'd worked so hard at. As soon as Mum left the kitchen, I sneaked that tray cloth out of the bin and hid it in my knickers. I was nervous as I ate tea, knowing that I would get into trouble if she found out. If Mum decided to cane me for anything and I had to pull my pants down, she'd see straight away. Fortunately she didn't cane me that day and as I got undressed at bedtime I managed to sneak the tray cloth into a secret hiding place in my bedroom. There was a gap underneath my wardrobe at a point where the shelves came down, hidden behind a little plinth. I put the tray cloth in there and next time Dad took me to Nan Casey's I brought it along and presented it to her instead.

'Vanessa, it's beautiful. I can't believe you did such a lovely piece of work as this. Are you sure it's for me? Thank you so much, darling.' She covered me with hugs and kisses as any normal mother might have done.

* * *

The Caseys were great animal lovers, who kept two dogs –
a red setter called Rusty and a dachshund called Fritz. I'd
been begging Dad to let me have a pet but Mum had
vetoed it, saying she would be the one who would have to
clear up after it. Towards the end of my first year at
school, though, Dad came home one night saying he had a
surprise for me, and he produced a cute little white bunny
rabbit with a twitchy nose and dark, sensitive eyes. I loved
it on sight. It was the best present I'd ever had.

'I'm going to build a hutch in the garden,' Dad
explained, 'and it will be your responsibility to keep it
clean, and to bring out food and fresh water every day. Do
you think you can manage that?'

'Yes, yes!' I cried.

'What are you going to call him?' he asked.

I thought for a moment and said 'Whirly.' I've got no
idea why – it was just a word that came into my head, but
Whirly he became.

I was assiduous at looking after Whirly. Dad brought
me bags of straw and sawdust and rabbit food every weekend and Mrs Plant would let me have carrot tops and
vegetable peelings to feed him. I would sit for hours on
end talking to Whirly, stroking and playing with him,
telling him all about my life. I felt calm and content out
there by the rabbit hutch. It was one of the few places in
my life where I did.

Chapter 9

By the age of six I had come to accept the fact that I heard voices in my head. I found them comforting now, in contrast to the terror they had inspired when I first heard them in my bedroom at night. The eyes had become shadowy faces that danced on darkened walls, in and out of the curtains. They began to appear in the daytime as well. Sometimes they urged me to be rebellious, like the time I told Grandma Pittam I didn't like her, but most of the time they seemed to give me good advice and help me to stay out of trouble.

'Keep out of your Mum's way,' they would say, or 'Pick up that block from the carpet before she sees it', or 'Don't argue back – it will only make things worse.'

I told Dad about the voices one time and he seemed very concerned about it. 'You should tell them to go away,' he advised.

'Why do the voices always talk to me when Mummy's going to be cruel?' I asked in all innocence.

'What do you mean?' he asked sharply, and I remembered that it had been a huge mistake to tell tales on Mum in the past.

I said, 'Sometimes Mummy's not very nice to me when you're not there. Can't you stay at home? Please, Daddy.'

He frowned and explained that he had to go to work to pay the bills. 'But I'm sure Mummy's only cross when you've been naughty. You just have to try harder to be a good girl, Lady Jane.'

Mum hated it if I mentioned the voices in my head to her. One night before I went to bed she took some small pieces of cotton wool and forced them inside my ears as far as they would go. 'That should stop your stupid voices,' she snapped. She claimed that sometimes I got a distant, glazed look on my face as though I was seeing something or listening to someone far far away, and it drove her to distraction.

When I told Nan Casey about the voices, I got quite a different response.

'Don't be afraid,' she told me. 'There is nothing to fear.' Then she said something that to me at the time seemed very strange. 'Your biggest threat is the people who are on this earth, not those who aren't. They can't hurt you.'

It was the first inkling I got that the voices came from real people who weren't on this earth, but the idea didn't scare me as much as it might have because I knew that, nine times out of ten, they were on my side, trying to protect me. Most were kind and caring, but they usually all had different opinions so it could be hard to decide which ones to trust.

* * *

It was Nan Casey who noticed that my hearing was deterio-rating, to the extent that I sometimes couldn't hear someone who was speaking across the room from me. At school I often failed to understand the teacher's instructions and I was too shy to put my hand up to ask for them to be repeated, so I'd get into trouble for not doing the work correctly.

I hadn't been to a doctor before that I could remember, although I suppose I must have seen one when my leg was broken at eighteen months. Nan Casey nagged and nagged Mum to get my hearing checked until at last she agreed. We went to a GP first, who shone a light in my ears and tutted. Using a pair of tweezers he reached in and extracted a small, hardened wad of cotton wool.

'Really, Mrs Casey,' he said. 'She shouldn't be putting things in her ears. It can cause a lot of damage.'

'Honestly,' Mum remonstrated with me. 'How many times have I told you not to do that?'

'But ...' I began, but her glare warned me to shut up.

The doctor looked at my throat next and remarked that my tonsils were very inflamed and that he would refer me to an ear, nose and throat specialist. Mum was not best pleased but there was nothing she could do about it. They'd have been suspicious if she hadn't taken me for the ENT appointment. The specialist I saw decided straight away that I needed an operation to remove my tonsils and adenoids, and that this would improve my hearing.

When the day came Mum took me into hospital, and I remember walking down the long, dim corridors that smelled of antiseptic. I had no idea what we were doing there and felt very intimidated. In the ward there were rows of narrow iron beds covered in starched white cotton sheets. A nurse in a pristine blue and white uniform and a big cap that was pinned at the back showed us to the bed I would occupy for the next three or four days. Mum watched over me as I got undressed and pulled on a hospital gown then clambered between the sheets. The ward seemed very noisy, with clanking trolleys and metal instruments over the buzz of voices. I could smell boiled cabbage, my least favourite food, which must have been served at lunch that day. It seemed like a bad omen.

I looked up at Mum in terror, desperately seeking reassurance, but instead she folded my clothes into the locker and said 'I'll be off, then.' She left without giving me a kiss, a hug or a kind word. I thought I was being left there for good, that she would never come back, and part of me wished this were the case. Other children had their parents sitting by their bedsides, telling them stories, playing cards, or letting them colour in with crayons. I felt very alone. The nurses were perfectly kind but they were always in a hurry with too much to do.

I have vivid memories of being wheeled down a corridor to the operating theatre and being lifted from the trolley on to a bed. A man in a white coat put a black rubber mask over my nose and mouth and told me to count backwards from ten to one. The sweet smell of gas got stronger and I think I only made it to eight before I conked out.

When I opened my eyes, the light was very bright. I felt thirsty and my throat felt as though it was full of broken glass. I asked a passing nurse if I could have a drink and she said no, that I was to go back to sleep again, but she would bring me something nice later on.

At teatime, when they brought the meals round, I was given jelly and ice cream − a huge treat. Mum never served puddings at home. I'd only had jelly and ice cream a couple of times before at Nan Casey's house. It hurt to swallow but I could let the ice cream melt in my mouth and trickle down my inflamed throat in a cool stream.

Evening visiting time came and I could see that every other child on the ward had a visitor except me. During my entire stay, neither Mum nor Dad came to visit me. I guessed that Dad must be too busy with work but I still scanned the groups of parents entering the ward as visiting hour began, hoping against hope that he might be there. I didn't have any books or toys with me but the nurses brought me some picture books to look at.

A few nurses asked where my parents were. Did they live very far away? And I felt embarrassed saying, 'No, Bentley Heath', as though I should be apologizing for their non-appearance.

On the day I was discharged I was told to dress myself. Mum and Dad couldn't pick me up, they'd told the hospital, so I was sent home in an ambulance, which was quite exciting – although I was disappointed they didn't turn on the siren. Back home, the ambulance man walked me to the front door, which was opened by Mrs Plant, the cleaner.

'Oh you poor dear,' she said, throwing her arms around me. 'What a rough time you've had. Come on in and you can lie on the sofa and tell me all about it.'

She was so sweet to me that morning that it almost upset me more, because the contrast was so great between her and my mother. If the hospital stay did nothing else, it gave me a glimpse into how other families lived, and the fact that mine was quite different from other people. This was something I would continue to ponder in the coming years, without having the power to do anything about it.

In my head, the voices were murmuring and I could make out what some of them were saying. They were wondering where my father was and when my mother would be home. I lay and listened to them and wondered what it all meant.

Chapter 10

During the school holidays, we were under Mum's feet again and I could tell she was irked by this. She'd got used to having a bit of freedom from us kids but it had been taken away from her for the next few weeks. She was still working as a dressmaker and often had to travel into Birmingham by train to buy fabric or haberdashery, so over the holidays she would have to take us with her. Usually she left Nigel and me to play at Dad's office in the electro-plating business, where Granddad Casey, Uncle Graham and Dad all made a fuss of us. I remember the sulphurous, rotten-egg smell of the place, which must have been a by-product of one of the processes there. Among other things, they electro-plated nibs for old-fashioned pens and Dad used to give me lots of extra ones to keep. Granddad kept a spinning top there as well as at home and we would play with that, or they gave us pens and paper to do drawings, or we were allowed to make long chains with paperclips.

This was infinitely preferable to being dragged round the shops with Mum. She never actually let me come into shops with her. Instead I would be given strict instructions to stand outside the door without moving and wait for her to come out again. They were usually fabric shops and she said I might touch the rolls of fabric with my sticky fingers and get her into trouble. I remember being very scared on these occasions, with so many strange adults milling around, and sometimes she seemed to take hours.

During the Easter holidays after my sixth birthday, I got a huge fright on the journey into town. Nigel wasn't with us because he was playing at a friend's house. Mum and I got on the train at Bentley Heath as usual. I was being as good as possible but I could sense she was in a testy mood. I'd already had a clip round the ear for dawdling as we walked to the station. We got on board and sat down in a carriage of our own. Soon after the train started moving Mum got up, saying 'Back in a moment. Stay right there.'

I sat neatly as I'd been told, with my hands on my lap, feet swinging back and forwards without reaching the ground. I looked out the window then glanced back at the corridor to see if Mum was returning. There was no sign of her. The train pulled into the next station and more people got on but still Mum didn't come back. I was so little and everyone else was so big. With mounting anxiety I got up and went to look up and down the corridor, but there was no sign of her. What if she forgot all about me and got off the train without me?

I began to hear voices in my head. 'You're lost, Vanessa, what are you going to do?' 'Tell someone where you live,' came another voice. I could remember our address – 39 Bentley Road – so I decided that if Mum didn't come back I would have to approach a guard at Birmingham Station and tell him I was lost. The voices continued, sometimes a mass of whispers like a breeze blowing through the leaves on a poplar tree, so indistinct I couldn't make out the words, then one voice would get through: 'Don't worry', or 'You're lost', or 'It'll be OK'. I had no idea who or what they were but I was getting used to hearing whispers in my head, usually when I was upset about something, and they didn't scare me any more.

The journey took around 45 minutes and by the time the train pulled into Birmingham New Street, where it terminated, I was tearful and shaking. I realized that I didn't have a ticket and the guard might shout at me for being on the train without one, as we'd seen happening to a boy some weeks earlier. I waited until all the other passengers had got off then I climbed down the steps on to the platform and looked around for a guard I could talk to. I'd just identified one and was nervously walking up to him when all of a sudden Mum appeared and grabbed me by the arm, her fingers digging in and bruising me.

'There you are! How dare you go wandering off when I told you to stay still!'

My eyes full of tears, I looked up at her face and I could see that far from being angry, she thought the whole thing was a huge joke.

'I thought you'd forgotten about me,' I said, the tears spilling over.

'If only I could,' she said spitefully. 'If only I could.'

She had obviously left me on my own just to give me a fright, and it certainly worked.

The guard came over to us. 'Is everything all right?' he asked.

'I don't suppose you'd like a little girl?' Mum said. 'You can have this one, but I warn you that she's very naughty. Maybe you can send her to work in the coal mines.'

'She's got pretty blue eyes.' The guard looked down at me sympathetically.

'Nonsense. Look at her! She's ugly as sin!' Mum marched off with me trailing in her wake, trying to grab hold of the fashionable swing coat she was wearing. I begged her to lift me up, scared of losing her again, but she ignored me. A tearful, snotty little girl trying to cling on to her favourite coat must have wound her up no end.

* * *

I wonder if she might have liked a pretty, sociable daughter she could show off to strangers like a fashion accessory, or if she would have preferred not to have had kids at all? All mothers have their days when the kids drive them crazy, with whining and being clingy and getting in the way. However, for some reason my very existence seemed to drive Mum crazy. She just couldn't bear me being around. At least once a week, usually more, God would tell her about some crime I had committed and I would be beaten and locked in the spider cupboard until bedtime.

* * *

When Nigel and I had been out at school all day, mealtimes became a flashpoint, an opportunity for Mum to take out the frustrations of her day. She played a despicable trick one night when I'd just finished eating a stew she'd made for dinner.

'Did you enjoy that?' she asked.

'Yes,' I said warily.

'Was it delicious? One of your favourite meals ever?'

'Em, yes.'

'That's interesting.' Mum's eyes glinted. 'Do you realize you've just been eating Whirly? I made a rabbit stew.'

Nigel reacted first, spitting out the last bite in his mouth. 'Ewwwuuh, that's disgusting.'

I jumped to my feet to run out into the back garden but Mum extended a hand to stop me. 'What do you say?'

'Please may I leave the table?' I mumbled, and she gave permission. I rushed straight out to the rabbit hutch and was devastated to find it empty. There was just a hollow in the straw where Whirly had been sleeping when I looked in on him that morning. The stew rose in my throat and I retched violently, and began to cry. Mum came out to watch, and Nigel followed close behind.

'How could you?' I demanded through my tears.

'You silly girl. It was only a stupid rabbit.'

'You shouldn't have done that, Mum. It's wrong. That was Nessa's rabbit, not yours,' Nigel complained.

'Shut up! I'm fed up with both of you. Get out of my sight. Go to your beds now.'

I lay in bed wide-awake, thinking of the bits of Whirly in my stomach and feeling utterly sickened. I remembered his twitchy nose and trusting eyes and the way he liked his head being stroked and I burst into a fresh wave of crying. I hoped against hope that Dad would come home that night so that I could tell him – he had bought Whirly for me after all – but he didn't appear. I hardly got a wink of sleep and crawled out of bed the next morning weighed down by grief.

I was sitting at the breakfast table unable to swallow a morsel of my cereal when Nigel burst in the back door looking excited. 'Nessa, guess what? Whirly's back. Come and see.'

We ran out to the hutch and sure enough, there he was, nose twitching, looking up to see if I had brought any carrot tops.

Mum was laughing her head off when we trooped back indoors. 'Got you!' she crowed. 'You should have seen your face when you thought you'd eaten him. That was hilarious!'

She was triumphant after each malicious victory of this kind. Far from infuriating her in the way I used to as a pre-schooler, I got the impression that she couldn't wait for me to get home from school so she could inflict her next sadistic punishment on me. Caning didn't give her the same satisfaction because although it still hurt, it didn't inspire the abject terror in me that it used to when I was younger. When she locked me in the spider cupboard now, I knew that the spiders weren't going to eat me up. I could just sit quietly, listening to the voices in my head while thinking my own thoughts. It took more ingenuity on Mum's part to make me cry.

But her next punishment would be the worst one she had ever inflicted on me.

Chapter 11

During the summer term of my first year at school, I got home one day to find a new window cleaner washing our windows. He shouted 'Hello, sweetheart!' at me as I walked up the path, which made me very self-conscious and embarrassed, especially since he'd taken his shirt off and I could see his naked, suntanned back. When he'd finished, he rapped on the front door and Mum tottered down the hall in her high heels to pay him. I'd seen her freshening up her lipstick in the kitchen first.

'I hope you've done an extra-special job for me,' she said coyly, head on one side.

'Course I have, darling,' he replied cheekily. 'I've always been one for the ladies, and you must have been a real looker in your day.'

I could sense Mum stiffening with fury. Even I could see that she would take this as a terrible insult.

She gave him his money without another word, slammed the door and disappeared into the dining room for a while. When she came out, there was a crackling energy around her and a scary expression on her face. She sent Nigel to the family room and called me into the kitchen where she was preparing dinner.

'I've got something very important to say to you,' she told me in an ominous voice, folding her arms and staring down at me. 'Stand straight with your arms by your sides.'

I obeyed.

'Someone has stolen something in this house and God tells me it was you.'

'I didn't, Mum. It wasn't me.'

'So you know what I'm talking about, do you?'

'N-n-no ...'

She took a deep breath and placed her hands on her hips. 'Mrs Ferguson came round for a fitting today. I made her some tea and went to the biscuit barrel to lay out a plate of biscuits and what do you think I found?'

I'd gone red, not because I was guilty of anything but just with nerves and fear of what was coming next. I shook my head slightly.

'One of the pink wafers was missing. The good ones that cost sixpence a packet. I couldn't believe my eyes. There's a thief in my own house. I didn't want to think it was true but I spoke to God this morning and he confirmed that you took the wafer.' She was quivering with self-righteousness, her eyes dark and staring.

'Mummy, it wasn't me.' I was terrified of being accused of this very serious-sounding crime. This was worse than dropping crumbs on the floor or getting a spot of paint on the sleeve of my school cardigan.

'Are you saying that God is a liar?' She was winding herself up, getting more enraged all the time. Behind her a pot of potatoes was boiling fiercely, spitting droplets of hot water on to the cooker top.

'N–n–no …'

'So you admit it's true. Do you know what the Bible says is the punishment for liars and thieves?'

I shook my head and stared at the ground, more scared than I could remember.

Mum looked at me with narrowed eyes for a moment, then she turned and lifted the pot of potatoes off the spiral electric ring, which glowed bright orange. Boiling water sloshed over the edge. She grabbed me viciously by the wrists, dragged me over to the cooker and placed my hands palm down on the ring, holding them there for a few seconds before letting them go.

I screamed in shock although I didn't feel the pain at first. Nigel came running in from the family room.

'What happened? Are you OK, Nessa?'

I couldn't speak. 'Get out!' Mum ordered him sharply. 'This doesn't concern you.' When he didn't immediately move, she screamed 'Go!' and took a step towards him in a threatening manner. He turned reluctantly and went back into the next room.

I looked down at the palms of my hands. The skin had gone all white where it had touched the searing heat and neat patterns of the rings had been transferred on to my palms and fingers. I could smell a sweetish smell like meat cooking on a barbecue. My hands felt strangely tight and it was hard to move my fingers. I just stared at them and started shaking.

'That should stop you next time you're thinking of thieving.' Mum's voice was quieter and gentler now, her rage dissipated. 'I'm doing this for your own good so you don't end up in jail one day. No daughter of mine is going to be a jailbird.'

I couldn't move or speak. I suppose I was in shock. I just stared at my hands.

'You'd better go to bed now,' Mum said, almost kindly. 'So long as you learn your lesson from this, we need say no more about it.'

As I walked slowly up the stairs, my hands were beginning to throb with a dull pain that got worse by the minute. I suppose the nerve endings had been damaged in the initial contact but as feeling returned I began to get very nauseous and dizzy. I crawled into bed, pushing my hands under the cold pillow in a vain attempt to cool them down. It hurt to have anything touching my palms, though, so I rested them on top of the covers and lay very still, very shocked. My teeth were chattering.

It was obvious to me that Mum had crossed some boundary and I was scared to death. If she could burn my hands like that, what wasn't she capable of?

When I closed my eyes, whispering voices came into my head: 'She shouldn't have done that'; 'You're not safe here'; 'You're not going to be able to do your schoolwork tomorrow'; 'You have to run away'.

I opened my eyes again because the room was spinning. I felt very cold and shivery, as if I had the flu. I lay on my back, trying to keep as still as possible. I was scared to move in case I was sick on the bed, which I knew would make Mum even madder.

An hour or so later, Nigel managed to sneak up to see how I was.

'Mum said you touched the cooker. Are you OK?'

I shook my head very slightly.

'Was it her?' he asked.

'She did it,' I whispered. 'She held my hands down on it.'

Nigel sat on the edge of the bed and looked at my upturned palms, with the fingers curled into claws. 'They look really bad, Nessa. It's all gooey under the skin.'

I shifted my head to look down. Huge blisters were rising on the whitened areas and oozing pus out the sides. 'It really hurts.' A few tears trickled down my cheeks but I didn't cry properly.

'I'll try to get help. If Dad comes home, I'll tell him what happened. Don't worry.'

I slipped in and out of a fevered sleep and wakened when the bedroom door opened and Dad came in and switched the light on. He was still wearing his grey outdoor coat so he'd obviously just arrived home. He put a hand on my hot forehead then gave a loud gasp when he saw the state of my swollen, weeping palms.

'For God's sake! What on earth were you playing at, Lady Jane? You know better than to touch a hot cooker.'

'Mummy did it,' I said dully, and for once he seemed to believe me.

He gave a sharp intake of breath and gently picked up one of my hands to look more closely. I winced.

'We've got to get this fixed,' he said, pulling back the bedcovers. 'Let's put your slippers and dressing gown on. I'm taking you to Nan Casey's.'

It hurt a lot getting my hands into the sleeves of the dressing gown. My arms felt stiff from the shoulders down. Dad was as gentle as possible. He found my pink fluffy slippers and put them on my feet then he picked me up and carried me down the stairs, being very careful not to let anything touch my damaged hands.

Mum came out of the kitchen and said, 'What do you think you're doing?'

'I'm taking her to my mother's. These hands need medical attention. Would you rather I called a doctor out here?'

'You're over-reacting, Derrick. She'll be right as rain in the morning.'

Dad just gave her a look and said, 'Muriel, you've gone too far.'

She shrugged her shoulders and went back into the kitchen.

* * *

I remember that drive very clearly. I sat in the front of the car beside Daddy, the street-lights flashing past outside. It felt very late because there was hardly any other traffic on the road. He seemed angry and didn't say anything except to ask occasionally if I was all right, or if I thought I was going to be sick. My hands were throbbing terribly now with pulses of white-hot pain, but I felt relief inside. Nan Casey would look after me. She would make it better.

When we got there and she opened the front door and held out her arms, my tears started to flow. I just cried and cried. Granddad phoned a friend of his who was a doctor in their village and he arrived at the house within ten minutes, despite the lateness of the hour. He was a kind-looking old man, about Granddad's age. He tutted and frowned when he saw the state of my hands but didn't ask me anything about how it had happened. I think they must have had a word with him beforehand.

I sat on Nan's lap while the doctor abraded some of the dead skin, which made me cry out in fresh pain, then he dressed my palms and gave Nan a prescription for various

creams to prevent infection as well as sterile gauze dressings and junior aspirin. I was to refrain from using my
hands at all, he said, and the dressings were to be changed
every morning.

While he worked, Nan, Dad and Granddad looked on.
Their silence somehow intensified the seriousness of the
situation. When the doctor left, Granddad made me some
hot milk to sip through a straw – it tasted funny because I
think he had put some painkillers in it – then Nan carried
me up to bed and tucked me in. I lay there, drifting in and
out of sleep, and I could hear the three of them arguing
downstairs but couldn't make out what they were saying.
At least I felt safe, though. Maybe now I would be allowed
to stay at Nan Casey's and I wouldn't have to live with
Mummy any more.

When I woke the next morning my hands were locked
rigid – I couldn't move them at all – and very, very sore.
Nan had to feed me my breakfast with a spoon, as if I was
a baby.

'Can I stay with you now?' I asked her.

'Don't worry. You're not going back there,' she said
with determination, hugging me fiercely.

This was a huge relief to me, but I still slipped into a
severe depression that lasted some weeks. It was as if I had
a huge weight pressing down on my shoulders and a lump
in my chest that made it hard to talk. I didn't enjoy any of
the things I used to like before, such as jelly or sweets, or
Granddad's spinning top. For the first time in my life, I
remember thinking that I wanted to die, and the only
thing that held me back was that Mum had told me that
when I died I would go to hell, where the big fire was.
'You'll just burn in agony for the rest of time,' she'd said. I

didn't want to go there, especially now I knew what burning felt like, but I genuinely wanted my life to be over. I felt weary and scared and very, very bleak.

Dad brought my schoolbooks over and Nan started giving me daily lessons at the kitchen table. I think she knew how depressed I was because she and Granddad went out of their way to bring me treats, entertain me and cheer me up. I heard them talking about me when they didn't realize I was listening, trying to think of ways to bring me out of the black hole I'd slipped into.

The turning point came one day when they took me to the farm down the road. A new family had recently moved in and they had a daughter, Fiona – known to all as Fifi – who was six, like me. We looked at each other shyly. She had blonde curly hair in bunches and a cheeky freckled nose. There were smears of mud all over her dungarees and I thought how much trouble I would have been in with Mum if I had got dirty like that.

'Have you ever fed lambs before?' Fifi's mother asked me. 'We've got a couple of orphans who need to be bottle-fed. Their mums didn't want them. Why don't you two go and do it?'

I looked down at my hands, which still had sterile dressings on them. 'You go and watch,' Nan said. 'You'll be able to help soon.'

Fifi's mother gave her a couple of big milk bottles with rubber teats on top. We ran out of the farmhouse and across the courtyard. Two funny, woolly, black-faced creatures pranced up to the gate on their spindly legs. Fifi upturned the bottles and pushed them through the bars of the gate. The lambs bleated with excitement and jostled each other as they tugged at the teats, slurping down the milk. In the next field, the other, bigger sheep burst into a chorus of bleating.

'Why didn't their mums want them?' I asked Fifi.

'They're the runts. Too small and too ugly. We tried to get another sheep to take them, one that didn't have any lambs, but it didn't work out so now we have to look after them till they're bigger. Their real mums would try to kill them if we put them back in the field.'

'Why would they do that?' I was all ears.

'They want to save their milk for the lambs they like, the ones they've chosen, and they don't want these little ones bothering them.'

I wondered if this was why Mum was so cruel to me – maybe she was just saving herself for Nigel, the child she really liked.

* * *

After that Fifi and I started seeing each other every day. The school summer holidays began and the days were long and sunny. Nan made us picnic lunches in the back garden, spreading out a huge checked cloth and covering it with little sandwiches, fairy cakes, dolly mixtures, biscuits and juice.

Fifi and I didn't talk much about anything – I certainly didn't tell her what had happened to my hands – but we had a warm friendship based on our mutual love of animals and the outdoors. She was my first-ever friend, apart from Nigel, and before long I was wakening in the morning actually looking forward to the day ahead.

Dad brought Nigel to visit and Fifi and I let him join in our adventures. My bandages were finally taken off and, although my hands remained stiff and I had to be careful to keep the skin from drying out, I could join in most of the games. Granddad bought us some fishing nets and we went fishing for minnows in a nearby stream. Every day we rode on the ponies and helped to groom them and muck out the stables. We collected the eggs and fed the lambs. I tried to milk a cow once but just couldn't get my hands to grip hard enough.

I didn't see Mum at all for two or three months and no one even mentioned her name, so I assumed I wouldn't ever have to see her again. But a knot of anxiety at the back of my mind told me that she was my mother after all, and it might not be as simple as that.

* * *

One evening towards the end of August, Dad came for supper at Nan's and he sat me down at the kitchen table for a little chat.

'Lady Jane, I know you've been having a lovely time here but school starts again next week and I'm afraid you have to go back.'

Instinctively I looked down at my hands. 'Where will I go to school?' I asked, already scared of the answer.

'Well, your old school of course.' Dad seemed hesitant. 'Mummy's missing you very much. It's time to come home.'

'No!' I yelled at the top of my voice. 'I won't! You can't make me!'

Nan came hurrying into the room. I think she might have been listening outside the door.

'You promised me, Nan,' I screamed at her, stamping my feet. 'You said I didn't have to go back.'

'Darling, I'm sorry but she is your mother. She wants you back and there's nothing I can do about it.'

'She doesn't want me. Please don't make me. I could go to Fifi's school and stay here with you.'

I cried and pleaded for ages but could tell that the decision had already been made by the grown-ups. Nan had tears in her eyes that she kept wiping away with the back of her hand. She and Dad wouldn't look at each other and I could sense there had been a big row between them. Granddad came and sat beside her and put his arm round her shoulders. There was nothing to be done. I was going home to Bentley Road, back to the lioness's den.

Chapter 12

When I got back from Nan Casey's, Mum ignored me at first. I started school at nine o'clock and came home at three and she put supper on the table and told us when it was bedtime. Nigel hovered protectively around me, trying his best never to leave me on my own in a room with her. Sometimes I caught her looking at me in a way that made me very nervous; it was as though she was just waiting for me to put a foot wrong. She knew I lived in mortal terror of her now and I think she got a sadistic enjoyment from that.

* * *

One Monday afternoon a few weeks later, Nigel was going to play with a friend of his after school so I walked home alone up the gully and through the back garden. Mum was testy from the moment I walked in the door.

'We should really put you on a diet,' she snarled. 'You've got even fatter over the summer. But mind you, losing weight wouldn't make you any less ugly. There's not a lot we can do about that.'

'Shall I get changed out of my school uniform?' I asked, nervous about making any moves without her say-so. I knew the mood she was in. Her face was spiteful and the air crackled with vitriol.

She had been hand-washing some of her nylon stockings and they were lying damp in a basin, coiled snakes of American tan colour. 'I've got a job for you first. I need these dried,' she said. 'You can stand and hold them in front of the fire in the family room.'

'Why don't you hang them on the line?' I asked timidly.

'Because I want you to do it. That's why, Miss Smart Aleck.'

The fire was blazing away in the family room despite the fact that it was a mild October day outside. I was apprehensive: I'd never been asked to do this particular task before and I wondered if she was going to play some kind of trick. Mum stood me in front of the fire, facing towards it and pulled my arms out straight in front of me; then she draped a stocking over each hand.

'Just stand like that,' she said, 'and when these are dry you can do the next pair.'

'OK,' I whispered.

She went back to the kitchen, leaving the basin of stockings on the rug beside me. My hands were beginning to smart as the heat irritated my old burns so I took a tiny step backwards. Even then I could feel my palms tightening up and I remembered what the doctor had said about not letting the skin dry out, but what could I do? I took another tiny step back.

When Mum returned she snapped at me, 'They'll never dry like that. You're too far away.'

She grasped my shoulders and pushed me further towards the flames and at that moment the stocking in my right hand caught fire. It happened so quickly that I had no chance to drop it. There was a crackling sound as it shrivelled back and melted on to the back of my hand. Branded by scorching, molten nylon, I screamed in agony.

'You stupid girl,' Mum snapped. She grabbed me by the wrist and pulled me to the kitchen to run cold water on the burn; then she wrapped my hand in a wet tea towel. I was howling with the pain.

'For goodness sake, stop your snivelling. It's your own fault for not being more careful. Don't you dare try to blame me for this the way you did with the cooker. Not a word or you'll regret it.'

I looked at her through my tears and saw a glint in her eye that terrified me. I'm not sure whether she had meant me to get burned but I suspect she did. I just felt utterly hopeless.

When Dad got home, Mum cornered him first and told him that I had been playing with one of her stockings in the family room and I had gone too close to the fire.

He unwrapped the tea towel to have a look at my hand. 'Lady Jane, what happened?'

'It was my own fault, Daddy,' I said in a dull voice, and caught a triumphant look in Mum's eye. 'I stood too close to the fire.'

Dad gave me a worried look but didn't question the story. He put a fresh dressing on my hand but this time the wound didn't heal quite so cleanly. There's a patch of scar tissue on my right hand that still shows up as a purply, discoloured area fifty years on from the stocking incident.

* * *

As the second year of primary school began, I was even more of a loner, too scared to raise my head above the parapet either at school or at home. When the teacher asked me a question I'd whisper the answer so that she'd end up having to ask me to repeat it several times. I felt under constant, self-imposed pressure to make my handwriting neater, to get all my sums right and to keep my desk tidy. At home, I tried as hard as I could to second-guess Mum's thoughts and do what she wanted before she even asked. I cleaned my plate at every meal, folded my clothes neatly when I changed into my nightie at bedtime and played without making any sounds that might disturb her. Surely if I did nothing wrong, I would be safe?

But the fact that I hadn't told on her after the stocking incident seemed to give Mum confidence that she could begin punishing me again. Before long, she was beating me with the bean cane or the washing tongs and inflicting other punishments when she felt like it (or when God told her to, which amounted to the same thing).

I could have endured any amount of beating and punishment if that is where it ended. But just before Christmas 1956, something terrible happened that was to inaugurate a whole new era of misery in my life.

Chapter 13

Living at home again meant that I had to start going back to Grandma and Grandpa Pittam's house. Every second Saturday, Mum, Nigel and I went to visit. While Grandma was as hostile as ever, Grandpa began to take more interest in me.

One day he asked if I would like to go upstairs with him to see his horology room. Grandpa had a workroom at home where he used to spend hours tinkering with old clock mechanisms.

'Would you like to see it, Vanessa? It's my very special place,' Grandpa said.

'Yes please,' I replied. I didn't know whether I wanted to see it or not, but Grandpa was being so nice to me that I felt I ought to say yes.

We went upstairs together. The room was filled with ticking, chiming, whirring, metallic wheels and cogs, every surface cluttered with disembowelled clock parts. The sounds were noisy and unsynchronized. Shafts of light pierced the window blinds and dust motes danced in the air. Grandpa showed me a pocket watch that he said was over a hundred years old, a big old clock with weighted balls underneath that set off a chiming mechanism, and a Swiss cuckoo clock on the wall. I didn't like that clock. I got a huge fright when the cuckoo popped out.

'I wish you would be my friend, Vanessa,' Grandpa said wistfully. 'I get very lonely because no one really loves me.'

I was delighted to be asked. 'I'll be your friend,' I assured him. I felt sorry for him because Grandma obviously wasn't much fun to be around.

'Does that mean you'll play with me?' he asked.

I was eager to please so I said, 'Yes, what do you want to play?'

'Come here and I'll show you.'

I hesitated. No matter how nice he was being, I hated getting close to him because of the cloying scent of his pipe tobacco and the scratchiness of his bristles when he kissed me. He sat down on a wooden stool and beckoned me over towards him. I walked slowly across.

'This game makes me very happy,' he said. 'You want to make me happy, don't you?'

He lifted the hem of my dress and brusquely yanked down my pants with his roughened, calloused hands.

'But I don't need a wee-wee,' I complained, pulling away from him, and I stamped my foot.

'Do you know what men use to do wee-wees?' he asked, and I saw that he had pulled out a brown, wrinkly piece of flesh from his trousers, just between his legs. 'Here, touch it.' He took my hand and placed it over the disgusting object. It was soft and squishy like a big fat slug and it twitched under my fingers.

I jerked away. 'I don't like doing that, Grandpa.'

'Don't you want to make me happy? I'll take you to see the budgies after.' His face was flushed and his eyes glassy.

Just then the workroom door opened and Grandma looked in. I jumped back guiltily, afraid she might be cross with me, but she didn't even glance my way. She looked down at Grandpa's thing hanging out of his trousers.

'Not here, Charles,' she said in a stony voice. 'That goes on downstairs, not upstairs.'

She turned on her heels and walked out, shutting the door firmly behind her.

Grandpa zipped up his trousers, giving me a lewd wink. 'We'd better follow orders. Pull up your pants. Let's go and see the birds now.'

Nigel had been looking for me downstairs and when he heard we were going to the aviary he asked if he could come along – to my huge relief and to Grandpa's evident annoyance. He was quite rough as he pushed me inside the aviary and flapped his hands to make the budgies flutter in panic around my head while I shrieked in fear.

* * *

On the way home that day, it was on the tip of my tongue to mention to Mum that Grandpa had pulled my pants down and got his thing out, but something stopped me. Had I done anything wrong? Or did all little girls do this with their granddads? I had no way of knowing. I hoped it had just been a one-off though. His thing was smelly, like old cheese, and it didn't feel very nice. But Grandma had seen and not been cross, so I supposed it must be all right.

* * *

The next time we visited, Grandpa came in while Nigel and I were sitting on the scratchy horsehair sofa.

'Hello, Vanessa,' he said in a wheedling voice. 'Are you going to be my friend today?'

I hesitated. I wanted to say no but it felt rude. Finally I mumbled, 'OK.'

'Would you like to come to the garage to play with me?'

'Can Nigel come too?'

'Not today. I just want you and me to be friends today but Nigel can come another time.'

'I don't want to come to the garage unless Nigel comes too,' I said stubbornly, and folded my arms.

'You're not being a very nice girl today,' he pouted childishly. 'I thought you were my friend.'

'I am ... but ...'

'All right then,' he agreed. 'Nigel can come too and we'll show him our special game.'

We got up warily and followed him to the garage, Nigel sensing my reluctance. Grandpa had brought down his wooden stool from the workroom upstairs and he sat on it, unzipped his trousers and pulled out his brown, wrinkly thing.

'This is a big sausage, isn't it?' he addressed Nigel. 'You'll have one of these yourself one day.'

'Eeuuwwh. It's horrible,' Nigel exclaimed, wrinkling his nose, and Grandpa laughed gruffly.

'No, it's not. It's natural. Come here, Vanessa, come and make me happy.'

I walked hesitantly towards him with my hands firmly behind my back. He pulled one arm out and placed my hand squarely over his thing. 'Nigel, this is what big boys do when they're just a little bit older than you. We all do it.' His hand moved rhythmically on top of mine and the wrinkly thing got bigger.

I looked at Nigel and we caught eyes but he didn't say anything. My face was hot and I felt like crying. Nigel went and got on the rocking horse and started to rock back and forwards, making that eerie creaking sound.

Grandpa's breathing had gone funny now. I stared straight out the window at the fence at the end of the garden. A bird had landed on it and I tried to pretend I was that bird, about to fly away into the sky. Suddenly Grandpa's brown thing jerked and something warm and sticky was all over my hand. I looked down and there was white stuff everywhere, like the tapioca we sometimes had at school dinners. I pulled my hand away.

'Hang on, sweetheart,' Grandpa said. 'Let me wipe that for you.' He pulled a big, crumpled hanky with oil stains on it from his trouser pocket and wiped my hand carefully, then he wiped the rest of the white stuff from between his legs. My hand still felt sticky and I could smell a funny, musty kind of smell.

'Who wants to come and see the budgies now?' he asked cheerfully.

I didn't answer but Nigel said, 'No thanks, Grandpa. Not today.'

'Don't you want to come, Vanessa?'

I shook my head, keeping my hand held out so that it didn't touch my clothes.

After he'd gone, Nigel looked at me. 'Are you OK, Nessa?' he asked.

I nodded. 'Yeah.'

'Do you want to play kings and queens?' he asked. 'We could go out into the garden.'

We didn't talk specifically about what had just happened that day. Neither of us knew words to describe it and I suppose we were embarrassed.

At teatime, I didn't want to use my sticky hand. I picked up the salmon and cucumber sandwich with my left hand and chewed it slowly, feeling sick to my stomach. I could still smell that funny smell in my nostrils and it seemed to be coming from my hand now. Back home, in the bath, I scrubbed and scrubbed my hand with soap and the nail-brush until it smelled clean again.

* * *

Next time we visited, Nigel and I told Grandpa in unison that we didn't want to play in the garage today, but Grandma overheard and told us we had to. 'On you go. Get out from under my feet.'

We had no choice – we had to go with him.

Grandpa sat down on his stool and unzipped his trousers and this time he asked Nigel first. 'Nigel, it's your turn to play the sausage game. Come over here and put your hand on it. That's all you have to do.'

Nigel said, 'No, it's dirty.'

Grandpa turned to me with a sickly smile. 'Come on, Vanessa,' he said. 'You do it then. You're my favourite. If you play these games with me, it will just make me love you more and more.'

Somehow he knew that was my Achilles heel. I wanted more than anything to be loved because of Mum constantly telling me I was unloveable. Maybe putting my hand on the thing between his legs wasn't too high a price to pay.

I don't know why Nigel seemed to have the strength to resist him but I didn't, not then. Perhaps Grandpa was scared to force him in case he had a fit. There was one time Grandpa made Nigel kneel in front of him and put the brown, stale-smelling penis in his mouth but Nigel sank his teeth into it, causing him to yelp in pain. I didn't. I let him move my head up and down, gagging and choking, a cheesy smell in my nostrils and a bitter taste in my mouth when the white liquid squirted out.

I began to hear the voices in my head when I was with Grandpa and I focused on them, straining to make out the words, concentrating hard, trying to take my mind away from what was physically happening to me.

'Hello, Vanessa, we're your friends,' they were saying to me. 'Don't worry; you're going to be fine.' 'We love you, Vanessa.'

Every second Saturday from then on, when we arrived at the Pittams' house, Grandpa would be waiting eagerly to lead me straight to the garage.

'That'll put him in a good mood for the week,' I heard Grandma saying to Mum once as he pulled me by the hand to the garage step.

So they must know about it – Mum too. I'd wondered about that. If they knew, it must mean this was a normal thing that little girls did with their grandfathers and I just had to put up with it.

The voices in my head gave conflicting advice. 'Don't go in the garage. Stay away from him,' one said, but then another advised 'It's just one of those things. It happens to lots of little girls,' and a third said, 'You're lucky it doesn't really hurt.' As usual, it was hard to know what to think.

Still, I hated the taste, the feel and the smell of it. It made me feel dirty and horrible, as though I was a disgusting person and it was all my own fault it was happening.

* * *

One of the saddest side-effects of this was that I began to avoid being alone with Granddad Casey when we were over at their house in Rugeley. I stopped going to band the pigeons with him or collect eggs for breakfast from the farm. I never asked him to spin the spinning top any more or play games with me and I avoided being alone in a room with him at all times. I have a clear memory of the hurt look in his eyes one time when he asked if I'd like to go for a walk and I said 'No, thanks' and ran to hide behind Nan.

He could have had no idea why I was behaving in that way after the close, jokey relationship we'd had before. I feel bad about it now. I just knew in my six-year-old head that it would break my heart if Granddad Casey asked me to stroke or suck the thing between his legs and I decided never to put myself in a position where that might conceivably happen.

Chapter 14

We visited our grandparents on alternate weekends, usually on Saturday afternoons when Dad was playing sport. Every second weekend when I was at Nan Casey's I'd run to the farm to find Fifi. We played skipping games, hopscotch, teachers or doctors and nurses; and we helped with farmyard chores or baked cakes in Nan's kitchen. Sometimes I looked at Fifi's happy little face and wondered if she had to put up with all the things I did – the beatings, being locked in a cupboard and the disgusting sausage games I had to play with Grandpa Pittam every other Saturday. I would have liked to talk to her about it all but I didn't know how to bring it up. Also, I was scared that it would make her think badly of me and maybe she wouldn't be my friend any more, so I said nothing and just enjoyed the hours of respite from my other cares.

My seventh birthday came and went. Mum never gave a birthday party for me, but it was just as well because Fifi remained my only friend so it would have been a very small party. Around this time Nigel and I were dropping hints to some of the adults we knew about what was going on at home, but it seemed that no one believed us.

One Sunday we were in the kitchen at Rugeley when Granddad came in with an armful of garden canes, ready to stake out some plants. Instinctively Nigel shouted 'Run! Nessa, run!'

I sprinted out the kitchen door and found a hiding place behind the sofa in the front room, my heart beating so hard I thought it would burst out of my chest.

'What on earth is wrong, young man? Is this a game of some kind?' Granddad asked him.

'Please don't beat Nessa,' Nigel asked.

Granddad called Nan into the room straight away and when she heard what had been said, she came to find me. I trusted her absolutely and knew for a fact that she would never have beaten me, so I let her lead me back into the kitchen, where Granddad's canes lay in an untidy heap on the floor. He looked very hurt and upset that I had been scared of him. He had no idea why I had changed so much in the way I was with him. Nan pulled me on to her lap on the rocking chair and wrapped her plump arms around me, kissing my hair.

'Now what are you two on about?' she asked. 'Will someone please explain?'

I said nothing, just stared down at my hands. After a while, Nigel said, 'Mummy beats Nessa with canes just like these. I thought Granddad was going to beat her.'

Nan and Granddad looked at each other in horror. 'Are you sure she beats you with canes?' Nan asked me directly, in a kind voice. She swivelled me on her lap so she was looking into my eyes. 'Is that really true?'

I nodded very slowly, feeling nervous. What if they told Mum? I no longer believed that any other adult could protect me from her so I had to look after myself, basically by staying out of trouble.

'No one is going to hit either of you here,' Nan told us firmly. 'It will never happen so you can stop worrying right now. Vanessa, how often has she hit you? Once? Or twice?' She looked at my face. 'More?'

'Lots, but please don't say anything, Nan,' I begged her. 'She'll be cross with me. It's only when God tells her to do it.'

'Is that so? I'll make sure she's not cross with you.' She looked angry but forced herself to smile at us. 'Now who wants a biscuit? It's a lovely day, so why don't the two of you go and help Granddad in the garden?'

Mum had been visiting one of her sisters who lived nearby and she was picking us up at five o'clock. I think Nan sent me to the garden so she could have a word in private but as soon as I heard the doorbell, I sneaked indoors and hid behind the kitchen door so I could eavesdrop on their chat.

Nan reiterated what Nigel and I had told her, and I heard Mum snort with derision. 'Unbelievable! That girl has the most fertile imagination. I don't know where she gets it from.'

'But Nigel backed up her story.'

'I'm afraid Vanessa has been teaching him to lie on her behalf. There have been quite a few instances of it recently. She's a very dramatic child.'

'She seemed scared of some canes Thomas was carrying. She's not that good an actress.'

'Honestly, Winifred, you can't seriously think I beat her with a cane. Where are the marks? She's making it all up, just like she makes up those stories about voices in her head. She's got a powerful imagination and sometimes the distinction gets blurred between truth and fantasy. We need to keep an eye on that.'

'She said that God tells you to punish her. Why would she say that?'

'I don't know why, but she's got this idea that God's people come to her bedroom at night because she's been naughty. As I said, she's a very imaginative child. Now, if you don't mind I have to get these kids home and bathed and into bed. It's getting late.'

I darted back into the garden so as not to be caught sneaking around. Nan said nothing more to me about it but I think she was watching out for cane marks from then on. If I stayed overnight, she always sponged me very carefully in the bath, and even when I just visited for the afternoon she often came to the toilet with me so she could surreptitiously have a look at my bottom when I pulled my pants down.

Of course, if she knew I was staying over at Nan's, Mum would make sure there weren't any marks to be seen. That's why Monday was always such a bad day for me. Not only was Mum in a vile mood after a day spent doing the washing, but she could also let loose with the cane, safe in the knowledge that the ugly purple stripes and bruising would be on the mend by the time I next went to the Caseys'.

* * *

There's an old saying that if you beat one devil out, you beat seven in. I walked on eggshells at home when Mum was around, but that didn't stop me making my small gestures of defiance, no matter how dangerous they were for me. One time I took a packet of raw jelly from the shelf in the spider cupboard. I absolutely loved jelly and Mum never made it for us. I sneaked that packet upstairs to my bedroom and hid it in the secret place under the wardrobe, then, when I dared, I could break off a chunk and put it under my tongue so it melted and filled my mouth with a sickly-sweet goo.

I was also getting a little bit braver about telling Dad what was going on at home – not that it did me any good. One evening, I told Dad about the spider cupboard. I'd said something cheeky to him and I instinctively put my hands over my head for protection.

'Are you going to lock me in the spider cupboard?' I asked.

'What do you mean?' he demanded sharply.

'That's where Mummy puts me when I've been naughty. She locks me in there.'

Dad took me by the hand into the kitchen, saying, 'Muriel, what's this about locking Lady Jane in a cupboard?'

I hung my head, afraid to meet her eye.

Mum let out a gay peal of laughter. 'Now I've heard everything,' she said. 'I suppose there are dragons and witches and a wicked wolf in there, and you prick your finger on a spindle and fall asleep for a hundred years?'

Mum was wearing a scarlet cocktail dress with a full skirt and she had on matching nail polish and high-heeled mules. She always got changed into something special on the evenings when Dad came home. She'd style her hair and retouch her makeup and slip on her high heels just before he walked through the door. I gazed at her. She looked so beautiful and her laugh was so pretty that of course Dad was going to believe her and not me. At that instant, I disliked him for being taken in by her. Why couldn't he see the truth?

'You mustn't tell lies, Lady Jane,' he admonished. 'It's not very nice. Don't you know the story of the little boy who cried wolf?'

I did know that story but the point was that no one had come running the first time I cried wolf. Even after my hands were burned, and at last they seemed to realize that I wasn't safe at home, I was sent straight back out to the same field again where the wolf was prowling. I didn't understand it. What would it take for everyone to open their eyes and see what Mum was doing?

* * *

Round about this time our class had some homework to do. We'd started writing a story at school and mine was about a little girl who had an imaginary friend. The task was to finish the story and bring it in to the teacher the next day. We hadn't had much homework before – just the occasional Janet and John reading book – so Mum asked what I was doing.

'Writing a story,' I told her.

'What's it about?' she asked, peering over my shoulder. A sentence caught her attention and she grabbed the jotter from me. My story was about a little girl whose Mummy was always cross. The Mummy used to beat the little girl with a stick and lock her up in a cupboard but even though it hurt, the little girl didn't mind so much because she had an imaginary friend who whispered comforting words and cheered her up.

'This is a terrible story!' Mum cried. 'You can't hand this in.' She ripped the offending pages clean out of the jotter and started tearing them to pieces.

I gasped and tried to grab them back. 'Mummy, the teacher will be cross with me. You've spoiled my jotter.'

'Nonsense. It just needs the torn bits trimmed off. Sit right there and don't move. Did the teacher look at it before you came home?'

'No,' I admitted.

She got some scrap paper from the kitchen cupboard, sat down and drafted out another story about a little girl who was very lonely so she invented an imaginary friend. Her mummy used to set out a plate of food and a glass of juice for the friend at dinner times and she'd always give the little girl two sweeties, so there was one for her friend. Then one day a new family moved in next-door and the little girl got friendly with the daughter and she forgot all about her imaginary friend.

When she'd finished, Mum handed it to me. 'Copy that in your homework jotter,' she demanded. 'I can't believe you've forgotten everything I've told you about not letting anyone at school find out how naughty you really are. They'll all hate you if they realize.'

'But the story wasn't about me,' I protested. 'It was about a little girl I made up.'

'Your story was totally wrong and you would have got into big trouble with the teacher if you had handed it in. Don't do it again!'

I sat and copied out the replacement story and Mum used her dressmaking scissors to tidy up the torn bits in my jotter. I thought at the time, although I didn't say so, that her story was much more boring than mine.

But my mother's next revelation was to prove a great deal more interesting.

Chapter 15

It was just a few days before my eighth birthday, and Nigel was almost nine, when Mum called us into the dining room one day after school and beckoned for us to sit down at the gleaming dark-wood table. This was virtually unprecedented and we glanced at each other nervously, unsure what to expect. Mum stood with her back to the window regarding us with a very serious expression.

'I've got something important to tell you both, which you should be old enough to understand now.' She paused for dramatic effect, looking from one to the other of us. 'The thing is that I'm not your real mummy, and Daddy is not your real daddy. You were both adopted when you were babies. We took you in so that you wouldn't have to stay in a children's home.'

'You're not our mummy?' Nigel sounded flabbergasted. I was too confused to say anything.

Mum nodded. 'That's right. I'm not.'

'What about Nan Casey? Is she our real Nan?' Nigel asked. I held my breath.

'No, she's not,' Mum said. 'None of your grandparents are blood relatives.'

I started to cry, because I wanted so much for Nan Casey to be my real Nan. I wanted more than anything to be allowed to go and live with her one day and not stay with Mum any more.

Nigel kept up the questioning. 'So who is our real Mum then?'

'You've got different mothers. Yours,' she nodded at Nigel, 'was a very pretty young girl but she had to give you up because she wasn't married. She cried and cried when it was time to hand you over and although she had no money, she made sure you were beautifully dressed. She begged me, "Please take care of him and love him as if he was your own."'

I was listening hard. 'What about Nessa's real mum?' Nigel asked.

'She was old and ugly. That's why Vanessa's so ugly now. People usually only pick the pretty babies from children's homes and she was left over because no one wanted her. They said to us, "You've already got one good-looking baby so please take this ugly girl to get her off our hands."'

I was sobbing now and a glance at Mum's malicious expression told me she was pleased with the effect she was having. This was yet another of her sadistic games.

'In fact,' Mum continued, in a speech that was openly racist, 'Vanessa's real father was a darkie. She's got black blood in her; that's why she always goes so dark-skinned if the sun comes out.'

It was true that I tanned very quickly and had a much darker skin tone than Nigel. Mum was always commenting on it.

'I just want you both to know that you owe a lot to your dad and me. We didn't have to take you on. I often wish I hadn't, because you're such a handful. If you're ever really naughty, I may just decide to take you back to the children's home and leave you there to rot with all the other naughty children no one wants.'

I considered this idea. It didn't sound all bad to me.

'What about our real mummies?' Nigel asked. 'Couldn't we go back to them?'

Mum smiled grimly. 'They don't want you. That's why they gave you away in the first place. They've probably got more children of their own now, their own families, and the last thing they want is some snivelling brats turning up on their doorsteps.' She looked at my tears in disgust. 'Oh, for goodness sake go and blow your nose. Get out of my sight. You know the truth now, so I don't have to tell you again.'

Nigel put his arm round me as we left the dining room. 'Nessa, it's good news because it means we're allowed to get married to each other when we're older. Brothers and sisters aren't really supposed to, but we can because we've got different parents.'

This speech didn't comfort me, though. There were two people in the world who tried to look after me – Nan Casey and Nigel – and I'd just found out that neither of them was my proper family. If only I could find my real mother one day. Surely she would love me, despite what Mum said? She'd have to, wouldn't she?

* * *

The conversation with Mum raised dozens of questions in my head, and explained a lot of things as well. When I asked Dad why he hadn't told me I was adopted, he said,

'It makes no difference. You're as special to me as any child could ever be. You're my Lady Jane and nothing will ever change that.'

'Can I see my real mum?' I asked him, and he said, 'You're too young. Enjoy being a little girl for now and we'll explain more to you later when you're old enough.'

The news made a kind of sense to me. No wonder Mum resented me if she hadn't wanted to adopt me in the first place. That's why I didn't look anything like her or Dad or Nigel, I realized. That's why I wasn't pretty. That's why Mum couldn't love me. I started to feel more detached from her and to plan ways I could get away from her. I thought quite a lot about going to live in a children's home, but I didn't think I would like it. It would be like being at school all the time, and maybe they would make me eat cabbage and boiled beef.

It occurred to me to wonder if I was being punished because my real mother had committed a sin. God punished sinners, didn't he? Was that why he kept telling Mum to beat me? The logic made sense to me although it seemed very unfair.

* * *

The day after the chat with Mum, I got home from school to find the door locked and no one home. I didn't have a key. Nigel had gone to play with a school friend so I sat down on the doorstep on my own. I was feeling so insecure after the adoption bombshell that it crossed my mind to wonder whether Mum had abandoned me. Maybe she'd never come back.

Aunt Edna from next-door popped her head out and called, 'Is your mum not back? I'm sure she'll be home soon, but why don't you come in and wait at mine?'

I hesitated, suspecting that I would probably get into trouble with Mum for this. I knew Aunt Edna and Mum had had a big row about something and didn't even speak any more, but Edna was so kind that I finally agreed. We went into her kitchen and I sat down on a little wooden stool while she got me a glass of squash. She opened the biscuit barrel and let me choose whatever I wanted. I had a chocolate bourbon, a custard cream and then a chocolate digestive.

'Are you all right, little one? You look a bit down.'

And so I told her about how my real mummy didn't want me and my adoptive mummy didn't love me and if I was naughty she might send me back to the children's home.

Aunt Edna's lips pursed very tightly and I thought I saw a glint of tears in her eyes. 'I wish you were my little girl,' she said. She'd never had children of her own. 'I would love you to pieces. I think you are just fantastic.'

I considered this option and said, 'I could ask Mummy if I could come and live with you.'

'No, no,' she said hurriedly. 'Don't do anything to make your mummy more angry, whatever you do. She's quite often angry with you, isn't she?'

'Yes,' I agreed. 'She can't stand the sight of me.'

'Does your mummy ever hurt you?' she asked, looking at me with sad eyes. 'Sometimes I hear you crying in the garden.'

I was wary. I always seemed to be disbelieved if I told adults about the beatings and the other punishments, and then Mummy got cross with me later. I chose my words with great care. 'Only if I'm very naughty, then God tells her to hurt me,' I said, thinking this was a fair assessment.

'How does she hurt you?'

I was beginning to feel very uncomfortable. 'Oh, you know, just hitting and stuff. With the bean cane on my bottom.'

'Does she hit you hard?'

'Hmm. Quite hard, I think. But only if I'm naughty.'

Edna gave me a big hug, and when we heard Mum coming home she let me sneak through her back garden into ours so I could pretend I had been there all the time.

It felt good to know that Aunt Edna had heard something of what went on at number 39 – it meant that she believed me. Knowing there was someone next-door I could talk to, and who said she wished I were her little girl, made me feel a tiny bit safer.

I suspect that Edna may have not been able to stop herself confronting Mum about what went on. If she did, it shows that she wasn't able to tolerate such cruelty going on within earshot and knowing that an innocent child was being beaten so viciously. I don't know what was said but the relationship between Edna and my mother deteriorated even further, to the point where they ignored each other entirely and walked past each other on the street in frosty silence.

Then even this small safety line was ripped away.

Chapter 16

During the summer holidays in 1958, the year I was eight, Mum began packing all our belongings into boxes, suitcases and tea chests.

'What's happening?' I asked.

'None of your business,' she said brusquely. 'You'll find out.'

My first, instinctive fear was that she, Dad and Nigel were moving somewhere else and they wouldn't take me with them.

'Are you going away?'

She gave me an exasperated look. 'We're all going, if you must know. We're moving house. We're leaving Bentley Road.'

'Where are we moving to?'

'I'm not answering your questions,' she said. 'It's because you've been so naughty that we have to move. God told me that you stole sweets from the corner shop down the road.'

This was nonsense, of course. I would never have dared. I braced myself for punishment for this supposed crime but none was forthcoming. Mum seemed distracted, and didn't pay us much attention.

The voices in my head were working overtime. 'You're going to the home for naughty children,' one said. 'No she's not, she's going to a very old house beside water.' 'It's far away, and no one lives nearby.' 'There's an old well in a lane by the garden.' 'Maybe they won't take her with them.'

It was hard to know what to believe.

I asked Dad if I was being taken to the children's home and he gave Mum a sharp look and snapped, 'No, of course not.'

It was obvious that the atmosphere was very strained between them. They were frequently snapping at each other, and I could hear raised voices at night as I lay in bed. The reasons for our move were never explained to us, but I sensed there was something odd about it. Hardly anyone I knew had moved away – it was much more common to stay in the area you came from and when you wanted a bigger house, you only went a couple of streets away. Now we would be further away from our families and from Dad's work and, in the event, Mum lost all her dressmaking clients because it was just too far for them to travel for fittings.

I had a feeling that one of the reasons for the move was because Mum didn't like Aunt Edna knowing about her punishment of us kids and that we had to get away from a place where someone knew the truth about what went on behind closed doors.

* * *

Arrangements for our house move continued. The ornaments, pictures, mirrors and rugs disappeared, along with most of my clothes and toys. On the morning the big, grey removal vans turned up outside, all that was left in the kitchen was one bowl each for Nigel and me to have cereal and a few cups and teaspoons so that Mum could make tea for the removal men.

Whirly was put into a cardboard box for the journey and his hutch dismantled to go in one of the vans. Nigel and I were sent into the back garden out of the way, and I sat beside Whirly's box, whispering reassuring words in case he was scared. One by one our sofas, beds, tables and chairs were carried out to the vans. Aunt Edna came into her back garden to say goodbye to us over the fence, and she had tears in her eyes.

'You two will look after each other, won't you? Remember, I'll be here if you ever need me.'

'Thank you, Aunt Edna,' I replied politely, though I had no idea how I would ever reach her if I needed her. 'Goodbye.'

'Goodbye, sweetheart.' She gave me a final kiss on the cheek and hurried back inside her house.

I felt nervous, but at the same time my head was buzzing with voices, all telling me different things, and I had a sense of excitement about the trip.

When everything was packed, Mum, Dad, Nigel, Whirly and I got into the car and waved goodbye to 39 Bentley Road. There was a sniffing sound and, looking over into the front seat, I realized Mum was crying. She was dabbing at her eyes with a handkerchief and desperately trying to control the sobs that slipped out. It was quite shocking. I had never in my life heard her crying before.

'What's wrong, Mummy?' I asked tentatively.

She didn't answer, so after a minute or so Dad said, 'Your mum's a bit sad to be leaving all her old friends behind. That's all.'

I pondered this for a while. I'd never known any of Mum's friends. She didn't have visitors except the ladies she made clothes for who came for fittings, and she never went out in the evenings. I'd never heard her chatting on the phone, the way Nan Casey did when we stayed there. Somehow I couldn't imagine Mum with proper friends.

Dad tried to make desultory attempts at conversation but Mum was not responding. She seemed quite cross with him – cross and sad and distant.

Nigel tried asking again, 'Dad, where are we going to live now?'

He hesitated before replying, and I butted in. 'I know where we're going.' The voices in my head had been telling me all about it for days now. 'It's a very old cottage and there's some water just beside it. There aren't many other houses nearby but there is a big garden with a well in the lane beside it. That's where we're going to live.'

Dad's foot jerked on the accelerator and the car lurched. 'Did you tell her that, Muriel?'

Mum turned round to glare at me. 'How did you know that? Who have you been talking to?'

I whispered my reply, nervous about their response. 'It was the voices in my head.'

'Don't lie!' Mum snapped. 'I'm fed up to the back teeth hearing about your bloody voices.' She turned to Dad. 'She must have overheard us talking about it, that's all.'

No, I didn't, I thought, but I was smart enough not to say it out loud. I had only spoken of the constant chatter of voices in my head a few times, without thinking. It had become a normal state of affairs to me – this varied commentary that went on in my head – and sometimes I forgot that it was best not to mention it. It used to drive Mum into a rage so I'd learned to keep quiet about my invisible companions.

* * *

We seemed to drive for ages but eventually we turned off the main roads into a setting that was much wilder and more rural. Straggling hedges grew by the roadside, separating us from wide-open expanses of fields. Up above, the sky seemed a brighter shade of blue than it had been closer to town, and wispy trails of cloud floated past. Nigel had fallen asleep, as he always did on long car journeys, and I sat quietly looking out the window and listening to my voices, which were very loud and almost continual that day.

'We'll play with you,' they said. 'No one else lives nearby but you'll always have us.' 'Don't tell your Mum about us. She doesn't understand.'

I wasn't sure if any other children heard voices like me. Nigel said he didn't. While Mum and Dad preferred it if I didn't talk about them, Nan Casey didn't mind hearing about them and had recently told me the voices I heard were those of angels, which was a very nice thought. I got the impression that maybe she had heard them as well.

Suddenly there was a thud and Nigel and I were nearly jolted off the seat; of course, no one wore seat belts in those days. Dad had turned on to a narrow, bumpy lane full of ruts and potholes. We turned a bend and there were four cottages: three small, pink-painted ones on the right, and a big, dilapidated one on the left exactly like the picture I had in my head. I immediately knew that was where we were going to live.

'Here we are, kids,' Dad said in a falsely jolly voice. 'This is Shernal Green, your new home.'

An old woman appeared in the doorway. 'Look!' I shouted in excitement. 'Nan Casey has come to welcome us.'

'What on earth are you talking about?' Mum asked sharply. 'There's no one here.'

'Oh,' I said, disappointed, because as we got closer I could see it wasn't Nan after all. 'It's another lady.' She was wearing a long, black dress and a white apron, and there was a lace-trimmed bonnet on her head. 'Who is she?'

Dad parked the car outside the gate. 'Who do you mean, Lady Jane?' he asked, peering round to see where I was pointing.

'There!' I gestured. 'She's standing in the doorway.' As I watched, she turned and walked back into the house, right through the closed front door. I blinked hard.

'There's no one there.' Dad frowned. 'Are you seeing things?'

'Did you see her?' I asked Nigel, and he shook his head.

Just then I heard more voices saying 'The new people are here – but have they got children?' and I gave a little shudder. I was used to the voices and I wasn't scared of them any more after my chat with Nan, but who was the woman who had walked through the door? Why could no one else see her? 'She used to live here,' a voice told me. 'A long time ago.'

The cottage had crumbling, redbrick walls, a red, tiled roof, lots of windows and a huge chimney-breast at either end. It looked as though it hadn't been inhabited for a long time, because the gate was hanging off its hinges, the garden was overgrown with nettles, and tall weeds were releasing white fluffy spores that floated through the air.

As we climbed out of the car, I saw the canal. About ten feet wide, it ran right alongside the house and through the isolated little hamlet. 'There's the water, just like I said,' I couldn't resist pointing out.

Dad had pulled a key-chain from his pocket. He selected one and walked up to the wooden porch to try it in the front door. It didn't work and he had to try every last key on the chain before getting the right one. I could tell it was making him a little bit bad-tempered. Mum stood back with her arms folded, obviously in a bad mood herself. I went to get Whirly's travelling box from the boot and he looked up at me as if to ask what was going on. Where were his hutch and his carrot tops?

Inside the house there was a large, musty hallway and I immediately felt as though the atmosphere was creepy. It was certainly very rundown, with crumbling plasterwork, wobbling banisters and a pervasive smell of damp. There was a lounge with an old fireplace to the right of the hall and a dining room to the left, and the kitchen and utility area ran right along the back of the house. Mum showed us our bedrooms and I was pleased that mine had a view of the canal from its window.

The furniture vans arrived and Nigel and I were sent out to play in the garden so the men didn't trip over us as they carried everything inside. It was a big garden, about an acre and a half, and when we walked into the lane outside, in front of the other cottages across the way, sure enough there was the old well I'd been told about by the voices. Some planks were balanced over the top but Nigel and I pulled them out of the way so we could drop stones down.

'One elephant, two elephants, three elephants, four elephants,' we recited before we heard the 'plop' way down below that told us the stone had hit the water.

There was a huge clump of hollyhocks at the top end of the garden and I eyed them warily because Dad had told me they were poisonous. Further round, behind the kitchen, there was a kind of enclosure that I later found out was an old pigsty. It was about ten-foot square with a corrugated tin roof, a mud floor and wooden picket fencing round about. The roof was tall enough that I could stand up in it – just – but Nigel had to stoop or he bumped his head.

Walking further, we spotted a huge water butt that collected run-off water from the roof and gutters. It had a little tap at the bottom so we played with that for a while, splashing each other and shrieking with laughter. Nigel had a thing about taps. Back in Bentley Road he'd often get into trouble with Mum for turning on taps to play with the water, then forgetting to turn them back off again.

We'd been told very firmly that we were to stay in the garden and not wander out near the canal, but the grown-ups were so busy that day that no one seemed to be keeping an eye on us. We'd never seen a canal close up before and here was one just at the end of our garden. Glancing back to make sure no one was watching from the house, we slipped through a small gap in the hedge. There were cycle tracks along the grass verge, then huge clumps of brown bulrushes before the water's edge. We sat down on a patch of grass and looked into the water. Much of it was overgrown with lime-green weeds that strained this way and that with the movement of the water. Between the patches of weeds that extended from either bank there was a dark blue-grey channel that looked very deep. As we watched, a silvery fish came up to the surface, gulped a fly and dived into the depths again.

It was very, very quiet. Just beyond the other cottages, there was a road but no cars drove along it. We couldn't hear any traffic sounds at all. There was a very distant mooing of cows, the buzzing of summer insects, the wind in the bulrushes, and the muffled voices of the men carrying furniture into our new house.

'Do you like it here?' Nigel asked me.

'Not sure,' I said. 'It's a bit creepy.' I couldn't put it into words but I felt instinctively that I would be less safe in such an isolated spot than I had been in the neat semi-detached house on Bentley Road, where we were surrounded by neighbours and with Edna next door.

'The garden's nice and big, though. And maybe Dad will let me go fishing in the canal.'

'Maybe,' I said doubtfully. A voice in my head was warning me something about Nigel and the canal but I couldn't make it out.

'Do you think we'll still see Nan Casey?' he asked, striking terror in my heart.

'Course! Why wouldn't we?'

'I think she's in the wrong direction. We're much further away from her house than we were before.'

I hadn't thought through all the repercussions of a house move. But perhaps it also meant that we were further from Grandma and Grandpa Pittam. I wouldn't mind that at all – I hated going there so much, and I was never allowed to escape the awful task of making Grandpa 'happy'.

But even if that was one good outcome of the move, we were still far from everything we knew.

'How will we get to school?' I asked.

'We'll have to start a new school,' Nigel guessed.

'I didn't see any schools on the way here.'

'S'pose there must be one somewhere.'

We sat gloomily for a while.

'Who was that lady you saw at the door, Nessa?' Nigel asked eventually.

'I dunno, I think maybe she used to live here.'

'Is she alive?'

I hadn't thought this through properly but now of course I could see that she wasn't, because she had walked through a locked door. 'No,' I told him.

'That means she's a ghost. You're lucky you can see ghosts. I wish I could.'

I can hear ghosts! I thought to myself. So that's what the voices are – they're people who were alive and have died. And I can see them too.

I wondered why I could see and hear them, and why they chose me to speak to. Was it a good thing or not? I knew that they couldn't hurt me, but they could still scare me. And I knew that this place was full of them.

When I went to bed that night, the air was thick with children's voices whispering to each other, and disembodied faces were dancing all over the walls. It was an eerie experience and there was no way I could sleep with all the activity in the room. Mum had hung my old curtains at the window but they didn't fit right across and I could see lights twinkling outside.

Curious, I went to the window to look out and there, to my horror, was the old woman who had stood in the doorway earlier – except now she was hovering a few feet above the canal. I screamed as loudly as I could until I heard footsteps clattering up the stairs. Mum burst into the room.

'Why are you not in bed?' she demanded.

'There's a ghost,' I said. 'The old woman. She's in the canal.'

Mum drew her hand right back and slapped me across the face with her full strength so that I fell and cracked my head on the bedside cabinet.

'Will you shut up about your voices and your ghosts or you'll be locked up in a funny farm one day! Don't you think I've got enough on my plate right now without dealing with you as well?'

She raised her hand to hit me again, so I scrambled into bed and pulled the eiderdown right up to my eyes.

'If I hear another murmur out of you tonight, I'll make you wish you'd never been born,' she threatened, then turned and walked out, slamming the door behind her.

I touched the sore place where my head had hit the cabinet and it was sticky with blood. Mum didn't realize that there had already been plenty of times in my life when

Punished

I wished with all my heart that I had never been born. The world was a scary, dangerous place for me and I could feel instinctively that it was about to get even scarier.

Chapter 17

When we first moved into Shernal Green, the cottage was virtually derelict. There was no running water so, until it was connected, Nigel and I had to carry in buckets of water from the well. Every room needed extensive plastering work and redecoration, so it was like living on a building site for the next few months. Mum was distracted, busy choosing paint colours, running up curtains and making endless cups of tea for the workmen.

Nigel and I started at Tibberton village school. To get there we had a one and a half mile walk down twisting country lanes to Oddingley parish hall, then a coach ride to Tibberton. At first I liked it. It was smaller than my last school and the teachers were very friendly and eager to help me settle in. I was further on in maths than the others in my class, and my reading was at the same standard, so I didn't have to worry about catching up. However, after we'd been there a couple of weeks Nigel had an epileptic fit in the classroom and I think it gave everyone quite a fright. They'd probably never seen anyone in that condition before, writhing on the floor, moaning and with saliva dribbling down his chin. No matter how many times I'd seen it, I never got used to it. I always panicked that he was going to choke and die.

Next day, as we approached school together someone shouted out, 'Hey, Loony Boy, are you going to have a fit today?'

'Ignore them,' I warned Nigel, but a small group of four or five boys and two girls crowded round us, jostling us and taunting, 'Loony Boy, Loony Boy!'

Nigel lost his temper and lashed out wildly. Unfortunately he hit the glasses one of the girls was wearing. They flew off and smashed on the ground and there was a communal gasp of shock.

'Look what you've done! You'll have to pay for these.'

'Leave him alone,' I said. 'It was your own fault. He can't help having epilepsy.'

'It speaks,' quipped one of the girls and they both giggled.

Nigel and I walked into school without saying anything more, but the friendly atmosphere had changed. From then on, the other kids gave us a wide berth because we were 'strange', not quite like them, and they didn't feel comfortable around us. As Nigel's sister, I was instantly tarred with the same brush as him. Faced with something they didn't understand, the children herded together to ostracize us.

* * *

Back at the cottage, Mum seemed to be permanently in a grumpy mood so I stayed out of her way as much as possible. Nigel often locked horns with her though. He was still her favourite and she indulged him in ways I could never expect but at the age of nine, going on ten, he was pushing his luck more and more. He'd make faces behind her back, leave taps running, trample mud on the floors and help himself to food from the pantry. Mum was so busy with the renovation work on the house that a lot of this slipped by unnoticed. Even I had more freedom than normal. When we'd been there a month, I'd hardly been punished at all and the bean cane hadn't been brought into the kitchen.

Dad was rarely there – he only ever appeared at weekends now – and Mum seemed sad and preoccupied. She often just heated a tin of beans and served them with tinned corned beef or Spam for our supper, rather than cooking a proper nutritious meal with vegetables. Sometimes she forgot to tell us it was bedtime and we stayed up till nine or even ten o'clock.

Given the relaxation of discipline, Nigel and I relaxed as well – him more than me. One day he got in from school and dropped his schoolbag in the hall before running into the kitchen to get a drink of juice. Mum was in the pantry deciding which cans she was going to heat for our tea.

'What do you think you're playing at?' she challenged him. Then her eagle eyes spotted the schoolbag right in the middle of the hall floor. 'Put the juice cup down and pick up your bag right away before one of the workmen falls over it and sues me.' Her tone was that of cold, nasty Mummy and I shrank back into a space beside the dresser, trying to make myself invisible.

'Get it yourself,' Nigel quipped, turning his back on her.

'Watch out!' I screamed seconds later as a tin of beans hurtled through the air. Nigel turned slightly and that move probably saved him from a serious concussion. The tin hit the wall at full speed, causing a huge chunk of plaster to fall out, then it ricocheted off his shoulder before crashing to the ground. He cried out in pain and shock. Mum stormed across the kitchen, grabbed him by the ear and marched him out to the hall, where she forced him to pick up the bag.

'Go up to your room! Get out of my sight!' she shouted at him and kicked his bottom, causing him to lurch forwards on to the stairs.

I considered my own position and decided to get out of her way, so I slipped out the back door and walked down the garden to an overgrown patch of lawn. I picked a long blade of grass and slit it with my thumbnail, then blew through it to create funny tunes, something Dad had shown me. I wondered if Nigel would be allowed to come out to play but thought it unlikely after that scene. He'd gone too far. Mum might have lightened up on our punishments in the new house but she was never going to put up with downright cheek like that.

When I reckoned it was teatime, I wandered back to the kitchen and peered in. No one was in the kitchen so I opened the door quietly and walked down the hall, poking my head round doors until I found Mum and Nigel in the sitting room. Nigel was lying on the sofa with a cloth on his forehead, his eyes closed. Mum was sitting in an armchair knitting, her needles clacking furiously.

'Your brother's had a fit,' she said. 'You'll have to get your own supper. There's some bread in the bread bin and leftover Spam in the fridge. Go and make a sandwich. You're old enough to feed yourself now.'

I looked at Nigel. His face was deathly white and he was so still I wasn't even sure he was breathing. 'Is he all right?' I asked.

'Of course he's not all right. He's got epilepsy,' Mum snapped. 'As if I don't have enough bloody trials in my life. Go on – don't you add to my worries tonight.'

I slipped off to the kitchen and made my sandwich, taking great care not to leave any crumbs on the tabletop. After I'd finished, I pulled a chair over to the sink and washed up my plate and knife then put them away. I was determined not to give her a single cause for complaint. The voices in my head were speaking to me again. 'He's not very well.' 'Maybe he needs a doctor.' 'Where's your dad? Why doesn't he come home?' 'Keep out of her way tonight. Put yourself to bed.'

I followed their advice and after supper I went up to the bathroom, brushed my teeth and washed my face and hands, then undressed and went to bed. All was silent in the house. I dozed off, then wakened with a start a couple of hours later. My first thought was to be worried about Nigel. I crept out to his room as quietly as I could, my heart in my mouth every time the floorboards creaked.

Nigel was tucked up in bed, his chest rising and falling peacefully, and I watched him for a while feeling a great rush of love for him. My brave, crazy big brother – imagine standing up to Mum like that! I was so relieved that he seemed to be all right again. But I was also aware that our holiday from Mum's ire was now over. Our bad, angry Mummy had returned.

* * *

Over the next few weeks Nigel was frequently absent from school. Mum said he wasn't feeling well but when I asked him he said he was fine, just a bit tired. They'd changed the medication he was taking to control the epilepsy and the new brand didn't seem to be agreeing with him so well.

I hated doing the walk to and from school on my own, especially as the nights got darker and more wintry. I was always afraid that someone was going to jump out from a hedge and attack me in the fading light. I developed a system of breaking down the journey into manageable chunks. When I walked along the side of the main road, I kept to the right on the way to school and the left on the way back. I ran full tilt along the twisty sections with tall, overgrown hedges on either side, then walked the parts that were more open, with fields stretching to the horizon. If I saw anyone coming towards me I'd duck behind a hedge and wait, completely still, until they'd passed, then I'd go back to my walking or running rhythm again.

One day it was raining hard as I walked home. I took my plastic Rainmate from my schoolbag and tied it over my head but the raindrops were still trickling down the back of my blazer. I accidentally splashed in a puddle that was deeper than I'd thought so my socks and shoes were wet through and that's what I was worrying about when I reached home. Mum would be furious.

I went to the back door first but it was locked and I couldn't see anyone through the glass. I went round to the front door but it was locked as well. I rang the doorbell but there was no answer, so I stood under the wooden porch for a while, thinking they'd be back any minute.

Mum had probably gone on the bus to take Nigel to the doctor, or to pick up some shopping.

The rain got heavier and heavier, huge drops splattering off the ground and spraying my legs. There was a leak somewhere in the porch awning and my blazer was getting drenched. I started shivering. Where could I shelter until they returned? We hadn't met the neighbours yet – I didn't even know their names – so I thought I'd better not knock on their doors. Instead, I decided to go and sit in the pigsty. I sprinted across the garden and through the little gate. The roof was watertight and the earth was dry so I sat down and hugged my knees to my chest, rocking back and forth to try and keep warm.

It was very dark and stars were twinkling in the sky when I saw car headlights coming down the lane. The rain had abated but I was still soaked to the skin and shivering with cold. When the car pulled up, both Mum and Dad got out and I was relieved. Mum wouldn't be able to punish me so harshly for getting wet if Dad was there. I crept round to the front door.

'Are you all right?' Dad called. He came up to put an arm round me. 'Christ, you're soaked. We got back as soon as we could.' He took his key out and unlocked the front door.

'Take your shoes and socks off and go straight up for a bath,' Mum ordered. 'Look at the state of you.'

'She won't have eaten, Muriel.'

'Bath first then I'll make her a snack.'

I was halfway up the stairs before it occurred to me to ask, 'Where's Nigel?' I turned round. They looked at each other awkwardly then Dad spoke.

'That's where we've been. You've probably noticed that Nigel's not been very well recently and we've been talking to the doctors, trying to decide what to do to give him the best chance of getting better.'

I felt as though my heart had stopped beating as Dad spoke, such a terrible sense of foreboding filled me from top to toe.

'Anyway, they decided it would be best to take him to live in a special school with other children who have problems like his. It's in a place called Surrey, quite a long way away from here, so your mum and I took him there today.'

'When's he coming back?' I asked, scarcely daring to breathe in case I missed a vital piece of information.

'Well, we don't know yet. It depends how he gets on. You have to be brave, Lady Jane. I know you're going to miss him but we all want what's best for him.'

Mum hadn't spoken. I looked at her now and caught just a glimpse of triumph in her expression. Nothing tangible, but I became convinced that this was all her doing and I hated her with a passion. She didn't like having a son with epilepsy. It embarrassed her. It was a burden for her to deal with his fits, and she didn't like being perceived by the outside world as having anything less than the perfect family. Now it was just going to be her and me. We caught eyes and I could see her thinking the same thing.

'When can I visit him?' I asked.

'We're not sure. Soon, I hope,' Dad said. 'You can write to him if you want to. I'll get you some envelopes and stamps and you can tell him everything that's happening here. He'd like that.'

'Go and get in your bath now,' Mum ordered. 'You're dripping on the stairs.'

Punished

I could barely raise the energy to climb the stairs and get in the bath. Every part of me felt heavy and exhausted. I missed my big brother so badly it was as though someone had stabbed me in the heart and ripped a great big gash through my chest. Now, for the first time, I was completely and utterly alone.

Chapter 18

'It's because you're not a nice child. You were a bad influence on him and that's why Nigel had to go to a special school. It's all your fault. You've only got yourself to blame.'

Mum was walking so fast, her stilettos clicking noisily on the pavement, that I was half-running to keep up with her. We were on our way to Grandma and Grandpa Pittam's house, which was the last place I felt like hurrying to. I was particularly apprehensive because it was the first time I'd ever been there without Nigel.

'You were always winding him up,' Mum continued. 'That's why he had the fits. If it wasn't for you he'd be able to lead a normal life and go to a normal school.'

I was eight and old enough to know this wasn't true, but I didn't contradict her. I said as little as possible to her these days, wary of accidentally making her cross. Without Nigel, I had no courage, no energy. I felt as though a part of me had been amputated, as though there was a huge, gaping space by my side. The only thing that kept me going was the hope that he'd be cured soon and he'd come back to live with us again. Surely it wouldn't be long.

At first, I wrote to him every day – about little things, like Whirly eating a tomato for the first time, and the way he sniffed it suspiciously for ages before taking a nibble; about what we had done at school and who'd got into trouble with the teacher that day; and I told him about what a cow Mum was being, since he was the only person in the world who understood what that meant.

After a few days, Dad suggested that it would save money on stamps if I wrote a bit to him every day but saved them up and just posted the letters once a week. I agreed reluctantly. I had to hide the unfinished letters in the secret hiding place under my wardrobe because I couldn't risk Mum finding them and reading what I had written about her.

Every morning when I heard the postman at the door, I ran downstairs to ask Mum if there was anything for me, but there never was. 'Why doesn't Nigel write to me?' I asked her.

'He's forgotten all about you by now, that's why,' she said spitefully.

When I asked Dad, he explained that Nigel wouldn't have stamps or anyone to post letters for him, and promised to see what he could do about that. I kept writing every week but I never got a single letter back from my brother. It was as if he had vanished into thin air.

* * *

When we arrived at the Pittams, Grandpa was waiting for me in the hall beside the grandfather clock. I felt the usual mixture of sickness and horror swirling in my stomach. I hated the very sight of him but I was absolutely powerless to stop the things that happened to me when I stepped into my grandparents' house. My grandmother must have known what was happening but I was still sent away with my grandfather every time we visited, to be forced to do things that made me retch and gag just to think about.

'You two go and play,' Grandma commanded. 'Your mum and I are going to have a cup of tea.'

Play – it sounded so innocent and childlike. I knew we weren't playing. Whatever it was we did belonged to a different world, an adult one, and I was terrified of it.

Grandpa was grinning as he held out a hand to lead me down the steps into the garage. 'I've got a new game today,' he said as he shut the door behind us. 'You'll like it. It's really fun.'

'I don't want to play today, Grandpa,' I said timidly. 'I'm not feeling very well.'

He sat on his wooden stool. 'Nonsense! Course you do! Come here!' He lifted my skirt and pulled my pants down, nuzzling my neck with his prickly chin. I jumped backwards as the bristles scratched me. Grandpa grabbed my arm to pull me to him. He put his rough, calloused fingers between my legs and began to probe there, hurting me.

I cried out, 'Stop it! That hurts!' and struggled to get away from his grip. My hand got caught in the chain of his fob watch, tearing it off his waistcoat.

'You little bastard. Who do you think you are?' he snarled, just managing to catch the watch before it crashed to the concrete floor. He slapped me across the face and I cried out again.

The garage door opened and Grandma looked in. She must have seen that my pants were around my ankles and

I was clutching my sore cheek. 'What's all the noise about?' she asked.

'She ripped my watch, nearly broke it,' Grandpa complained, holding it out to show her.

'You'd better behave yourself,' Grandma told me sternly. 'Do what your Grandpa says or you'll be in big trouble with me.' She slammed the door shut again.

Grandpa grabbed my arm roughly and twisted it up my back; then he dragged me over to the rocking horse. By pulling my arm upwards, he forced me to bend over it and lifted up my skirt. 'Stay there,' he growled, and I didn't dare move, although I felt very exposed with my bottom all bare like that, just as when Mum beat me with the bean cane.

Grandpa pulled his wooden stool over so that he was sitting just behind me and he stuck his fingers between my legs again. I whimpered with pain as he put his finger in my bottom; it felt as though he was splitting me open, but I was too scared to struggle now in case the pain got worse.

I heard him unzip his trousers then he gave a low moan. I think he was stroking his thing, while his fat fingers continued to push inside me, splitting and bruising me.

'Don't worry, Vanessa, it's going to be all right. You'll be fine. I'm here. I'll look after you.'

I lifted my head ever so slightly and was startled to see a fuzzy figure of a beautiful blonde spirit lady in a long, white dress. She obviously wasn't human because she was shimmering, not solid, and she hovered a few inches off the floor over by the garage door. 'Don't be afraid,' she said, and I wasn't. She had loving eyes and was smiling at me warmly. Grandpa couldn't see her. I just gazed in awe. 'It will soon be over,' she murmured in her musical voice.

Sure enough, I soon felt the jerking movements and heard the throaty groan that Grandpa gave when his white stuff came out. He stopped jabbing me with his fingers and got out a hanky to clean himself up. I stayed bent over the rocking horse, unable to move while he sat so close behind me.

'There, wasn't that fun?' he asked, patting my bottom. 'Didn't you like it?'

'No,' I said quietly.

'You will. All the girls do.' He pulled the stool back to let me stand up. 'Here – put your pants on and we'll go and look at the birds.' He was cheerful now, pleased with himself. I hated him passionately at that moment. The blonde spirit lady faded into mist.

I stood up and pulled my dress down. There was a throbbing pain between my legs that made it difficult to move. I looked down and saw that some blood had trickled down my legs. 'I'm bleeding,' I told him. 'You hurt me.'

'Don't worry. That's perfectly normal,' he said. 'I'll just get Grandma to clean you up.' He walked over to the garage door and called, 'Elsie? Vanessa got a bit dirty and she needs a clean. Can you fill the tub?'

He turned back to me. 'You stay here and your grandma will see to you.' He bent down, held my head tightly between his hands, and kissed me hard on the lips, forcing my teeth into the inside of my lip. His breath stank with a rancid, gassy odour.

I waited, and soon Grandma appeared carrying the corrugated iron tub. Mum followed close behind with a bucket of water in one hand and a cigarette in the other. I blanched, remembering the time Grandma scrubbed me raw in that tub with a scrubbing brush and caustic soap.

I walked over to them very gingerly, with tiny baby steps, so as not to chafe the swollen bits between my legs. Mum looked me in the eye with a wry, mildly curious expression, then poured her bucket of water into the tub and turned away again.

'What did she say to him?' Mum asked, obviously carrying on the tail end of a previous conversation with Grandma.

Grandma brought through another bucket of water and poured it into the tub. 'That she knew her rights and he wasn't going to get away with it. She'd go over his head to the manager if need be. That shut him up.' Grandma turned to me. 'Take your dress off. Here's a flannel. You should be old enough to wash yourself now.'

'So did she get her money back?' Mum asked. 'I hope she didn't give in.' She lifted me into the freezing water and I winced.

Grandma passed me a bar of soap and I lathered carefully and washed myself thoroughly between my legs, soaking away all the streaks of blood. The icy water provided a welcome numbness for my sore bits. Mum and Grandma stood in the garage doorway carrying on their conversation but I could feel their eyes on me, waiting to tell me off if I did one thing wrong.

'Every penny. It just goes to show, doesn't it?'

'She's a right one. You've got to hand it to her.'

When I was finished, Grandma handed me a frayed, scratchy old towel. I knew it was more than my life was worth to drip water through the house, so I dried myself very carefully, standing on one leg to rub each foot in turn.

Mum and Grandma carried on talking to each other as I pulled my vest over my head, put on my pants, dress, socks and shoes and went through to the front room to sit quietly on the horsehair sofa. I didn't want to join Grandpa at the aviary. I missed Nigel so badly it was like a physical pain in my chest, much worse than the aching between my legs. I felt I could have put up with anything if only he was sitting there beside me, taking my hand and saying 'Don't worry, Nessa, I'll look after you.'

Who was the spirit lady in the garage? I wondered.

'Your guardian angel,' a voice whispered to me. 'She'll be there whenever you need her. She'll just appear.' Another voice asked, 'Why didn't you say no? I'd have said no.' 'She can't say no,' a third chipped in. 'He'll just force her to do it.' I sat listening as various different voices gave their opinions on my situation.

When it was time to go home, Mum came to get me. I was sitting absolutely still, trying not to think about the dull uncomfortable ache in my tummy, low down, like a bruise on the inside, or the fact that I still felt dirty down there despite my wash in the tub.

'You've got a face like a wet weekend,' she said. 'I hope you're not going to be moping all the way home or your face will trip you up.' She turned to Grandma and kissed her on the cheek. 'Bye, Mum. Say bye to Dad for me. I can't be bothered traipsing all the way out the back.'

On the bus on the way home, I was desperate for Mum to ask me what had happened. I wanted to tell her that Grandpa had made my bottom bleed and it was still very sore, but she kept talking about the price of school uniforms and complaining that I was growing so fast my school skirt was already too short.

She must know, I told myself. She helped Grandma put me in the bath. She saw where it hurt me. She must know and she thinks it's all right.

Was it all right? I knew, with utter and complete certainty, that it wasn't. There was no way that what Grandpa Pittam had done to me was normal. If it was, then why had Granddad Casey never done such a thing? Why hadn't Dad?

It was wrong. It was bad. I knew that, and I was sure that Mum knew it too. Sometimes I would plead with her with my eyes as Grandpa led me off to the garage, but she just ignored me. I was too scared to ask her directly about what Grandpa was doing to me and she never brought it up. It was something that wasn't talked about. That contributed to my feeling of shame and a sense that it was all my own fault for not being a loveable girl.

Dad was waiting to pick us up at the bus stop and his jollity was almost more than I could bear. 'Did you have a good time then? Salmon and cucumber sandwiches, I'll be bound.'

'Of course,' Mum laughed, rolling her eyes. 'No surprises there. How was the cricket? Did you win?'

Why didn't I just open my mouth and tell Dad what had happened? I didn't think he would believe me, that's why. Mum would tell him it was my lively imagination at work again. As soon as we got back to Shernal Green I ran out into the back garden to cuddle Whirly and told him all about it. His eyes met mine and he looked sad and sorry and very sympathetic. But there was nothing anyone could do about it.

* * *

As Nigel had predicted, we didn't go to Nan Casey's as frequently as before. It was a long drive right round the outskirts of Birmingham from south to north, which took well over an hour and a half – more if the traffic was heavy. Visits dwindled to once a month, but Mum and I continued to go to her parents every second weekend and sometimes two weekends in a row, because they were on our side of town and only a bus ride away from Shernal Green.

Once, urged by the voices in my head, I tried to resist Grandpa. When he bent down to kiss me, I swung my fist towards his face, knocking the monocle from his eye. He reached out to grab me and I pushed him away as hard as I could, crying, 'Leave me alone!'

'You want to play rough, do you? You stupid little girl, I'll show you rough.' He shoved me so that I fell over on to the floor, then he manhandled me until he had stripped all my clothes off. I heard my blouse rip a little at the sleeve and panicked about what Mum would say. Grandpa rolled my vest into a little ball and forced it inside my mouth, then he pulled the belt from his trousers and began to beat me with it.

I writhed around on the concrete floor trying to avoid the blows, which landed on my arms, legs, back and bottom, causing stripes of stinging pain. That wasn't working so I huddled myself into a ball, with my hands over my head, whimpering.

'Have you had enough?' he gloated, and I could hear the same tone Mum used when she was beating me: amusement, pleasure, excitement. He delivered one last, vicious blow to my bottom then pulled me to my feet. I felt weak, as though my legs wouldn't support me.

He sat down on the wooden stool, took his thing out of his trousers and then lifted me up so that I was sitting on his lap with my legs to either side of him. His thing was touching my private parts. It was a disgusting feeling. I wriggled to get away and he seemed to like that, because he chuckled. He put his fingers inside me, rubbing roughly, and then he did something else that I didn't understand. He hawked loudly, spat in his hand and rubbed the spit between my legs. He repeated this, still fumbling around with his rough fingers, then I felt an agonizing pain as if I was being ripped open from front to back. I tried to scream but couldn't because of the vest in my mouth and then I think I passed out.

When I came round, I was lying naked on the garage floor. I looked up and the beautiful angel was floating nearby and gazing sympathetically down at me. Pulses of pain shook my body all the way from my legs up to my chest and I could feel that I was sticky with blood between my legs. Grandpa wasn't there any more but soon Grandma arrived carrying the tub.

'Come on, then. Let's get you cleaned up.'

'You have to tell someone,' the angel was saying. 'This is not right. He's injuring you. You need help.'

But the woman who should have been protecting me from this was calmly filing her nails in the garage door-way.

'Get in the water,' Mum snapped at me. 'And hurry up. We haven't got all day.'

Surely it must be wrong for Grandpa to hurt me so much that I passed out. But I felt that it was my fault somehow. I was a misfit, the black sheep of the family, the ugly duckling, and I needed to go through these ordeals to gain acceptance. This is what I deserved for being dirty and unloveable. If I could only put up with the abuse for long enough, I hoped I would win their love one day. I just wished it didn't hurt quite so much.

* * *

That was the first time that Grandpa raped me. He had, of course, been working up towards it ever since he had first started touching me, when I was only six years old. Now, at the age of eight and three-quarters, he seemed to think I was old enough to take him, and from then on he always finished our sessions by pushing his horrible thing inside me, even though it hurt me so much that I often fainted.

Over the next few months, Grandpa's games became more and more perverted. He tied my arms behind my back, blindfolded me and penetrated me in every possible way. He beat me, kissed me and sometimes he held and stroked me like a lover.

'This will make me love you, Vanessa,' he assured me as he raped me over and over again. 'I love you more every time we do it.'

I, on the other hand, grew to hate him with a fierce, white-hot hatred that I still carry around to this day. I don't think I will ever get rid of it for the rest of my life.

Chapter 19

I saw less of Dad at Shernal Green than ever before. His commute to and from work took longer than it had from Bentley Heath so he stayed away during the week. He came home on Friday nights, only to leave again on Monday morning with a small bag of clothes. I asked Mum where he was during the week and she said, 'With the other woman!' and laughed wryly.

'What other woman?'

'Nosey parker.' She tapped the side of her nose. 'You're too young to understand. It's something for grown-ups.

Was she telling the truth? Was there really another woman? Or was it one of her snide, throwaway comments? I could never tell with her – she was such an accomplished game player that I couldn't distinguish between her bluffs and her rare moments of honesty.

On Saturdays, I usually spent the day with Dad, helping him to tame the wilderness of the cottage's huge garden. He dug up the weeds then rolled out long strips of pristine green turf on the bare, freshly dug soil. My job was to plant spring bulbs – snowdrops, crocuses, daffodils and tulips.

While he was gardening, Dad would stop to chat with the people in the other cottages, especially Mrs Black, a large old lady whose flesh wobbled like blancmange as she walked. They often gave each other cuttings from plants and asked each other's advice about insecticides and fertilizers and soil acidity.

While Dad got on well with everyone in the lane, Mum kept the neighbours at arm's length, just nodding hello as she passed. One day, Mrs Black witnessed an incident that made relations between Mum and her decidedly more chilly. I was out throwing stones down into the well and had lifted the planks off the top for a better view. Mum crept up behind me. I half-turned as she drew near but wasn't quick enough to get out of the way. She grabbed my arm and pushed me hard in the small of the back so that I fell forward over the wall. My shoulder joint wrenched backwards and I would have toppled down into the chasm if she hadn't kept hold of my arm.

I screamed, of course, and seconds later Mrs Black came running out of her kitchen.

'What on earth are you doing?' she shouted.

'Oh hello,' Mum said in her poshest voice. 'How are you?'

Mrs Black bent over, out of breath from her run. 'You nearly pushed the child down the well. I saw you,' she panted.

'I wouldn't have let go,' Mum soothed. 'I was just trying to teach her a lesson about how dangerous it is to lean over wells. You've got no idea how mischievous she can be.'

Mrs Black peered at us through her glasses and frowned. 'She could have slipped and she would never have come out of there alive. That well is more than fifty feet deep. You really should be more careful.'

'Thanks for your concern, I'm sure.' Mum was snippy now. 'But I think I know how to handle my own daughter.'

I tried to catch eyes with Mrs Black and convey an apology with my expression but I could tell she was horrified by Mum's actions. She just said 'Good day to you', and turned to walk back to her kitchen. I hoped she would mention to Dad what she had seen but I don't think she did. I suppose she didn't want to get involved.

* * *

Soon after that incident, on a Saturday morning, I went out to Whirly's hutch to feed him and I found him lying stiff and cold in his bed. 'Dad!' I shrieked and he came running from the kitchen. We lifted him up but he was floppy and definitely dead.

'Poor old Whirly,' Dad sympathized. 'He must have caught a virus or something. We'll make a nice grave for him and you can decorate it with flowers.'

'But I want Whirly back! He was my only friend in the world.' I was distraught. It seemed every human being I loved was taken away from me somehow and now my pet rabbit was gone as well. I might have a guardian angel who came to me in those awful moments when Grandpa was playing his games with me, but I couldn't hug her, or take solace in the warmth of her body. Whirly's fur had absorbed more of my tears than I could count.

After breakfast, Dad dug the grave and we put Whirly in a cardboard box with some carrots and straw and lowered him into it, while I sobbed my heart out.

'OK, Lady Jane? I have to go out now but when I come back I'll bring a special surprise for you.' He gave me a hug. 'Just you wait.'

He was gone for a couple of hours and when he came back he was carrying a little squirming thing in his big hands. I couldn't see at first what it was. 'Here you go!' He held it out, and I gasped with delight. It was a little black and white collie puppy with a twitching black nose and eager, pleading eyes.

'I'm going to call her Janie,' I said, kissing her soft fur. 'Thank you so much, Dad.'

He had bought her a little bed to go in the kitchen, a supply of dog food and he gave me a book from the library explaining how to train puppies. I was nervous about showing her to Mum, but in fact she seemed to like Janie from the start, reaching out to give her a stroke and showing me a corner of the kitchen where I could place her bed.

It was strange watching Mum being affectionate towards my new puppy; it was a side of her I'd never seen before and it made me wish, briefly, that she could be like that with me. But mostly I'd given up hope of her ever being nice to me. My main goal was to somehow track down my real mother one day, in the hope that she would let me go to live with her instead.

I loved Dad to pieces but I no longer believed that he would ever protect me from Mum. There had been too many occasions when he'd taken her word rather than mine. Since we'd moved to Shernal Green, I could sense that he and Mum weren't getting on very well. She'd stopped being so girly and flirtatious with him, replacing it with a cool politeness, and I often felt that he was just playing the happy families act with us over weekend meals.

'I married the wrong man,' Mum told me around this time. 'Lots of men would have killed to marry me, one in particular, and I made a mistake when I chose your dad.'

Once, as we worked in the garden, I asked Dad if everything was all right, and he said yes, of course, it was fine. 'I've got a lot of business worries right now,' he said. 'But aren't we lucky we've got this beautiful new house to live in?'

He was pretending, so I pretended to him as well: school was OK, I said, and yes, I was making friends. And I never mentioned to him what was happening to me when Mum and I went to the Pittams' house on Saturday afternoons. It was a terrible secret that I kept to myself. I could not bear to think about it and shut it out of my mind as much as I could. Even the voices didn't speak about it when it wasn't happening.

* * *

Once the decorative work around the cottage was finished, Mum's mood deteriorated and she redirected her energy to making my life a misery. A new stick was placed in the utility room just off the kitchen and Mum began talking to God again and beating me for misdemeanours as 'He' directed. I'm sure she was bored. She had no sewing work to do any more, so she spent her days keeping up with the housework, playing with Janie, knitting, or painting watercolours of flowers, a new hobby she had taken up. She didn't have a car so she was very isolated during the week when Dad was away. Public transport was a rare, infrequent commodity round Shernal Green. Dad drove her to Droitwich to do the shopping every Saturday morning and he sat in the car reading the paper while she got everything she needed. I usually stayed with him, reading my book, or sometimes he bought me a comic.

As I got older and bigger, Mum's temper flare-ups became more vicious. While she always stopped short of injuring me to the point where she would have had to call an ambulance, she seemed to get more out of control each time and I was never sure that she wouldn't actually kill me. Sometimes I could tell when an explosion was coming – if she broke a nail or ripped her stockings, for example – but other times it came out of the blue. I think punishing me provided a temporary relief from the tedium of her life and the frustrations of her marriage. It was just the two of us now – there were no neighbours close enough to hear, no Nigel and no Dad, most of the time. All her rage and pent-up despair came rolling out of her, expressing itself in a wild violence towards me. Barely a day went by when I didn't get beaten and my backside and thighs were permanently bruised and raw. After beating me, as I lay whimpering and groaning with the pain, she would sit down, light a cigarette and sigh. She always seemed calmer, as if something fighting inside her had been resolved.

Hurting me was the only thing that could make her feel better.

Chapter 20

In December 1958, when we'd been in the cottage for about five months, I was bringing Mum a box of eggs from the fridge while she cooked supper and I accidentally dropped them. I don't know why – they just slipped from my grasp. A tight band of fear constricted my chest as I bent down to see if any of them had survived unbroken.

Suddenly Mum grabbed me by the hair, twisting her fingers deep into the roots so she had a good grip, and she lifted my face till it was inches from hers, hissing: 'You ugly, stupid brat. Do you think we're made of money? I'm fed up to the back teeth with your clumsiness.'

She battered my head against the kitchen wall again and again, using each crash to punctuate her invective. 'You're the bane' – crash – 'of my life.' – crash – 'Without you I'd be' – crash – 'working in the fashion industry' – crash – 'and going out with my friends to parties' – crash – 'instead of which' – crash – 'I'm stuck in the middle of nowhere' – crash – 'with an ugly brat' – crash – 'who does her best to wind me up.'

She let go of my hair and I fell to the floor, stunned.

'Is this it?' I wondered. 'Is she going to kill me this time?' I considered trying to make a run for it and get across the lane to Mrs Black's but I was too dizzy to stand up.

'I don't want you in my house,' Mum screamed. 'Get out!' She pointed at the back door. 'If you know what's good for you, you won't come back till morning.'

Although the days were unseasonably sunny, there was a sharp frost in the air when the sun went down and the nights were bitterly cold. I had no time to grab a coat or jacket. I was just wearing a pair of crimplene trousers, a thin sweater and a hand-knitted cardigan.

I stood outside the kitchen door for a while, hoping that Mum would relent at some stage, but she made her own supper and took it on a tray through to the sitting room to watch our newly acquired television set. My head was thumping and my eyes couldn't seem to focus properly; everything looked blurred. I was worried that Mum might have damaged something in my head with all the blows. I drank some water from the water butt but it made me feel nauseous, so I sat down on the back step and rested my head on my knees, holding my aching temples between my hands.

A couple of hours later Mum came back into the kitchen. She glanced out and saw me sitting there and I looked up pleadingly, but her face was expressionless. She turned and walked away, switching the kitchen light off behind her. She put off all the lights on the ground floor and then I saw her bedroom light come on. I was shivering with cold in my bones, and sickened by the dull, pulsing pain in my head.

I tried the kitchen door again but it was firmly locked. The front door was locked as well. I walked round the house checking to see if any windows were open a crack but there were none I could have climbed through. Half an hour later Mum's light went out and the cottage was in complete blackness. There was only a sliver of moon that night so the darkness was almost absolute. I couldn't see any flicker of light over at Mrs Black's cottage. The only thing I could think of was to go into the pigsty, where I had sheltered the day Nigel was taken away to school.

Dad now kept the lawnmower and some of his gardening tools in the pigsty, so I made myself a space between them and lay down, wrapping the cardigan around me as tightly as I could. Outside an owl hooted and although I'd heard that owl before from inside the house, it was scary to think that the only thing separating me from its sharp beak and claws was a tin roof and a picket fence.

'Go to sleep, Vanessa,' a spirit voice said. 'We'll look after you. You're safe here.'

I nodded off but was wakened some time later by a snuffling noise and a sense that there was something nearby, just on the other side of the fence. The creature sounded as though it was digging at the soil beneath the fence, trying to make its way inside.

'Go away,' I said loudly, my voice shaking with fear. The snuffling and digging stopped. 'Get out of here!' I yelled and I heard the creature pattering away. I crept over to the doorway to look out and saw two white streaks waddling off into the undergrowth. They were badgers, slightly bigger and rounder than Janie.

It took me ages to get back to sleep after that. I knew that badgers wouldn't do me any harm, but what other wild animals might be out there? Wolves? Snakes? Wild cats? I racked my brains to think of potential dangers. In reality, the greatest danger I faced was hypothermia. I was so cold that I had lost feeling in my arms and legs and it was difficult to move them; they felt numb and heavy, as if they didn't belong to me. My head still pounded with a dull, regular pulse in the temples and another, deeper ache right at the back of my eyes. I felt nauseous, but not the kind of nausea that would be helped by actually being sick. I curled up on the ground again, trying to stay alert for unusual noises.

I must have dozed off because when I awoke it was morning. A mist hovered over the grass outside and low sunlight sparkled on the frost. I clung on to the fence and hauled myself to my feet, then stumbled stiffly across the grass to the kitchen door. Mum was inside, sipping a cup of tea at the table. Tentatively I tried the door handle and found it was unlocked now.

Mum regarded me calmly. 'Have a good night, did you? You're filthy. You'd better take your clothes off and have a wash at the water butt before you come into my house.'

'I'm freezing,' I told her, my jaw so stiff with cold that I could barely speak.

'Wash first, then you can come in.'

There was no point in arguing. I stripped off my clothes, turned on the tap under the water butt and splashed my skin, washing my grimy face and hands carefully.

Mum came to the door to supervise. 'You'll have to wash your hair. It's caked with mud. Here.' She reached over to the sink and handed me a bottle of washing-up liquid to use as shampoo.

She lit a cigarette and stood with one hand on her hip, watching, as I bent double to rinse my hair under the tap. I was shuddering convulsively. The cold water intensified my headache. It felt as though my skull had shrunk and was pressing against my brain. My fingers were too numb to rub effectively but I did my best, knowing it would be far worse if she decided to help me.

When I had finished, Mum threw me an old kitchen towel, the one I used for drying Janie after we'd been out for a walk together in the rain.

'Don't dare drip on my kitchen floor,' she barked. 'Hurry up now or you'll be late for school.'

I've got no idea how I got through that school day. I hugged the radiators at breaktime, trying to get some warmth back into my bones. I must have been very pale and I felt dazed and unwell but none of the teachers noticed. My stomach was gurgling loudly, which made some of my classmates giggle during morning lessons, but then I wolfed down my school lunch so quickly that I felt sick all over again.

When I got home that afternoon, I could tell Mum was pleased with herself. 'It's much more peaceful in the house at night without you moping around, muttering away about your stupid voices when you should be asleep.' She shoved a plate of supper into my hands. 'There you go. Why not take this outside to eat? If you're going to behave like an animal, I might as well treat you like one.'

* * *

From then on for the next four years, I was forced to spend at least one night a week in the pigsty and many of my meals were eaten outdoors. If I tried to resist, as I often did as I got older, she manhandled me out of the door and bolted it behind me. After a while, I came to accept the situation as almost normal.

The spirits kept me company and made me feel less scared out there. There was a little girl with one arm who became a particular friend. She taught me how to play games like 'I Spy', and she told me little jokes to try and make me laugh.

My guardian angel was motherly towards me, giving me advice. 'Bring an old coat outdoors and leave it here so you can keep warm,' she'd say. 'Don't worry about that noise. It's a fox looking for food but he can't get through the fence.'

Sometimes I saw the old spirit woman who had been on the porch the day we arrived at Shernal Green but she just looked at me sadly, without speaking. Between them, the spirits kept me sane on those cold and lonely nights, and I felt they were protecting me in their own way.

As my guardian angel had advised, I brought out an extra sweater, an old coat and a blanket to hide in the pigsty. I also stockpiled a pack of biscuits, some sweets and a bottle of juice for my nights outdoors. One Saturday Dad spotted my provisions when he was getting his spade out.

'Is that your secret hiding place, Lady Jane?' he grinned. 'Don't worry – I won't disturb it. Your secret's safe with me.'

I looked up at him and decided to tell him the truth, but without any real hope that he would believe me.

'Mum makes me spend the night out here sometimes,' I told him, my voice flat and expressionless.

He looked annoyed. 'Don't be so ridiculous. Of course she doesn't. Why on earth do you say these things? It just makes everyone cross with you.'

I didn't say any more. He was so convinced I was a liar that there was no point in arguing. I felt sad that he didn't know me better or question why I would make up a bizarre story like that. He didn't want to see problems so he didn't.

I must have had a fairly robust constitution because I survived my nights outdoors without succumbing to serious illness, although I did get one distressing health condition. The skin on my arms, chest and scalp developed thick, red patches with silvery flakes of dead skin on top. They itched infuriatingly then bled when I scratched them.

It was Nan Casey who diagnosed the problem on one of my increasingly rare visits to her house. 'You poor wee thing,' she sympathized. 'It's psoriasis. It must be really uncomfortable.'

She got some lotion from the chemists and applied it to all the angry, irritable patches, but as soon as I got back to Shernal Green Mum threw the lotion in the bin. She didn't care about the maddening discomfort I suffered – in fact, she enjoyed it.

And she was about to get a partner in crime, who enjoyed seeing me suffer just as much as she did.

Chapter 21

One day, a friend of Mum's called Auntie Pat came to stay. I'd never heard of her before and couldn't decide what to make of her at first. She was a short woman with a pointy, witch-like nose and a ruddy complexion. She spoke in a slurred voice that was sometimes difficult to understand, and she bumped into furniture a lot. There was a fruity, pungent smell about her, which I realized after a while was gin. She guzzled gin from morning to night and wherever she was sitting, there was always a bottle nearby.

'Why is she here?' I asked Dad.

'She's a friend of your mother's family. She's not very well and she needs people to look after her,' he explained. 'Usually she stays with your mum's sister Dorrie, but Dorrie needs a break so she's coming to live with us for a couple of weeks.'

I hoped that Mum would have to stop being so cruel to me with a witness in the house but it soon became apparent that wasn't going to be the case. Auntie Pat was delighted to become Mum's partner in crime, quite happy to laugh at Mum's cruelties and lash out at me herself given half a chance. She was usually drunk, making it easy to duck out the way, but she caught me a few clips round the head when I wasn't looking.

An unpleasant side-effect of Auntie Pat's alcoholism was that she wet her bed most nights, and it became my job to change her sheets and put the soiled ones in the washing machine.

'It's the very least you owe me after all the times I changed your sheets when you were younger. Not just sheets – your pants, skirts, socks, everything. It's time for you to pull your weight round here,' Mum told me.

My duties already included washing the kitchen floor, vacuuming the stairs and doing the dishes after dinner every night, but this new task was by far the most unpleasant. I couldn't bear the acrid stench of the urine as I stripped the wet sheet from the bed. Sometimes there were streaks of yellowy vomit encrusted on the pillowcase as well. If it had soaked through into the mattress, I had to bring a brush and a bucket of soapy water and scrub away the stain. The soap seemed to exacerbate the psoriasis on my hands and they would be inflamed and painful after-wards. Meanwhile, Pat would stomp around the room acting as if it was all my fault.

'Get a move on, brat. I need to get changed and I'm not doing it with you here. Move that face away from me!'

I was filled with fury, thinking, why don't you change your nasty sheets yourself, then, you horrible old woman? But I knew better than to say as much out loud. I'd put her sheets in the big twin-tub washing machine and set it to run, and then hurry off to school, inevitably late and with the unmistakeable scent of urine still stinging my nostrils.

* * *

One evening, Mum and Auntie Pat were particularly raucous when I got home from school and I got the impression they'd both been drinking for a while. The gin bottle on the kitchen table was nearly empty and the ashtray between them was overflowing with lipstick-smeared cigarette butts.

'Look what the cat dragged in,' Mum snorted when she saw me. She poked me in the stomach. 'It's getting fatter and uglier every day.'

'Send her outside,' Pat suggested. 'We don't want her sour face spoiling our drinkies.'

'Yes, out you get,' Mum agreed.

'Please can I go to the bathroom first?' I asked.

They looked at one another and grinned spitefully. 'No. Go outside. Now.' Mum commanded.

'I've got an idea,' Auntie Pat suggested brightly. She lurched to her feet, staggered across the floor and pulled a tumbler from the cupboard. 'Pee into that, and bring it to the back door when you're finished.'

I looked at Mum. She shrugged. 'You heard her. Do what you're told.' They both sniggered.

I took the tumbler and went out into the garden. Janie followed me so I bent down and rubbed her tummy and she jumped up with glee, always grateful for any attention. Did I really have to pee in the tumbler? What were they going to do with it?

'Get a move on!' Mum yelled out the door.

Sighing, I moved round the corner of the house, pulled down my pants and tights and tried to squat over the tumbler. I was permanently swollen and sore between my legs now and I had a smelly discharge that streaked my pants. It stung as I peed into the tumbler, and some spilled on my fingers, irritating a patch of psoriasis there. I pulled my pants and tights up again and washed my hands at the water butt.

'Is that you done?' Mum called. 'Where's the tumbler?'

I shuffled to the back door and handed it to her. She put it on the side by the sink.

'What are we going to do with it?' Pat asked. 'How about a pregnancy test? You could see if the little slut has been up to anything she shouldn't be.'

Mum chortled. 'She's only just started her monthlies. She couldn't be pregnant.'

I was startled by this suggestion. At the time, I was very unclear about how pregnancies occurred. I'd heard somewhere that the man's seed had to get inside the lady's egg, but I had no idea how that happened. Vaguely I suppose I was aware that what Grandpa was doing to me had something to do with the facts of life, but the mechanics were very muddled in my head. Where was my egg kept? And where were his seeds? How did they come together to make a baby?

'Nah, she's not pregnant,' Auntie Pat said. 'What boy would look at her with that face? It's all blubber in her belly, not babies.' She suddenly touched her forehead to signify that she'd had an idea. 'I know! Why don't we make her drink her pee? It's supposed to be good for you. I read about it in a magazine.'

'Really?' Mum looked dubious.

'It's supposed to cure all kinds of illnesses. Maybe it would get rid of that revolting rash she's always clawing away at.'

Mum suddenly seemed tickled by the idea. 'Well, why not? Vanessa, drink your pee. Gulp it down. It's good for you, Pat says.'

I screwed up my face. 'Mum, I can't. Please don't make me.'

Mum stood up menacingly and lurched towards the back door. She held out the tumbler, her hand shaking so that some wee spilled on my school shoe. She grabbed my hair to hold my head in place.

'Drink it!' she growled, bringing the tumbler to my lips and breathing alcohol fumes in my face.

I kept my lips pressed tightly together, so she forced my head down towards it and a little more spilled on my blazer.

'Do as your mother says,' Auntie Pat ordered, taking a huge slurp of her gin.

'Drink it now or I'll beat you black and blue,' Mum hissed. 'I'll flay you alive. Drink!' She yanked my hair again and I took a sip of the still warm, cloudy urine. Instantly I began to retch. The taste wasn't too bad – slightly vegetable, with a chalky aftertaste – but it was the thought of what I was consuming that turned my stomach.

'If you're sick, we'll make you drink ours as well,' Auntie Pat cackled.

Mum wasn't laughing any more. This was serious. 'Drink!' she commanded and I took another sip. Mum tipped the bottom of the tumbler. 'More!' she said.

I just gave in. I couldn't fight the two of them together. I glugged down the entire tumbler of my own urine, then held a hand over my mouth as waves of retching convulsed my diaphragm, threatening to bring the whole lot back up again.

'Stand there!' Mum ordered, pointing to the corner of the kitchen. 'If you throw it up, we'll just make you drink more.'

'Disgusting,' Pat crowed. 'She really is repulsive, isn't she?'

I stood, trying to listen for some comforting spirit voices but I couldn't find any that day. It was probably because Mum and Auntie Pat were in the room, their alcohol-fuelled sadistic gaiety blocking any spiritual atmosphere. My cheeks felt hot and my stomach was churning but I was determined not to give them the satis-faction of seeing me throw up or burst into tears. At last Mum gave me permission to leave the room and do my homework. I headed straight for the bathroom to brush and rinse my teeth over and over again, trying to get rid of the taste that coated my mouth and tongue.

Although I did not suffer any ill effects from this ex-perience, the emotional abuse battered away at what remained of my spirit. It was hard enough to resist Mum and escape her fury when she was on her own. With Pat to encourage her, she was even more impossible. What else would they do to me? Where would it all end?

Pat left after a couple of weeks, as Dad had promised, and I was delighted to see the back of her. She was a mean-spirited woman, who treated me like an animal and brought out the worst side of Mum as well. I could sense Dad couldn't stand her either because he kept well out of the way when she was around. The morning after she left, he was there at breakfast time and seemed to be in a very jolly mood.

'Have you ever made pie clits, Lady Jane?' he asked. 'It's a Casey family tradition and I'm going to show you how.

Then you can make them for me in future and the custom will be carried on to a whole new generation.'

First of all he got me to sprinkle some yeast and sugar on to a warm milk and water mixture and we set it aside. Then I had to sift the flour and salt into a bowl and make a well in the middle. When the yeast was ready, I mixed it all together with a big wooden spoon, and Dad dropped dollops of the paste into special ring shapes he'd laid in the hot frying pan. I stood on a chair to watch as lots of little bubbles rose up on the surface of the pie clits and burst, leaving holes like craters on the surface of the Moon.

When the first one was ready, Dad lifted it out and buttered it for me. 'Have a taste. What do you think?'

It was delicious – warm, buttery, soggy and chewy all at once. I took another bite and a dribble of butter escaped and dripped down the front of my cardigan. I gasped. 'Oh no!'

'What is it?' Dad asked and turned round to see me staring in dismay at the mark. 'Not to worry, it'll come out in the wash.'

'But Mummy gets angry if I get my clothes dirty.'

He put his head to one side thoughtfully. 'All children get dirty sometimes. It's part of what being young is all about. They just need to get cleaned up afterwards. Now, are you ready for another delicious pie clit?'

I took one because I could see how much it meant to him, but I was cautious not to let any butter drip from it this time. Mum came into the kitchen, looked at what we were doing and sighed loudly.

'Not the bloody pie clits!' she moaned. 'You Caseys think you're so special with your secret recipes and traditions passed through the generations like you're the royal family or something. It's just a bloody crumpet, for God's sake.'

She stormed out of the kitchen, slamming the door. Dad stared down into the pan and didn't comment.

Chapter 22

I never knew what 'games' Grandpa Pittam would have in mind when I visited. I'd long ago stopped trying to resist him. He kept a huge tub of Vaseline in the garage that he'd plaster on whenever he wanted to penetrate me because I was too tight and swollen to make it possible otherwise. Cuts in my delicate tissue often didn't heal from one session to the next and ripped open again at his lunging. My psoriasis always flared up when I went there, making my skin agony to the touch.

While he had his way, I focused hard on my spirit world. I'd realized I could have conversations with the spirits inside my head without talking out loud. They heard what I wanted to say if I just thought it, and the only problem was that I often got several voices clamouring to speak to me at once, making it hard to separate one from the other.

Certain characters were regulars: my guardian angel, of course; the one-armed girl, whom I now called Polly Poppet; and a wise old spirit called the Clown. My guardian angel brought the Clown to meet me one day and explained that he would be with me for the rest of my life.

'Always listen to him carefully,' she said. 'Never doubt his word. He is the special spirit who has been assigned to guide you in this world.'

I could see him very clearly, unlike many other spirits who were just vague, misty forms I could only hear. The Clown was quite short and dressed like a court jester of old, in a multi-coloured jacket. He had a warm smile that reached his eyes and I was pleased to meet him, although I had no idea how important he would become to me.

Listening to spirits and concentrating hard, I could project myself away from the pain in my body. I no longer smelled the stale, horrid smell of Grandpa or felt his scratchy bristles or calloused workman's fingers. The ugly panting sound he made in his throat faded into the background.

I sometimes imagined I was floating outside my body, up near the garage roof or even higher into the sky. When I looked down, I could make out the shape of a white-haired old man pounding away at a little girl's naked body, and I felt sorry for her in the abstract. I wished I could save her but at the same time I knew I couldn't.

Sometimes it was worse after he finished, when Grandma filled the tub and made me get in it. If she were in a bad mood, she'd bring out the old scrubbing brush and the pink disinfectant soap and scrub away at my skin until the patches of psoriasis were raw and bleeding.

It still broke my heart that Mum watched without comment. One time, when I had some bad bruises on my inner thighs from Grandpa's belt buckle, I thought I caught a flicker of recognition, even sympathy, in her eyes before she turned away and lit a cigarette. The thought flitted through my mind that perhaps this had happened to her as a child. Did she have to do these things with her daddy? But she was still flirty and affectionate around him, whereas I had grown to hate him passionately.

* * *

From time to time, I considered telling someone what was happening to me. Nan Casey was the obvious person but I'd look at her kind, smiling face and wouldn't be able to get the words out. What if she didn't believe me? Mum kept telling her that I was a liar with a vivid imagination. I couldn't bear it if I told her and she thought I was making it up. Besides, if I told Nan and she mentioned to Mum what I'd said, my life would be a living hell.

There was another thing: I couldn't bear to put my experiences into words because somehow that made it all the more real and shocking. I had learned that Grandpa's 'thing' was called a penis, and the white stuff was called sperm. Sometimes I tried rehearsing in my head what I would say if I told someone but it sounded so strange that I almost didn't believe it myself.

I considered telling someone my own age rather than an adult, just to find out whether this happened to other girls as well. I hardly ever saw Fifi any more because she had her own group of friends and was seldom around on the occasional days when I visited Rugeley. I didn't have any close friends at school but there were a few girls I talked to about homework and pets and skipping. In the end, shame stopped me from speaking to them. Although I knew, because the spirits had told me, that what Grandpa was doing was wrong and wicked, I felt ashamed and dirty myself because I let him do it. I worried that my contemporaries might be repulsed if they knew I'd had an old man's wrinkly penis inside me. When I did at last tell someone, I made an interesting choice of confessor: someone who would listen without asking any questions.

Dad's youngest sister, Gilly, was a kind, pretty woman who worked from home as a hairdresser. She was married to a lovely man named Roy and they had a daughter, Alison, about my age, who had Down's syndrome and a range of serious disabilities. A chubby blonde child, Alison couldn't walk or talk but she was extremely affectionate and loving to me and I liked playing with her. I rarely saw them – perhaps only once a year – but one weekend in January 1959 I was dropped off to spend a few days at their house while Mum and Dad went to Surrey to visit Nigel.

On the Saturday morning, Aunt Gilly had hairdressing clients coming in and out but she gave Alison and me some rollers, kirby grips and combs so that we could style our dollies' hair. We were told we could sit in the corner of her workroom so long as we kept reasonably quiet. My doll had long blonde hair and first I rolled it up into a bun and changed her into a silvery evening dress. Alison beamed at me and gave me a hug. Then I braided pigtails into her doll's hair and dressed her in some jeans and a checked shirt.

I decided I wanted to wash my doll's hair so I took her through to the bathroom and rinsed it under the tap. The evening dress was getting wet so I took it off and my attention was caught by the lack of genital features – between the doll's legs was just smooth, unbroken plastic.

I wished I could be like that and then Grandpa wouldn't be able to play his games with me. I was thoughtful as I wandered back through to sit with Alison on the work-room floor. Gilly was chatting to her client about a new car.

'Alison,' I began tentatively, keeping my voice low, 'when you go to Granddad's, does he make you play with his thing?'

She looked at me puzzled, not understanding.

'You know. The thing between his legs. His penis.'

She shook her head, no idea what I meant. Her big eyes were watching me in a concerned, utterly trusting way that encouraged me to say more.

'When I go to Grandpa Pittam's he puts his thing in my bottom there and there.' I pointed to the places on the doll. 'And sometimes he puts it in my mouth too.'

She continued to watch me intently.

'He makes me do it. He forces me to sit on his lap or he makes me bend over the rocking horse and then pushes it in me.' I showed her again on the doll. 'In there and in there.' I took my finger and rammed it hard against the plastic. 'Then he pushes it in and out like that.'

I had been talking in a very low voice but suddenly I became aware that Aunt Gilly had gone quiet. I turned round and she was looking at me with a most peculiar expression on her face. Fear gripped me. Had she over-heard?

'Could you hold on just a minute?' she asked her client, and turned to me and held out her hand. 'Can I have a word with you in the other room, Vanessa? You stay there, Alison.'

She took my hand very gently and led me back to the kitchen. My heart was beating hard and I had a big lump in my throat and tears behind my eyes. I was very scared of what was coming next.

Aunt Gilly sat me down at the table and gave me a cup of juice. Then she sat beside me, her face very close to mine. 'I heard you telling Alison about someone putting his thing inside you.' She stroked my hair back from my face and looked me in the eyes. 'Who did that, Vanessa?'

I was so terrified I could barely speak. 'Grandpa Pittam,' I whispered.

'It must have hurt a lot,' she said, and I nodded. 'Does he do it often?'

'Every time I visit them.'

Gilly had tears in her eyes. She kept stroking my hair. 'How long has he been doing it? What age were you when it started?'

I'd thought about this before and knew the answer. 'I was six the first time he played his games with me, because it was just after my hands got burned. But it got worse after Nigel went away.'

'That's a long time,' she gasped, and then she held out her arms and gave me a big hug, stroking my back. Not once, for a second, did she question whether I was telling the truth or not. She believed me completely, and that was an incredible feeling for me.

'We're going to fix this. It's not right,' she told me firmly. 'Don't worry. It's going to stop now.'

She got up and went to the telephone in the corner of the kitchen. She phoned her husband Roy first of all and spoke briefly and urgently. 'I need you to come home as soon as possible to watch Alison. It's important … I'll tell you later. There's something I've got to do.'

It was a black telephone with a long, curly flex and she was winding it round her fingers as she spoke, keeping one eye on me the whole time.

She pressed down the little buttons to get a dialling tone then rang another number, putting her fingers into the holes on the dial then letting them slide round with a clicking noise. 'Hello, Mum? It's Gilly. Look, there's an emergency. Roy's on his way home then I'm coming over to yours with Vanessa. Wait for us. Don't go out.'

It took me a minute to work out who she was talking to then I was overjoyed to realize that Gilly's mum was Nan Casey. She confirmed it a minute later. 'I just have to finish off the client in the front room and wait for Roy to come home, then I'll take you over to your Nan's,' she said. 'I want you to tell her everything you've told me. We're going to help you, OK?'

'Mummy will be cross with me,' I said.

'No, she won't,' Gilly told me firmly. 'We'll explain to her. No one's going to be cross with you, my love.' She kissed my cheek and she smelled sweet, like flowers. Her lips were lovely and soft.

When we got to Nan Casey's house, Gilly asked me to sit and play with the toys in the playroom while she had a quick word with Nan in the kitchen. I picked up the spinning top in a desultory manner but didn't spin it. Instead I sat, utterly still, listening hard, too nervous to go and eavesdrop at the door but desperate to know what they were saying. I was worried that Nan Casey wouldn't believe me, and on the other hand I was scared that she would, because what would happen then? I heard a little scream at one point and it made goose bumps stand up on my skin.

It wasn't long before Nan came into the playroom. She sat down on the floor beside me and pulled me into her arms for a big hug. I could see she'd been crying and I could hear tears in her voice. 'Nessa, why didn't you tell me?' she asked.

'I thought you wouldn't believe me,' I mumbled.

'Of course I'd believe you. I've always believed you. You're not a liar. Besides, no child your age should know about these things. Can you bear to show me what he does to you?'

My tears started to flow and I wasn't very articulate but I showed her the places he put his penis in me, and I told her about the way he blindfolded me and tied my hands behind my back and beat me with his belt. She was sobbing out loud and holding me so tightly she was nearly squashing me. 'My poor baby,' she said, over and over again.

'Nan, please don't tell Mummy. She'll be cross with me.'

Nan shook her head. 'She won't be cross, my love. She'll be very, very sad to hear about this.'

It was on the tip of my tongue to say 'She already knows' – but I didn't, because I couldn't say for sure that she knew. I just assumed she must.

Gilly brought in a tray with some tea and cakes, and orange squash for me, and Nan went to make a telephone call. When she came back, she told me: 'Do you remember that nice doctor who fixed your hands when they got burned? He's going to come up to visit you and see if you're OK. It won't hurt, and I'll be with you the whole time,' she added, seeing my panicked expression. 'Then as soon as your dad gets back this evening we'll ask him to come over here and have a chat.'

'Not Mum?' I asked quickly.

'No. We'll talk to your dad first then we'll decide what to do. But you'll stay here with me tonight no matter what. Is that OK?'

I nodded.

The doctor came that afternoon and he was very gentle but it upset me when I realized he wanted me to take my pants off so he could look at me down there. I sat on Nan's lap with her arms round me while he examined the scarred, torn bits and took a swab of my discharge. He asked me to pee in a little jar and I was alarmed, remembering when Mum and Auntie Pat made me drink my own urine, but he explained that it was just so he could test if anything was wrong with me. It turned out that I had a urinary tract infection and a nasty dose of thrush, and he said there was damage to the cervix. The doctor prescribed medication to deal with these complaints and also gave me a prescription for some pills to help ease my psoriasis. He didn't ask any questions. I assume Nan and Granddad had explained the situation to him and assured him they were dealing with it.

It was dark outside and I had gone to bed by the time Dad arrived, on his own. I was wide-awake though, my mind whizzing through all the possible outcomes. Gilly had gone home, but Dad, Nan and Granddad went into the front room and I crept out in my nightdress to sit on the stairs and listen. The door was closed so I could only make out the words when voices were raised.

Dad shouted 'How dare you!' then I heard Granddad sounding uncharacteristically fierce as he said, 'You do not talk to us like that in this house.' The strangest thing was that at one point I thought I could hear Dad sobbing. It was a loud wailing sound punctuated by gasps for air and it upset me a lot. I wanted to go and comfort him. I must have fallen asleep on the stairs listening to the murmur of their voices, because I vaguely remember Nan carrying me back to bed some time later.

Dad stayed overnight in the house and when I saw him next day over breakfast he seemed very subdued and shame-faced. He didn't refer directly to what he'd been told, but he said, 'Lady Jane, Nan and Granddad and I have agreed that it's best if you never go to the Pittams' house again. You don't have to see them any more. Would you like that?'

'Yes.' I nodded. 'But what will Mummy say? I don't want Mummy to smack me.'

'Mummy won't smack you, I promise. I'll explain every-thing to her.'

'Do I have to go back to the cottage?' I pleaded. 'Can't I stay here with Nan? Or with Aunt Gilly?'

'Nan's too old to look after a little girl all the time. She's got her own life to lead. And Gilly has enough on her plate dealing with Alison. Besides, Mum and I would be too lonely without you. We want our Lady Jane to live with us.'

'Couldn't I go and find my real mummy? I'd come back and visit you sometimes.'

'It's just not possible,' Dad said, looking very troubled. 'But everything will be fine now. You'll see. Mummy won't be cross with you.'

I looked down into my porridge feeling worried. I knew she was going to be cross; I was sure of it. But at least I didn't have to see Grandpa Pittam any more. I sensed that this was the end of the matter and it would not be mentioned again. No family would want this kind of thing to be known and talked about, so it would be kept private and dealt with behind closed doors. There was not even a whisper of the idea that the police should be brought in. Charles Pittam would escape punishment for his crimes.

We all went to church together that morning and Dad and I stayed for Sunday lunch then we drove back to Shernal Green. He chatted on the way about how well Nigel was doing and he asked me about school, but he didn't say anything about what Grandpa Pittam had been doing to me. I think he was embarrassed.

When we arrived at the cottage, I went to find Janie and took her out to the garden to play. I saw Mum and Dad sitting at the kitchen table and Mum was smoking heavily, lighting one cigarette from the end of the last one, but I didn't hear raised voices. Did she pretend to be surprised when he told her I'd been abused by her father? I expect she tried to claim it wasn't true, that I was making it all up. But Dad stuck to the deal he'd agreed with Nan Casey, and Mum had no choice but to accept it.

Over supper that evening she gave me a few sharp looks but all she said was: 'Your Dad and I have agreed that when I visit my mum and dad's on Saturday afternoons, you'll stay with him. Is that what you want?' Her tone was cool and I could sense danger. For the first time, I became aware of a reddish glow around her, something I now refer to as an aura. The Clown spirit taught me that the colour of a person's aura reflects their moods and true feelings as well as their basic character.

'Yes,' I said, staring down at my lap.

'Well, that's that then,' she said. But I knew it wasn't.

Chapter 23

The next day I woke up to find it had snowed in the night. The garden was a sparkling wonderland of low sunlight twinkling on heavily laden branches. The canal had frozen over and the lawn was a pristine carpet, except for one set of footprints leading through the snow – probably that hungry old fox, I guessed.

I didn't see Mum at breakfast time. I got myself wrapped up warmly, ate some cereal and headed off down the lane. Lots of children didn't come into school that day because roads were blocked and the buses weren't running. It was a fun day because the teachers played games with us; we did quizzes and colouring in and listened to stories instead of normal lessons. At four o'clock I tramped home along the darkening lanes, my feet dragging. This would be the first time I'd been on my own with Mum since I'd dropped my bombshell at the weekend. I wasn't sure how she was going to react but I was very apprehensive.

I slipped in the front door as quietly as I could but she was listening for me in the kitchen and already had her revenge prepared.

'Come in here,' she ordered. 'Take off your boots and tights.'

I obeyed. The red aura around her was strong and pulsating. She opened the back door and I saw the blue bucket in the middle of the lawn. It was filled with water and there was a film of ice over the top.

'Go and stand in the bucket,' she ordered.

'Mum, I can't. I'll freeze.'

'If you don't go I'll make you. Is that what you want?'

Still I cowered, so she grabbed me by the hair and dragged me out the back door on to the snowy ground. 'Get in the bucket!' She hit me across the head. 'Now!' She hit me again.

I raised one foot and shuddered with shock as I lowered it through the crackling ice into the freezing water.

'And the other!' Mum hit me again, so I put the other foot in and immediately started shivering violently.

'How dare you accuse my father of all those things? You little bitch. You're not fit to kiss the ground he walks on.'

'But, Mum, he did them. You saw him,' I said, and she hit me so hard I fell out of the bucket into the snow.

'Get back in there.' She hauled me up and forced me back into the icy water. 'I'm going to make your life a bloody misery. Up to now it's been a picnic. You mark my words.'

It seemed like ages that she made me stand in that bucket but it was probably only ten minutes or so. My toes quickly went completely numb, and I began shivering compulsively. Although it was only four-thirty, the moon and stars were out and the owl was hooting as if it was midnight. I had visions of losing my toes to frostbite, like a mountaineer I had read about at school.

When at last Mum allowed me back into the kitchen, my feet were a purply-red colour. She had filled a basin with warm water and told me to step into it, and I did so unthinkingly. The pain was agonizing as circulation returned to the damaged tissues and I jumped straight back out again.

'Get in there now!' Mum forced me back in.

I nearly fainted with the indescribable, raw pain. I developed chilblains on my toes that chafed against my shoes and made me limp on the walk to and from school all that week and the next. However, my punishments for telling on Grandpa Pittam were by no means over. I was beaten with a big stick, made to sleep in the pigsty despite the fact there was snow on the ground, and I frequently went without dinner in the next couple of weeks.

It was terrible and I suffered a great deal – but knowing I would never have to see my grandfather again made it bearable for me. It was over, at last.

* * *

Mum went to visit her parents alone the following Saturday afternoon – no one seemed to think it strange that she still wanted to visit the parent who had committed such horrors on her daughter, but she must have maintained the pretence that she didn't believe me. Dad and I dropped her at the bus stop and picked her up on her return, and I could tell she was incensed when she got back, just itching to punish me. There were some clips round the ear and vicious pinches, but my real punishment had to wait till the Monday after school when Dad wasn't around.

I crept home to find Mum cooking dinner. There was a big stick laid out on the table, ready to beat me with.

'Come in here!' she ordered. I stood, looking at the floor, trying not to think about the beating that was coming. 'Grandpa told me on Saturday that you've broken his heart. How could you do that to an old man? He's very ill, he's got heart problems and it's all because of you.' She was shoogling sausages in the frying pan.

With Nan Casey and Aunt Gilly behind me, I felt more able to stand my ground. 'How could he do these things to me? He shouldn't have done them, Mum.'

'You don't even know what you're talking about. You just make up lie after lie. He probably hasn't got long to live and you spread these malicious rumours to poison his last years.'

'But he's evil. I hate him.'

Mum lifted the frying pan in temper and jabbed it at me. I tried to duck but it caught me across the left cheekbone and sent me flying to the ground. The sausages fell out. Mum picked up the stick and started whacking my legs with it. I curled up foetal style, clutching my cheek. I could feel that it was badly hurt but didn't dare take my hand away to check.

Mum continued to hit me with the stick as hard as she could, screaming, 'You bitch! You lying bitch.' When she got into a frenzy like this there was no option but to let her work it out. I didn't cry, although the blows stung my bottom and the backs of my thighs. I was more worried about the pain in my cheek and a dizziness and nausea I recognized from previous occasions when she'd hit me especially hard on the head.

When Mum had beaten me enough to work off her adrenaline, she dropped the stick and kicked me hard on the bottom. 'Get up now and clean yourself up. What a disgusting mess.'

She sat down at the kitchen table and I heard the click of her lighter and a sucking noise as she inhaled. I lifted my head slowly, and that's when I realized my face was burned quite badly. The skin was tight and already blistering.

'Wash your face,' she instructed.

I staggered to the kitchen sink and rinsed my face and hands, but my cheekbone hurt badly where the pan had hit it.

'Mum, I think the bone might be broken. It feels very bad.'

'Of course it's not broken. Don't be ridiculous. Go out into the garden and don't come in again until you've stopped being so rude about my father.'

I went to sit in the pigsty. I wanted to feel safe, in a place where there was only one entrance and no one could sneak up behind me. I also wanted to talk to the spirits.

'Keep splashing it with water,' my guardian angel said, appearing as a warm glow in the corner. 'Try to be calm.' 'She's going to have a scar,' another voice commented. 'And a black eye,' said a third. 'Look, it's coming up already.'

My head was pounding so I lay down on one of the old sweaters I kept out there, pulled a coat on top of me and fell asleep for a while. When I woke it was pitch black. A single light was on in Mum's bedroom but there was no sign of Dad's car and I didn't feel safe enough to go back into the cottage without him there so I decided to spend the night outside. It felt good to have a bit of self-determination instead of meekly obeying Mum's orders all the time. I ate a couple of biscuits, drank some juice then settled down to sleep for the night. Most of the nocturnal creatures were hibernating so I slept without interruption. Also, I was probably concussed, and that could have contributed to a deeper than normal sleep.

When I awoke the next morning, I was stiff with cold and my cheek was throbbing, but my mind was working overtime. I needed to find somewhere else to live, because if I stayed at the cottage Mum would end up killing me. We seemed to be in a cycle where the violence was getting more extreme and I hated to think where it might end. It was time to find my real mother now but I didn't know how to go about tracking her down. The only thing I could think was that maybe Nan Casey would be able to help.

Dad had recently started giving me pocket money of a shilling every Saturday. I'd been saving it up and had almost a pound now. I resolved to save more money then use it to run away from home. I'd find out about the buses first and make my way to Nan Casey's and throw myself on her mercy. She'd believed me about Grandpa Pittam's abuse, so surely I should be able to convince her about what Mum was doing to me?

* * *

When I saw the kitchen light come on, I got up and made my way shakily to the back door. I washed my face and hands at the water butt. The left side of my face felt oddly swollen and I couldn't see properly through my left eye. When I opened the back door to ask for a towel, Mum was visibly shocked at my appearance.

'Look at the state of you!'

'Can I come in and get dressed for school?'

'You'll need a clean shirt and cardigan. You've got those all dirty.'

I went upstairs to change and when I looked in the bathroom mirror I saw what Mum had been shocked about. My left eye was swollen up like a golf ball, blackish red in colour, and there was a burn about two inches long just over my cheekbone, where the flesh was red and shiny. I looked like a hideous goblin from a picture book.

Mum had laid out some cereal for me. 'If anyone asks, you were running across the kitchen when you tripped and your face hit the frying pan.'

I considered this and supposed it was a plausible story. 'What about Dad? What will I tell him?'

'He won't be back till the weekend. We'll see how it looks by then.'

'Where is he?' I asked, feeling brave. I had a hold of sorts over Mum while I was sporting such a dramatic injury. She knew I could easily blurt out the truth to a sympathetic teacher, if I chose – and who would Dad believe if I told him about it next weekend?

'The usual place,' Mum said. 'Eat your breakfast and go to school.'

'Where's the usual place?'

'Mind your own business.'

Was he with his other woman again? Or was there something else I was not being told about? I had no way of finding out.

* * *

After school that day I checked the bus stop and noted that buses left for Worcester every hour at ten past the hour. If I caught one of those buses then surely there would be another one in Worcester that would take me on to Birmingham then another that would take me north to Rugeley? It occurred to me that I had better try and find a note of Nan's phone number so that I could call her and say I was coming. It would be terrible to arrive and find she wasn't even there.

Mum had a tiny address book that she kept in her handbag. However, the bag was usually lying somewhere in the room where she was sitting so it wasn't easy to get hold of. I bided my time and a few days later, when we were watching the news on television, Mum left the room to make herself a cup of tea. Fingers trembling, I unzipped the top of the bag and pulled out her little floral notebook. Nan's number was under 'C' for Casey. I didn't have a pencil handy to write it down, so I just memorized it: '764 823'. I slipped the book back into the bag and zipped up the top again, trying to position it at precisely the same angle as it had been before. My heart was beating loudly but Mum didn't suspect a thing when she came back into the room. As soon as I got the chance, I slipped out to the hall and scribbled the number on a piece of paper, which I put in my blazer pocket.

Dad came home on the Friday night and was horrified to see the state of my eye. Mum got her story in first, as always.

'It gave me the fright of my life,' Mum told him before I could say anything. 'Her hands were in her pockets as usual, and she tripped over just as I was moving the pan off the heat. She fell headfirst on to it. What a mess it all was.'

Dad was examining the mark. 'You're going to have a scar there, Lady Jane.' He stroked my hair. 'Still, I suppose scars add character. You do look a sight.'

'Thanks a lot,' I said gruffly. Mum smiled, triumphant that yet again I hadn't told on her.

I couldn't help wondering why Dad didn't question my injuries more closely, especially as they appeared just after Grandpa's abuse had been revealed. But I knew that he always refrained from challenging Mum about anything for fear she would blow up. These days they would no doubt have admitted their mistake and divorced, but it simply wasn't an option at the time, so they lived almost separate lives and whenever Dad did come home, he'd escape again out to the pub straight after dinner.

Dad gave me my pocket money on the Saturday and I added it to my savings, which I kept in the hiding place under the wardrobe. I decided to run away on Monday, because Mondays had always been Mum's cruellest days and I couldn't face another scene like the frying pan one.

* * *

On Monday morning, I sneaked my money into my schoolbag, along with a spare sweater and pants and my toothbrush. I was worried that Mum might see it bulging as I left for school but she didn't comment. I was only a hundred yards down the lane when I felt in my blazer pocket for Nan's phone number and found it wasn't there. I searched the other pocket, and the inside zipped one, but it had gone. Mum must have emptied my pockets over the weekend. Had she seen the number there? If so, I could be in huge trouble when I got home.

I considered just catching the bus after school anyway, but didn't dare without Nan's number. I racked my brains but could no longer remember it. All I needed was another evening when I could get access to Mum's address book and I would run away the following day. However, when I got home that evening, Mum grabbed my bag from me as soon as I walked in the door and opened it.

'Planning to escape, were you? You wouldn't have got far with a toothbrush, a cardigan and a pair of pants.'

I kept quiet.

'Were you thinking of going to your Nan's?' She had a nasty tone to her voice that made me wary. 'Well, you'd have been out of luck because she's in hospital. She's got pneumonia.'

'What's pneumonia?'

'It's when your lungs fill up with fluid and you can't breathe any more.'

I hardly dared ask the next question. 'Is she going to be all right?'

Mum snorted. 'The old battleaxe? Knowing her she'll outlast us all.'

'Can I go and visit her?'

'They don't allow children in the hospital – especially fat, ugly ones with horrible scars on their face. Your dad's going tomorrow so if you want to write her a note I suppose I could get it to him.'

I sat at the kitchen table drafting several versions of the note, but in the end all I wrote was: 'Dear Nan, I love you very much. Please get well soon. Love from Vanessa xxx.' I gave it to Mum and she tucked it away in her handbag promising to pass it on.

The next night when I got home from school, I asked immediately how Nan was.

'I haven't heard yet. Your dad hasn't been home.'

'Did you give him my note for Nan?'

'Oops!' Mum covered her mouth with a perfectly manicured hand in a mocking fashion. 'I forgot. I'll do it next time.' She laughed sadistically at my expression. 'Dad will be home on Saturday so you can give it to him then.'

'Can I post it to her at the hospital?'

'No, I'm not wasting a perfectly good stamp on something like that.'

All week I felt anxious. The spirits weren't telling me anything specific but they weren't allaying my fears either.

* * *

At breakfast on Saturday morning, Dad was very subdued. When I asked how Nan was getting on, he just said, 'The doctors are doing their best.' He spread marmalade on his toast but then only took a couple of bites and seemed to forget about it.

Suddenly the phone rang and we all jumped. No one ever phoned that house. I couldn't remember the last time I'd heard it ring. Dad walked over to the dresser to pick it up and stood with his back to us.

'Derrick Casey here … I see … I understand … Yes, this afternoon … Of course. Thank you.'

He hung up and kicked the wall so hard I knew it must have hurt his foot, then he leaned his forehead against the dresser. Without turning to look at us, he said in a muffled voice 'She's gone' then he hurried out of the room. I heard his footsteps limping up the stairs.

Mum and I looked at each other. 'So whose house are you going to run away to now? Don't think I didn't know about your little scheme.'

I wasn't quite sure yet what I'd just heard. 'Is Nan ... is she dead?' I asked.

'Yep!' Mum said brightly. 'She's dead and gone and you won't be seeing her ever again.'

I scraped my chair back and ran outside to the pigsty to talk to the spirits. I felt gripped by a worse sense of panic than I'd ever experienced in my life. It was as though I couldn't breathe; no oxygen was getting through my lungs. I was light-headed and my heart was beating so hard I wondered if I was having a heart attack.

'She's at peace now,' my guardian angel told me. 'But this is not the end. Don't worry because you will see her again. Remember everything we have been teaching you.'

I hugged my knees to my chest and rocked back and forwards on my bottom. The Clown came to talk to me. 'You're on a journey,' he said, 'and this is going to take you forward to the next stage. It will test your belief at times but I know you will come through.'

I heard Dad's car leaving and many hours later, when it was dark, I heard him coming back again. He came out to the pigsty to find me.

'Lady Jane, you have to come in. Mummy's made some supper and she says you haven't eaten since breakfast. Come on now.'

I didn't move, just kept rocking. I couldn't stop thinking that I would never hear her voice again or see the loving expression in her eyes when she looked at me. It was an unbearable feeling.

'Your Nan wouldn't want you to be miserable on her account. Just think how much she loved you and wanted you to be happy. It's your duty now, in memory of her, to look after yourself. Will you try? For Nan's sake?' He stretched out his hand.

I got to my feet and let him lead me back to the kitchen for supper, but I didn't say anything at all during the meal and afterwards I just went straight up to bed. The world felt black and empty. I had no future, nothing to look forward to any more. I'd lost my only place of safety, the only person who was on my side.

Chapter 24

*B*ack in 1959 it wasn't understood that children experience grief just as powerfully as adults – perhaps more so, because they can't intellectualize it at all. Everyone kept telling me to be a good girl because Dad was so upset, yet I felt that my heart had split in two. It was an intense physical pain combined with feelings of severe panic as I contemplated the emptiness of the future without her. She'd been my only hope of escape from Mum's cruelty and now that hope was gone.

I wanted to go and see Nan's body but I wasn't allowed, and then I begged to go to the funeral so that I could say goodbye, but it was unusual for children to attend funerals in those days and Mum forbade it. I was sent to school as normal that day, aware that Mum and Dad were dressed in dark suits and sombre hats, ready to pay their respects.

I only saw Granddad Casey once after Nan died, when we went up to Rugeley one Saturday afternoon. He seemed utterly shattered, as though a great sense of exhaustion had settled on him. The house and garden were massive for one man to manage, albeit with domestic help, and he didn't even try. He sat in Nan's rocking chair, his thoughts miles away, and although I tried to cheer him up by making an effort to chat about school and my vegetable garden and the spring flowers that were coming out, I could tell I wasn't getting through to him.

I understood exactly how he felt because I felt the same way. I carried on doing what was required – getting dressed, washing, eating what was put in front of me, answering the teachers' questions at school, doing my homework, enduring Mum's behaviour, going to bed – but I did no more. I kept to myself at school more than ever, standing alone in the corner of the playground each break-time, and at home I spent most of my time in the garden, talking to spirits.

* * *

The garden was a magical place for me. It was huge and Dad had only managed to tame a fraction of it, so there were wilderness patches of long grass, dandelions and wildflowers, and that was where I imagined the fairies lived. In my fantasies, I saw them prancing around with apple blossom on their heads and filmy clothes made out of gossamer. Spirit children would often join me in my imagination games, ringing a little bell to signal their arrival. They played tricks on me, sometimes tinkling the bell in one direction and appearing from completely the opposite way. At other times, the Clown came to teach me about the spirit world, and he explained more about how I would be able to use my ability to communicate with spirits in order to do good in the world, such as helping people to heal – but first I had to start to heal myself.

'You must develop a new way of seeing,' he explained. 'A third eye that will let you look all the way into people's hearts and minds.'

I didn't understand what he meant back then, but I noticed that I was becoming more intuitive at reading people's auras. Mum's angry red aura softened and became tinged with blue when she was petting Janie, or if Dad told her how pretty she was looking. I could see when a teacher at school was having a bad day, or when Dad's grief at the loss of his mother was most overwhelming, from the changes in the colours surrounding them.

I wasn't aware how obvious my withdrawal from the world was to those around me until Mum and Dad got a letter from the school asking them to come in and talk to my form teacher, Miss Stewart. Mum didn't go – she never went to any school events – but Dad took the after-noon off work to attend the meeting, which was at the end of the school day. I waited for him on a bench outside so that I could get a lift home. I had no idea what the meeting was about but I wasn't particularly worried because I knew I hadn't done anything wrong. Miss Stewart wasn't angry with me; on the contrary, she had been particularly warm and kind recently.

When Dad came out of the school, his shoulders were hunched forward and I could tell from his aura that he was feeling very sad. I stood up as he approached the bench and he put his arms round me and gave me a bear hug. He held me for while without moving, then said gruffly, 'We'd better get in the car, Lady Jane, or your mum will wonder what's happened to us.'

As we drove, he told me what Miss Stewart had said and I listened in silence. 'She says that you never talk to any of the other pupils and if they ask you to join in their games you just shake your head and walk away. Is that right?'

I thought about this for a while and then nodded. Yes, it was.

'In class discussions you never speak unless asked a direct question by a teacher and even then you answer in as few words as possible. She says you were always shy but that you've been much more withdrawn in the last couple of months. Is it because you're missing Nan Casey?'

Tears filled my eyes and started trickling down my cheeks and when I looked at Dad his eyes were watery as well. This released something in me and I sobbed and sobbed. It felt as though there was an oval-shaped pebble lodged in my throat and it hurt to cry. My muscles ached and the tears stung my eyes. There's healing crying that makes you feel better afterwards and there's bitterly sad crying that makes you feel worse, and mine was somewhere between the two. But it was good to sit there in solidarity with Dad, both of us engulfed by the same emotions.

'She was a magnificent woman,' he said shakily, 'and she loved you with all her heart and soul. You and Nigel were her first grandchildren and you had a special place in her heart.' He paused. 'It's hard to explain this but just because her body is no longer on this earth, it doesn't mean you've lost that love she gave you. It's still there, and it's yours for the rest of your life.'

'I know,' I said in a very small voice. The Clown had explained this to me. She had loved me in a way that meant I would always have that love. I firmly believe that this is one of the main things that helped me to survive my childhood.

'You and I have to stick together from now on,' Dad said as we approached the cottage. 'We need to spend more time together at weekends, sorting out the garden and going for walks and being each other's friend. I'm sorry I haven't been there for you as much as I should have. I think we can both help each other to get through this. Will you be my friend?'

I nodded but couldn't speak because of the pebble lodged in my throat. I felt very sad but I also felt a tiny bit of hope for the first time since Nan died.

* * *

The next Saturday, Dad came downstairs for breakfast and announced that he and I were having a planting day. In a big patch at one end of the garden we had already planted potatoes, peas, beans, carrots and cabbage. We had also put in some apple and pear trees, making a miniature orchard area. That morning Dad gave me my own little garden, about ten feet square, and gave me some lettuce, pea, bean and radish seeds. He told me I was responsible for planting, weeding and watering it.

I made furrows with a rake and sprinkled the seeds along them then covered them up with loose soil. Meanwhile, Dad created a fruit garden over near the orchard, where he drove in stakes for the raspberries and gooseberries to climb around. We worked hard all morning then, after lunch, he suggested we went for a walk through the lanes and across the fields. As we walked, he talked to me about the flora and fauna around us.

'That's a hedgehog burrow,' he said. 'Did you know that hedgehogs get their name because they root around looking for food in the same way that hogs do?' He gave a snorting impression that made me laugh.

'That's part of a robin's egg,' he said, picking up a broken piece of shell that was pale blue with reddish speckles. 'Some are blue and some are plain white.'

On our Saturday afternoon walks, I learned about all the wildflowers in the region. I loved the fabulous names, like lady's bedstraw, Devil's bit scabious, dogwood, corn cockle, toadflax, candytuft and shrubby veronica. Dad taught me how to tell the difference between hornbeam and beech trees, and that woodpeckers are especially partial to ash trees. He pointed out dragonflies and hoverflies, hairstreak butterflies and fritillaries. I drank it all in and never forgot a single thing he told me from one walk to the next.

One Saturday our walk took us by a pub called Pear Tree Lodge, which was a couple of miles from home.

'I could murder a pint,' Dad said. 'Do you fancy stopping for a drink? We can sit outside on the bench here.'

I nodded. I still wasn't talking very much. Dad went inside and when he came back out he presented me with a bottle of a new drink I'd never tried before – ginger beer. I felt very grown up. Wasn't beer something that only adults were supposed to drink? I had a sip and it tasted completely different from orange squash or any other drink I'd had before. It was sweet but the ginger gave it a kick and the bubbles made my tongue tingle. I decided I was going to like it and took another swallow.

Dad produced two packets of crisps with their little blue paper twist of salt inside. 'It's a race,' he announced. 'Let's see who can open their salt, sprinkle it on the crisps and put the paper down on the table again first. One, two, three – go!'

I suspect that Dad let me win, but nevertheless, I was still revelling in my victory when a lady suddenly appeared beside us. 'Hello, Derrick,' she said in a soft voice.

'Well, Margery, hello. How nice to see you. Won't you join us?' Dad turned to me. 'Lady Jane, this is Margery Wyatt, an old friend of mine. She lives just near here in Pear Tree Cottage.'

'Hello, Lady Jane,' said the lady with a warm smile. 'How nice to meet you.'

I liked Margery immediately. I suppose she must have been about the same age as Mum but her hair was dark and her features softer. There were laughter lines at the corners of her blue eyes, something my mother would never develop because she seldom laughed. I liked the colours Margery wore – aubergine, petrol blue, moss green – and the stylish way she put outfits together with some beads or a belt or a pair of earrings accentuating the colour scheme. Her aura was a kind, peaceful, bluey-green colour and she had a real gentleness about her.

She stayed chatting with us for almost an hour, and I found her very easy company. She included me in the conversation in a friendly way and she didn't seem upset if I failed to reply.

On the way home, Dad said to me, 'You won't mention meeting Margery to your mum, will you? Women can be a bit funny about that kind of thing.'

I shook my head. I wouldn't have dreamed of it.

After that, we saw Margery quite often. If we walked to the Pear Tree Lodge, more often than not she came and joined us for a drink. I loved listening to her talk. There was something she said once that really struck a chord with me. She said, 'It's not what's on the outside that matters; it's on the inside, what's in your heart and soul, that counts in the long run.' As a child who had been brought up to think of beauty as the most important quality, one which I was totally lacking, this was a revealing new concept and it made me take notice of Margery when she was around.

I was surprised to hear she had never got married; she seemed so pleasant and calm that if I were a man I'd have wanted to marry her. I wished I could see her more often but I didn't know how to go about it, so we just sat companionably enjoying a drink outside the Pear Tree from time to time.

Meeting Margery was a lovely secret that Dad and I shared together, in contrast to all the bitter, nasty secrets that Mum and I had kept over the years.

* * *

On Sunday mornings, Dad and I walked over the fields to Hadzor parish church, where I went to Sunday school and he attended the main service. Through the lessons there, I began to realize just what a skewed version of religion Mum had been feeding me over the years. I learned that God loves everyone, even sinners of the worst kind. I learned about Heaven, and how any sinners who repent will be allowed in. I read a book about some nuns living in a convent, and how they fed the wild animals in the convent garden every day, and a little germ of an idea was planted in me. If I lived in a convent, I wouldn't have to talk to other people or make friends or get a job. I could just pray and bake bread and feed the animals, like the nuns in the book. I wished I could talk to Nan Casey about this idea; she would have known how I could go about it. I felt sure she would have approved. I hoped that she would come to me in the spirit world and tell me herself but there was no sign of her among the many voices I heard.

I looked forward to going to Sunday school, but I was uncomfortable when the teachers tried to initiate discussions amongst the pupils. I was well aware how much less sophisticated I was than the other eleven-year-olds there. One day we were talking about our hobbies and the others cited pop music, fashion, dancing, watching TV and reading magazines. I had never heard any pop music, wore clothes made by Mum, and wasn't allowed to watch television after seven in the evening.

'What about you, Vanessa?' the teacher asked. 'What are your hobbies?'

I couldn't think of any. There was a long pause and all the others turned to look at me. I think someone sniggered. I found it very hard to think of things to say at the best of times. 'Gardening,' I said finally.

'What a wonderful hobby!' the teacher exclaimed. 'Growing new plants and flowers is a great way to be in touch with God's universe. Congratulations to you.'

The others turned away, raising their eyebrows and whispering, underlining what a social outcast I was. I didn't care. I was only interested in talking to spirits, not real people.

Chapter 25

That summer, when Janie was not quite a year old, I made a huge mistake by letting her off the leash while we were out for a walk. I didn't realize that she could be on heat so young. The encounter with one of the farm dogs only took seconds but soon after she was walking round with a huge, swollen belly. I felt very guilty because Dad told me that she was really too young to be carrying babies.

About fourteen weeks later, I woke early when I heard a high-pitched yelping sound coming from downstairs. I rushed down to the kitchen in my dressing gown and found Janie lying on her side on the floor, giving birth. One tiny pup, all covered in blood and mucus, had already slithered out and Janie was licking it clean. It wriggled, eyes closed, like a skinned rabbit, only a few inches long. I could tell Janie was exhausted but as I watched a contraction seized her body and another pup slid out squirming.

I didn't know what to do and I didn't dare wake Mum to ask, so I shut the kitchen door and got some warm water to help wash the pups as they arrived. Janie looked up at me and I was sure she was grateful. It felt as though we understood and trusted each other at that moment – a genuine communion between human and animal. I brought her water bowl over but she was too tired to lift her head to drink. The first pups managed to latch on to her nipples, and then there was another contraction as the third pup arrived. All in all, six came out, the last one much smaller than the rest. I looked at the clock. It was still only seven in the morning, an hour before I had to leave for school.

Auntie Pat was staying again and while she was there I usually got myself up and made my own breakfast because she and Mum liked to sleep off their hangovers. I worried about leaving the pups on their own, though. Could I pretend to be sick and stay off school? That would never work. Mum made me go to school with raging temperatures and hacking coughs. She wouldn't dream of letting me have a day off.

I cleaned up all the mess on the floor around Janie and tidied her bed to make it as comfortable as I could. The pups were wriggling around her belly, trying to find a nipple, yapping in high squeaky tones and clambering over each other – feet in ears, heads in bottoms, mouths chewing legs. Janie lay in a state of blissful exhaustion, occasionally lifting her head to lick one or to drag it back towards her if it was wandering too near the edge of the bed.

I was dressed and ready for school when Mum appeared in the kitchen, red-eyed and slow. 'Look, Janie's had her pups. Aren't they cute?'

She didn't even look at them. 'You'd better hurry up. Don't be late for school.'

'Mum, please will you look after them for me? Don't let anything happen to them?' I had visions of Auntie Pat

staggering and falling on top of them, or even being deliberately cruel. She was without scruples as far as I could see.

'Go to school,' she snapped, filling the kettle. 'And come
straight home afterwards. No dawdling around.'

She didn't need to ask this. As soon as the bell rang at
four o'clock, I grabbed my schoolbag and ran full pelt
down the lanes, only stopping when the stitch in my side
stabbed too powerfully or my lungs just couldn't take in
any more oxygen. I was home in record time and ran
straight into the kitchen, where Janie was more alert now,
tending her pups like the proudest mother in the world. I
picked one up and stroked its belly and it yelped with
excitement and tried to gnaw my hand. Janie seemed to
trust me because she looked on unalarmed as I played with
her babies. Mum and Auntie Pat were in the sitting room
so I took a huge risk and stole a slice of cold meat from the
fridge and fed it to Janie. She needed to get her strength
back. Janie gulped it back, just as the sitting room door
opened.

'Time to deal with our little problem,' Mum announced,
and I looked up, wondering what she meant. 'Can you
fetch the big blue bucket from the pigsty and fill it with
water?'

'What for?' I asked.

'Never you mind. Just do it. Bring it to the back door.'

My mind was turning over the possibilities as I filled
the bucket. Did she want me to scrub the back step? Wash
the windows? What did she mean about our 'little problem'?

I heaved the full bucket to the back door and Mum
appeared carrying a dark green shopping bag. Yapping
sounds were coming from the top of it.

'Is that the puppies?' I asked, alarmed. 'What are you doing with them?'

'I'm going to teach you an important lesson today,' Mum said calmly. 'It was your fault that Janie got pregnant because you let her off the leash when you shouldn't have done. Now you have to deal with the consequences. What did you think we were going to do? We've got a dog already. We can't take on another six.'

'I'll find good homes for them.' I hadn't yet worked out what she intended but I was panicking. 'I'll ask around at school. I'll put a notice on the board. I could put an ad in the local paper.'

'I'm afraid not. It would take too long and I'd have to put up with them pissing and crapping all over my house in the meantime. It's not going to happen. It's your responsibility to put them out of their misery by drowning them.'

'No!' I wailed. 'Mum, no, please. Don't make me. You can't do this.' I became hysterical and Mum slapped me hard across the face then lifted the first puppy from the shopping bag and held it out to me. I took it from her because I could tell she was hurting it the way she was squeezing it round the middle, making it yelp. I cupped it in my hands and stroked its soft head with a finger, blinded by tears.

Mum put the shopping bag on the ground, grabbed my arm so tightly that her fingernails were digging into my flesh, and then forced my hand, holding the puppy, down into the freezing water in the blue bucket. My fingers relaxed and the puppy struggled clear, yelping with fright as it tried desperately to swim to safety. Mum grabbed my wrists this time and forced both of my hands down on the puppy's head so that it was trapped underwater.

I was screaming, 'No! Stop! Let go! Mum, please don't,' but to no avail. The little legs kicked frantically as the pup fought as hard as it could for life. Then it stopped kicking and went limp and I knew that it was dead.

Mum released her grip on my hands, lifted the body out of the water and threw it on the grass. She reached into the shopping bag and handed me the next puppy. I kissed its little face and it licked me on the lips, before Mum grabbed my wrists and forced me to hold it underwater until it stopped struggling. I was sobbing so hard my chest ached and I could hardly see for tears. I began to pray, in my head, for the souls of these little pups, who were only twelve hours old. I couldn't fight Mum – she was much stronger than me – but I made sure that I kissed each pup gently before Mum grabbed my wrists and forced me to murder it.

When the last one lay lifeless on the pile on the grass, Mum grabbed the back of my hair. 'I think you should see what it feels like,' she said; then she forced my head down into the bucket and held it underwater. I didn't struggle at first. I felt complete hopelessness. I was ready to die at that moment – in fact, I wanted to. After a minute or so, a biological survival instinct set in and I fought to lift my head, but she held me down with incredible strength. Time telescoped. I've got no idea how long I was underwater but it felt interminable. Suddenly she let go and I lifted my head to take a great gasp of air, and realized with despair that I was still alive.

'Now bury them,' Mum ordered. 'I don't want to see them again. I hope you've learned your lesson from this and won't let Janie off the lead any more. If she gets pregnant again, it will be her we drown next time.'

I prayed to God the whole time as I dug a communal grave for the puppies down at the wilder end of the garden, near the hollyhocks. 'Please bless their souls and welcome them to Heaven,' I prayed. 'Please let Nan Casey look after them.' I worried that they hadn't been christened, but surely that wouldn't matter for dogs? I laid them side by side, all cuddled up to each other, then I picked some wildflowers and scattered them on top. I felt as though I would die of grief when it was time to start pouring spadefuls of soil back on top of them. Even though I was sure they were no longer breathing, I worried that they might wake up in the dark, cold earth, and be unable to get out.

Just when I was at my lowest point, my guardian angel appeared over the hollyhocks and spoke to me kindly. 'Don't worry, Vanessa, they didn't suffer. The Lord has welcomed them to His kingdom and their souls are saved.'

'I killed them,' I told her. 'I'm a murderess.'

'You were not to blame,' she said, and reached out a hand towards me as she shimmered faintly in the dusk.

I made a cross by tying two sticks together with a long blade of grass and I sprinkled more daisies and buttercups on top of the little mound, then I sat keeping vigil, unwilling to leave them on their own.

'Supper's ready!' Mum called from the kitchen door. 'It's getting cold.'

With leaden limbs, I walked back into the kitchen. The first thing I noticed was that Janie wasn't in her basket.

'Where's she gone? Where's Janie?' I cried, panicking that she had been drowned as well.

Mum looked amused. 'Keep your hair on. She's around somewhere.'

I found Janie out in the hall searching frantically for her babies. She sniffed in every corner, pushed her nose under each piece of furniture, walked round every single room then started back at the beginning again. For days she kept looking, long into the night. Several times I picked her up and looked her in the eyes and tried to explain and apologize, but as soon as I put her down she would start looking again. I felt horrible, sickening, overwhelming guilt. I was a murderess. I had killed six of God's creatures.

* * *

The following Saturday, I told Dad about it but he didn't seem to understand my grief.

'It was the most practical solution, Lady Jane. Maybe Mum shouldn't have made you watch, but if you consider yourself an animal lover, you have to do cruel things sometimes in order to be kind in the long run.'

'She made me do it, Dad. I had to drown them myself.'

He frowned. 'Well, I expect she thought it was for the best.'

In my heart I closed a door and moved just a little bit further away from him. Although I adored my father, I knew that he had let me down badly over the years. He had been given so many chances to open his eyes and see the truth but somehow, he couldn't do it. Even when I'd been badly injured by my mother, he had allowed it to continue by pretending to himself that it was nothing to do with him and that my mother could not be as bad as she seemed. When I'd truly needed help, he'd given it to me, but only up to a point. He wasn't prepared to stand up to her. In an awful way, he had to choose between the two of us – and he chose her.

But this was one of the times when I saw that my father was in the wrong. He wasn't just fooling himself. I knew that what I had been forced to do to those puppies hadn't been right. If only Dad was around a little more often he would see what life was like for me, living in an isolated cottage with a woman who hated me so bitterly that it seemed she would stop at nothing to make me suffer. The only thing that kept me going was the thought that one day I would find my real mother and she would love me and look after me and she wouldn't let anyone treat me cruelly ever again.

Chapter 26

Most of the spirits I encountered around Shernal Green were friendly, but one night I came across one who wasn't. It was foggy outside and I crept downstairs in the middle of the night to get a drink of water. There was a peculiar, bluish light coming through the windows into the hall, caused by the effects of moonlight on the fog. I shivered a little, sensing something in the dark by the banisters, and next thing I knew I was being shaken violently.

I screamed as hard as I could and kept screaming. The shaking only continued for maybe twenty seconds but it felt a lot longer, then I crumpled like a rag doll on the floor. I knew I had encountered a malign spirit. The Clown whispered to me that it had been trying to get inside me but couldn't. I lay shaking on the hall floor. Up above I heard Mum's footsteps. She came charging down the stairs, clip-clopping in her high-heeled slippers.

'What on earth happened? Did you fall?'

I took a deep breath and tried to get up. 'It was an evil spirit,' I told her. 'It attacked me.'

I suppose I wasn't expecting sympathy but what happened next still came as a shock. Mum lifted her hand

and slapped me full force around the head. As I stood, stunned, she slapped me again.

'Your bloody spirits! I've had it up to here with your weird mumblings and eccentric behaviour.' She slapped me again. 'I will not put up with this any longer.' Another slap. 'Do you hear me?' She hit me so hard this time that I lost my balance and fell, cracking my head on the banister. I lay there dazed, barely conscious. 'I'm going to have a word with your father. I think you are genuinely mad and we should get you committed to a mental hospital where you can be with your own kind of people. I don't want you in my house any more.'

She clattered back up the stairs and slammed her bedroom door self-righteously. I lay there for a long time, feeling very giddy, then I made my way through to the kitchen where I placed a cool, damp cloth over my head where it had hit the banister. I could feel the familiar throbbing headache starting so I did something very daring. I knew Mum kept a pack of aspirins in her handbag so I crept into the sitting room, opened her bag and stole one, aware that I would be in big trouble if she found out. When I'd swallowed it and drunk some water, I crawled back upstairs to bed.

Mum must have spoken to Dad the very next day because he came to pick me up from school. I liked being in the car with him. I felt safe and comfortable there, but I wasn't entirely happy about what he had to say.

'Your mum thinks you have a mental illness and that's what is making you see all these spirits. I think it's not so serious, that you're lonely and these are your imaginary friends.' He glanced across to see how I would respond to this but I didn't say anything. I was thinking about how

Mum had got Nigel put away in a special school when his behaviour got too much for her, and I was sure that's what she was planning to do with me now.

'At any rate, we've decided you should talk to a doctor who specializes in the mind. A psychiatrist, that is. You can explain to him what's going on in your head and maybe he'll be able to help you get better.'

I rubbed my nose, which was suddenly itchy. 'I don't want to get better, Dad. I love talking to spirits.'

'You're nearly twelve. Soon you'll be a teenager. You need to make friends and go out and start communicating with people your own age again. This has gone on for too long.'

'It's only three years since Nan Casey passed over,' I whispered.

Dad sighed. 'But you weren't very sociable before that. I think these spirits of yours prevent you making friends in the real world.'

'I don't want to make friends. I want to be a nun and take a vow of silence so I can live in a convent forever and no one will bother me.' The Sunday school teacher had found me a couple of other books about nuns and the more I read, the more I was attracted to the idea. To have an excuse for a solitary life seemed perfect to me. I also liked the thought of wearing a veil so that no one could grab my hair and yank it at the roots. The suggestion seemed to make Dad very angry though.

'That's the most ridiculous thing I ever heard. You're not going to be a nun. The sooner we get you to a psychiatrist, the better.'

I turned to look out of the car window. I didn't like the sound of this at all. Still, I supposed that if I were sent to a mental institution, at least it would get me away from home. That had to be a bonus.

* * *

On the day of my appointment with the psychiatrist, Mum and Dad drove me to Powick hospital, a big, old, redbrick building on the other side of Worcester, where they specialized in mental illness. I felt very apprehensive in the car on the way there because I knew they were trying to take away my communication with the spirit world. I also knew I wasn't going to lie about it. The Clown had explained to me that I should never deny my gift, no matter how hard it was to tell the truth.

We were directed to a waiting room with curved wooden chairs on metal legs. There was a pungent, institutional smell. I looked round shyly at the other occupants, wondering what they were doing there. There was a dark-haired woman who was hugging herself and staring at the ground, and her aura was one of deep sadness. An elderly man kept pacing up and down, turning with military precision when he reached one side of the room and retracing his steps back to the other. Mum and Dad were called in to talk to my psychiatrist first and while they were away, the pacing man hissed at me, 'The bombs are coming!'

I sat, picking at the skin beside my fingernails and trying not to meet anyone's eye. I heard the tinkle of a bell and some child spirits came to visit me. 'Refuse to talk to him,' one suggested. 'Stick your fingers in your ears so you can't hear what he says.' Another disagreed. 'He won't do you any harm. You might as well cooperate or you'll get into trouble.'

At last Mum and Dad emerged. 'Your turn now, Lady Jane,' Dad said and he led me to the door of a consulting room and gestured for me to enter. 'This is Dr Armstrong. Just answer all his questions and we'll see you outside in half an hour.'

I saw an old man with neatly combed grey hair and thick glasses sitting behind a big wooden desk with a blotter on top. He nodded that I should sit down in the chair opposite him. Over his shoulder there was a shadowy figure of a very old woman floating a few inches off the floor, but he didn't seem to be aware of her.

'Hello, Vanessa. How are you feeling today?' he asked. His voice was stern and I didn't like the way he peered down his nose at me.

'Fine,' I mumbled.

'Can you tell me what age you are?'

'Eleven and three-quarters.'

He wrote something down on the pad in front of him. 'Do you know why your parents have brought you here today?'

'Yes.'

'Could you tell me why you think that is?'

'They don't like it when I talk to spirits.'

He nodded. 'Tell me about those spirits. Who are they, and how do you talk to them?'

'Just in my head. All kinds of spirits.' At that point, the woman behind him introduced herself and told me she was his mother. She said to ask him about her engagement ring.

'Can you give me an example?' he was asking, so I told him what I'd just heard, that his mother was standing behind him and wanted to know about her ring. He looked startled and turned quickly but of course he couldn't see anything there.

'How clearly do you see people?' he asked.

'Sometimes I just see their heads and sometimes it's the whole body. Some are quite fuzzy and others are very clear but they're always hovering just off the floor.'

'What does my mother look like?' he asked, so I described the way her hair was rolled into a bun and she had a mole on her left cheek and she stooped slightly. He frowned and made more notes on his pad.

His mother had faded away now so I examined the room instead. It was dark and gloomy with big heavy drapes at the windows and books piled everywhere. You could see imprints on the shag-pile carpet where people had walked. There was a leather chair with studs in it like drawing pins and I concentrated on counting them.

Suddenly Dr Armstrong hit the desk with a ruler and I jumped. 'You're not paying attention, Vanessa. I asked if you want to get well again and stop seeing these spirits.'

'No.' I shook my head. 'I don't want to stop. I like spirits better than I like people.'

'How are you ever going to fit in the world when you are doing this very strange thing? Don't you want to have a normal happy life with a husband and children?'

'No. I want to be a nun.'

'Are you Catholic?' he asked, looking at his notes in surprise.

'No.'

'Nuns have to be Catholic,' he told me and I reddened, because I hadn't even known that. He began telling me about the monastic lifestyle, painting a grim picture of early mornings getting up in the dark and washing in freezing cold water, the same food day in day out, and constant praying wearing out your knees.

'Do you still want to be a nun?' Dr Armstrong finished.

'Yes I do,' I said stubbornly. What else was there to be, after all? I would just become a Catholic, if that was what I had to do.

'I wonder if you are just feeling upset about your grand-mother dying and that is making you shy away from the world.'

I shrugged. I didn't want to talk to him about Nan – it was none of his business how badly I was missing her – so I consciously blocked his words. I tuned into the spirit world instead and listened to the cacophony of voices of spirits who had a connection with this hospital.

As the session progressed, I could see his aura redden-ing and could sense that he was losing patience with me. At the same time, I became more and more uncooperative, giving the briefest answers I thought I could get away with. Finally, he called Mum and Dad back into the room and told them that he would need to see me again, that he couldn't rule out psychiatric illness at this stage but that he suspected I was just stubborn and wanted to be a martyr.

'That's what I've said all along,' Mum claimed. I didn't point out that she was the one who had said I was mentally ill.

In the car on the way home, both Mum and Dad nagged at me, saying I had to give up these imaginary conversa-tions. If I heard voices in future, I was to ignore them. It was time for me to grow up, they said. In return, I said as little as possible.

* * *

I saw that psychiatrist on and off over the next two years but I didn't give him any more information than he'd had at the first appointment and I could sense he found our sessions boring. Finally he discharged me, giving Mum and Dad the advice that they should just let me be a martyr if I wanted to be.

'Why not let her try monastic life?' he suggested. 'She'll soon grow tired of it.'

'Over my dead body,' Dad growled, but I didn't listen.

My plans to become a nun were the only thing that kept me sane during that dark period and I spent many hours daydreaming about the simplicity of the life I would lead, protected behind the monastery walls, surrounded by kind, older women who grew vegetables and fed wild animals. I wanted to be one of them more than anything. I just had to find a way.

Chapter 27

I n September 1962, I started at Pershore High School
wearing my brand new navy skirt, navy and mid-blue
striped tie and a crisp white shirt. After the village school
it seemed huge and frightening, but I soon realized that
the sheer size made it easier to slip into the background
and be anonymous. I was definitely not one of the 'in'
crowd, especially after Mum chopped my hair into a crude
boyish crop, but that suited me just fine.

From the beginning I was in the top set for maths, and I
also did well at history, religious education and domestic
science. The games teacher enlisted me in the netball team
and I loved playing, but unfortunately I could never make
it to the matches in the evenings and at weekends because
it was too far to travel and Dad usually wasn't around to
give me a lift.

I started singing in the choir at Hadzor church and
found I had a certain talent for it. I only needed to hear a
piece of music once to remember it and although I didn't
have the strongest voice in the world, I had a tuneful
soprano and they were happy to include me in the choir.
The hall where we practised backed on to a monastery

called St Joseph's and for the first time I got to see some real monks going about their daily life. Watching their graceful movements and their kind, calm expressions reinforced my desire for monastic life. I wanted their solitude, stillness and serenity. I had a chat with the choirmaster, whose name was Graham, and I told him my plans.

'You're obviously a very spiritual person,' he said thoughtfully, 'and I can see that it would suit you in some ways, but you must finish your education first. Get the best qualifications you can so that you will have more to contribute to whatever community you end up in.'

I liked and trusted Graham and on one occasion I decided to tell him about my communication with the spirit world. He looked very taken aback and didn't reply for a while, then he said: 'I think you need to keep this to yourself. There aren't many people who will understand what you are saying, yet they will be quick to judge you harshly.'

I was beginning to realize he was right. The psychiatrist had shown me that I certainly couldn't expect understanding from any conventional sources, such as the medical profession. I still hoped that when I entered a convent the others there would welcome my links with spirit and appreciate the insights it could bring.

* * *

My world was expanding in those years and I began to make a few tentative friendships and come out of my shell a little bit. In particular, I got to know the Howard children who lived on the farm on the other side of the canal from us. David, Stephen and Shirley were older than me but we shared the same tortuous journey to school every weekday morning, with a mile and a half walk to Oddingley parish hall where the coach picked us up, followed by the opposite on the return journey home in the evening, so we soon got to know each other pretty well. Before long, I was being invited to the farm at weekends and after school to play in the straw, help tend the animals, or – my favourite thing of all – to exercise the horses they kept. I loved those horses to pieces, especially a black and white one called Pinball, and I was soon a proficient rider, often seen trotting round the lanes and fields of Shernal Green.

I always got covered in mud, manure and animal hair when I went to the farm and I knew I would be in huge trouble with Mum if I had gone home like that, so I became crafty. I sneaked out an extra set of clothes and kept it in a barn at the Howards' so that I could leave my dirty clothes behind for next time and go home looking pristine. I think Mrs Howard must have had some idea what was going on at home because I would sometimes arrive at the barn to find that the dirty clothes I'd left there the last time had been laundered. It could only have been her. When I saw her in the yard I tried to thank her, but she just smiled and winked and told me not to mention it.

* * *

One spring day after I turned thirteen, I got home from school to find Mum with a nasty expression on her face and a cruel red glow to her aura.

'Janie's been shot,' she told me. 'Your precious dog must have been worrying the lambs. Mr Richards at the top farm rang to say he's got her up there.'

'Is she dead?' I asked quickly.

'Not quite, but as good as.'

I started running upstairs to change out of my school uniform, knowing Mum would never let me go up to the farm wearing it, even in an emergency. Halfway up, I turned back suspiciously. 'How did she get out of the house?'

Mum shrugged. 'She must have escaped when I was out in the garden.'

'You left the back door open?' I was horrified. Mum, Dad and I had discussed over and over again that although Janie was very well trained, she needed to be kept indoors or on a leash during lambing season. Any farmer seeing a stray collie in his field would take a pot shot at that time of year.

Mum gave her malicious smile and I knew she'd done it deliberately. I got changed as quickly as I could and rushed over to the Richards' to find Janie lying, barely breathing, on some blankets on their kitchen floor.

'I'm so sorry, love,' Mr Richards said. 'I'd no idea she was your dog until I got up close and read the collar. She was not fifteen yards from my lambs so I couldn't take the risk. We've called the vet and he's on his way.'

I crouched down to whisper to her, trying not to look at the dark blood matting her coat. She didn't seem to know I was there.

The bullet was lodged in her back and although it had missed her spinal cord, she'd lost a lot of blood. The vet decided to operate on the spot rather than risk the bullet moving around if he tried to take her to the surgery. I held her head in my hands and tried to speak calmly to her as he cut the bullet out and cleaned up the wound. Once she was stabilized, he lifted her into his car and drove us slowly back to the cottage, then we carried her to her bed in the kitchen. I could see Mum wasn't pleased at this turn of events – she would no doubt be worried about blood on her kitchen floor – but she was pleasant and chatty with the vet, asking questions about what we could do to help Janie as if she really cared.

At first, Janie barely lifted her head off the bed, sleeping most of the time and wakening only to whimper when the painkillers wore off. As soon as I got home from school I'd sit on the floor beside her, talking to her.

One afternoon the Clown came and suggested that I tried to heal her by placing my hands directly over the wound, a few inches above it. The first time I did this, I felt the strangest tingling sensation in my hands and a real sense of heat radiating between my palms and the wound.

'Imagine that you are drawing out the pain and sending it into the atmosphere, at the same time sending in your own good healing energy,' the Clown instructed, and I swear I could feel this happening. I began to hold my hands over the wound morning and evening, focusing all my thoughts on Janie's recovery.

'What are you doing?' Dad asked.

'I'm sending all my nice energy into Janie to make her well,' I told him, and he looked puzzled but didn't try to stop me.

Just a week later, Janie was up and walking around again, albeit tentatively. It was the first time I learned that

I had healing powers and I was very excited about it and keen to find other creatures I could practise on.

'Don't ever abuse your powers,' the Clown cautioned. 'Only use them wisely or you may lose them. You'll know when the time is right to heal because I will tell you.'

In fact, it wasn't for many years, until adulthood, that I would understand how powerful those powers could be and learn how to use them responsibly.

Chapter 28

The following Saturday, Dad said he was driving Mum to Droitwich to do some shopping, and I could come along if I wanted.

Janie's old collar had got soaked in blood so I decided to use some of my pocket money to buy her a new one. There was a good pet shop in Droitwich where I was sure to be able to find a good one. I ran upstairs to retrieve my pocket money stash from under the wardrobe. There should have been several pounds there. I slid my fingers beneath the ledge but couldn't feel anything. I moved my hand along from side to side then I laid my head down on the floor so I could peer underneath. The money had gone. I noticed indentations in the carpet that showed the wardrobe had been pulled out from the wall and put back in a slightly different position. Mum must have been spring-cleaning behind it and she'd come across my secret hiding place.

I marched through to her bedroom, where she was smartening herself up for shopping. She had on pink lipstick and a burgundy raincoat and she was just bending down to put on a pair of burgundy slingbacks with high stiletto heels.

'Where's my pocket money?' I demanded, made brave by the knowledge that Dad was downstairs so she couldn't punish me – or so I thought.

'What money?' She smiled slyly and I knew she had taken it.

'The money that was under my wardrobe. You've taken it and I want it back.'

'Are you calling me a thief?' she asked in a dangerous tone of voice.

'If you don't give my money back then yes, you are a thief.'

Mum lifted her right hand, still holding the stiletto. I raised my arms to protect my head from the blow and felt an excruciating pain as the pointed heel pierced my left elbow between the bones. I sank to my knees on the carpet and the shoe fell to the floor.

'That will teach you to fling accusations around.'

I felt breathless with the pain. I cradled my lower arm, trying hard not to faint.

'Are you girls ready yet?' Dad called from the bottom of the stairs.

'Vanessa's not coming. She's not feeling well,' Mum shouted back. 'I'll be down in just a sec.' She turned to me with a grim smile. 'You'd better go to your bed and think about the importance of being polite to your elders.'

'I can't move my hand. It's all pins and needles.'

'Stop making such a song and dance about it. As far as your Dad's concerned, you fell and landed with your elbow on the shoe. You'd better not tell him any different or there's more where that came from.'

She picked up her shoe and inspected the heel for blood, then slipped it on and whisked out of the room. Her head reappeared round the door a few seconds later to hiss 'Don't you dare bleed on my carpet.' Then she was gone.

I got up slowly, feeling sick with the pain, and went to the bathroom to survey the damage. Because of the position of the puncture wound, I could only see it clearly in the mirror. There was a hole, maybe quarter of an inch deep, and it was bleeding but not profusely. The main problem appeared to be damage to the nerve that passed between the bones there, because I kept getting shooting pains from my shoulder to my fingertips and it was hard to move my fingers.

I put a plaster over the wound and fashioned a sling from an old scarf, then I went out to sit in the garden for the afternoon, playing with Janie and talking to spirits. When Mum and Dad got back, it was obvious she had already told him her version of the story.

'What a crazy accident, Lady Jane! You must try to stop being so clumsy.' He patted me on the head. 'Maybe we should start calling you Calamity Jane.'

I didn't bother to contradict him. There never seemed any point. I knew what I had to do and that was stay out of Mum's way as much as possible until I was old enough to leave home. I could endure the regular beatings and the nights in the pigsty, and I reckoned I could get through most things Mum could dream up so long as she didn't actually kill me some time. And, to be honest, I didn't much care if she did.

* * *

In summer 1963, Grandpa Pittam's heart problems worsened and he became seriously ill.

Mum was evidently upset and was always dashing over to visit him in hospital whenever she could. This meant I frequently had to wait in the pigsty when I got home from school before she returned to let me in the house. She wouldn't give me a door key, saying, 'I can't trust you in the house on your own. You'd probably go and steal biscuits from the biscuit barrel.'

From the way Mum spoke to me, it was as if it was my fault Grandpa was ill and nothing to do with the heart problems.

'You destroyed him. He's never been the same since you made up your lies. Woe betide you if he dies. God will never forgive you, and neither will I.'

'Mum, you know it's not lies,' I protested. 'You were right there smoking your cigarettes and Grandma said "That will make him happy for the week."'

'Don't be so ridiculous!' she snapped and turned away.

She returned from one visit and told me, 'I asked Dad if he could forgive you today and he said no. He said he never loved you and never would. He thinks you are a self-ish, ungrateful bastard.'

'What's a bastard?' I asked.

'Someone shameful whose parents weren't married when they were born. Just like you. Someone mean and horrible.'

I felt completely unmoved by this. I had wanted Grandpa dead. I didn't like living in a world where I might turn a corner one day and find him standing there with his creepy monocle, stale tobacco smell and leering expression.

One afternoon, Mum came home red-eyed and shaking.

'He's dead,' she whispered when she saw me. 'He's passed away.'

I felt nothing but a sense of triumph that suddenly turned into a surge of bitter hatred. It burst out of me before I could stop it. 'I hate him and I hate Grandma too!'

Instantly I was reeling under the force of the slap Mum gave me. It was true, though. I had thought I might feel a sense of relief when he passed over but my hatred burned as fiercely as ever. Mum was distraught, and took to lying on the sofa sobbing for hours on end, and I felt no sympathy; if anything, I felt angry with her that she was mourning such a monster.

There was an article in the newspaper that weekend about stepfathers who murder their partner's children, after a horrible case that had been in the news all week. Dad read out some of it to Mum and me at the breakfast table: '"These men are often childlike themselves and resent their wife's attention to another man's children but they're not intelligent enough to analyse their own motives. Testosterone, the male hormone, takes over and makes them lash out in anger."'

'Grandpa Pittam was like that,' I said. 'He lashed out at Nigel and me.'

Mum gave a strangled scream then burst into tears, covering her face with her hands. Dad leapt to his feet to put an arm round her, glaring angrily at me. 'That was cruel and insensitive,' he rebuked. 'Can't you see your mother's in mourning? Remember how you felt when Nan Casey died and try to be a bit nicer.'

I scraped my chair back and ran out into the garden. How could he compare Grandpa Pittam to Nan Casey? Why did no one seem to see what a monster that old man had been? It seemed as though Dad had just forgotten the horrors I'd been put through. Had he ever known the true extent of it? Aunt Gilly knew that Grandpa had put his penis in me, but I had no way of knowing what Dad had eventually been told.

More painful, though, was that he could use the past tense when talking about my grief for Nan. It was so raw and recent. Sometimes it felt as though I missed her more every day.

* * *

A couple of weeks after Grandpa Pittam died, I was lying in bed one night when I saw a strange light coming through the curtains. I went to the window and looked out to see a bright spirit hovering over the canal. It was just a light at first but then it began to take on a fuzzy shape. I sensed it was a very important visitation before I could make out who the figure was, and then I gasped out loud. The spirit floated up from the canal. I stepped backwards and seconds later Nan Casey came in through the closed bedroom window. The expression on her face was calm and very beautiful.

'I've been wanting to come and see you to make sure that you're all right. You must have known I would come some time.'

Over the years since she died I had often hoped she would, but didn't dare believe it could be true. As I watched, her outline was becoming clearer until it could almost have been the real person in the room, apart from a luminescent glow around her.

'I've been watching over you and trying to keep you safe. I'm glad you are free from Charles Pittam now but it doesn't mean things will be easy for you. Your life will always be a rollercoaster but remember that you are a strong person. You will be challenged but there won't be anything you can't cope with.'

The figure was starting to pulsate and fade and I reached out a hand. 'Please don't go. Stay a while longer.'

'I'll be back very soon. I love you so much,' she said as she disappeared.

Choked with emotion I climbed back into bed and noticed a single yellow cowslip on the bedside table. That was the first flower that Nan and I had ever pressed together and we both loved them. From then on, whenever Nan visited me she always left behind a cowslip as a present.

I started to worry that Grandpa Pittam's spirit might come to visit, but I was reassured by the Clown that he wouldn't. It is only the people who love you who come back to find you.

Chapter 29

By second year at high school, I'd started hanging round with a crowd of kids outside the village hall after school, buying sweets or swapping magazines or just chatting. It was a way of avoiding going home, so that I had less time to pass in the cottage on my own with Mum. I hovered on the fringes of the group, and only set off for my walk home when the others had dispersed. Mum never worried if I was late. I don't think she would have bothered to call the police or send out a search party if I hadn't turned up at all. It would have suited her right down to the ground.

On 15 November 1963, after the others had headed for their own houses, I was walking home in the dark when all of a sudden a vivid picture appeared in front of me. There was an open-topped black car with flags waving from little flagpoles at the corners. There were two men in the front, and in the back there was a man and a very pretty lady. The picture became clearer and I could see that the flags had lines going across and some stars. The word 'president' came into my head. Suddenly there was a loud bang then another bang and lots of screaming and I saw the man die. Part of his head was blown clean away. I wanted to stop the movie that was running in my head but I didn't know how. It was very disturbing, like a vivid nightmare except that I was wide awake.

I ran the rest of the way home. It was a Friday so Dad was there.

'Where have you been, Lady Jane? I was just coming out to look for you. I thought you'd got lost.'

I was breathless. 'Dad, a man is going to be killed. I think he's a president. What country has stars on their flag and lines across it?'

'America, of course.'

'Well, I think the president of America is going to get shot. I just saw it in a picture.'

'Oh, for God's sake,' Dad said crossly. 'Of course you didn't. I thought we'd told you to ignore all the voices and visions and silly things you see in your head.'

It felt very important that I convinced him that day in case he could do something to prevent this terrible murder.

'Dad, my voices and visions tell me the truth. For example, I can tell you something you didn't know I knew. For your twenty-first birthday, Nan gave you a golf club and a blue and white tankard, and you accidentally dropped the tankard on the floor and smashed it.'

'How did you know that?'

'Nan told me recently. Dad, she comes to visit me. I can see her and hear her just as clearly as I'm seeing and hearing you now.'

Dad sat down on a chair and clasped his head in his hands. 'You can't possibly be seeing Nan. She's dead. She's in Heaven. You might be seeing her in your imagination, because you have a very strong imagination, but you must-n't think that it's her because it's not.'

'So how did I know about the tankard?'

'She must have told you while she was alive and you're just remembering it now.'

That definitely wasn't the case. I couldn't think how to get through to him, but I was very worried about the president I had seen being shot. I overheard him telling Mum about my premonition while I listened outside the door.

'There she goes again. Do you have any idea how scary it is for me being trapped in the house with her all week when you're not here? She's a lunatic. I can't believe the psychiatrist didn't put her away. If only you were here, you'd see for yourself. She's on her best behaviour for you at weekends.'

Dad gave a huge, heartfelt sigh. 'Muriel, you know the deal. I thought it suited both of us.'

'Things change, Derrick. I never thought it would go on for this long.'

'It was your idea in the first place. Don't tell me you've changed the way you feel?'

There was a pause and Mum said, 'No, absolutely not.'

'Well then,' he replied, and she turned on her heel and walked away.

Once again, I began speculating about where Dad went during the week. I'd tried asking the spirits but they weren't any help to me at all. On one of our Saturday walks, I plucked up the courage to ask Dad if he had another lady.

He laughed, gruffly, and looked away. 'Where on earth did you get that idea from? Silly girl. Oh look! There's a jenny wren. They're my favourite bird. What's yours?'

I persevered. 'So when you're not here in the week, where do you spend the night?'

'Here and there. It depends on business. Why does it matter? I'm with you at weekends, aren't I?'

'What if I wanted to phone you in the week?'

'You can always get me at the office during the day.'

So I never really got an answer to the lady friend question and after a while I gave up. He obviously didn't want me to know.

The following Friday, 22 November, I got home late again. As I opened the front door, Dad called to me from the lounge.

'Come in here.' His tone was quite sharp.

Mum and Dad were sitting watching the television news. The newsreader announced that there was breaking news from America, that President Kennedy had been shot. No one knew how serious it was but he had been rushed to hospital where surgeons were operating.

'He's dead already,' I said. 'He died in the car.'

Mum and Dad looked at each other, and I could see fear in their expressions. It wasn't the President dying they were afraid of. They were scared of me, especially next morning when the news bulletins confirmed that I was right.

A few weeks later some footage showing the assassination was released and I couldn't believe my eyes. It was exactly the picture I had seen while walking along the lanes. A big open-topped car with three men and a pretty lady and flags, and as we watched there was a loud bang, and another, and the man in the back seat collapsed. The woman tried to clamber over the back of the car to escape and a security man jumped on and grabbed hold of her as the car sped off. I watched mesmerized.

It shook me up to realize just how accurate my premonitions could be. It brought a whole new responsibility that I would have to work out how to deal with over the years.

Chapter 30

O ne day, very near the end of my second year at Pershore High School, I got home around six o'clock. I was hungry and hoping I wasn't too late for some supper. I hung my blazer in the cloakroom and dropped my schoolbag and walked through to the kitchen – then I stopped dead. There was a tall, dark-haired youth standing by the back door. He had traces of facial hair, a Beatles-style haircut and long, lanky arms and legs.

'Nigel!' I cried and ran over to hug him. He seemed embarrassed but hugged me back in a stiff kind of manner. Mum sat at the kitchen table smoking and watching us intently.

'Are you back to stay?' I asked.

'Yeah, I'm fifteen so I've left school now.' His voice was unrecognizable – much deeper, and his accent had changed somehow. It sounded posher to me.

'Are you going to stay here?'

'For now. I'm going to get a job.'

'You look different.' His hair, which had been dark blond when I last saw him, was now definitely brown, and his eyes were deeper set and smaller.

'So do you. What happened to your hair?'

I'd had long hair with bunches when he went away and now I had the shaggy boy's crop Mum had given me. I glanced at her before replying briefly, 'I had it cut.' I wanted to talk to him in private. 'You coming out to the garden? Do you want to see my vegetable patch?'

'Yeah.' Nigel shrugged.

'Be quick, now,' Mum warned. 'Supper will be on the table in five minutes.'

I felt unaccountably shy around my big brother after not seeing or hearing from him for six whole years, and I could tell he felt awkward with me as well. I showed him my vegetables and we walked round the rest of the garden not saying much at all, until I burst out: 'Why didn't you write to me? Didn't you get my letters? I wrote to you every week.'

'I did!' He was surprised. 'I wrote back. Not as much as you, but I certainly wrote. Didn't you get any of them at all?'

He wasn't lying, I knew that. Nigel was never a liar.

'Mum!' I exclaimed. 'She must have taken them.' She couldn't bear our closeness. She had always been trying to pull us apart since we were young children.

'Would she really have taken my letters though?'

'Oh, yeah. She was the one who usually got to the post first. Why didn't I think of that?'

'Is she still as mean to you as she used to be?'

We slipped down to the canal and sat by the waterside.

'You don't know the half of it.' I told him about sleeping in the pigsty and showed him the scars from the frying pan in my face and the stiletto in my elbow. Then I told him about how the sexual abuse with Grandpa Pittam got worse after he had gone and how Aunt Gilly finally found out when I was eleven. 'You were lucky he didn't do all those disgusting things to you,' I said.

'Oh, he did.' Nigel stared off into the distance across the canal. 'Just a few times, but he did.' He pulled up a handful of grass and started shredding it in his hands.

'But I thought you always fought him off?'

'It happened three times when you weren't in the garage. It was disgusting. He was a bastard. If he wasn't dead already, I'd go round and kill him.' Nigel threw his shredded handful of grass into the canal. 'Why didn't you tell anyone what was going on with you?'

'Sometimes I tried to, not often. They hardly ever believed me. Dad loves Mum, you know. He doesn't see how cruel she is.'

'They always seemed very jolly when they came to visit me. That kind of false jolliness you put on when visiting someone in hospital.'

'What was it like there?'

'OK, I guess. Nothing special. I made some good friends.'

'What did you do all the time?'

'Normal stuff. We had lessons and homework and sport. I'm not a bad spin bowler now. In the evenings we watched TV and stuff. It's just a boarding school where they have medical staff to keep an eye on you. I don't know why I had to stay over the school holidays as well though – most of the other boys went home, but I was kept in so it was kind of lonely. Mum and Dad always said that it was because I needed special care that they couldn't give me – but lots of boys much sicker than me got to go home in the holidays. Maybe they just couldn't be bothered.'

'I really missed you. It was terrible without you.'

'I missed you too, Nessa. I don't know why I had to go there. I used to argue with Mum and Dad when they visited, begging them to bring me back, but they always said I was in the best place.' He sighed.

We could hear Mum shouting in the distance, her voice carrying on the summer breeze, and we stood up to go back indoors. At that moment, I saw a vivid picture of Nigel rolling into the canal and floating face down, unconscious. It was horrible.

'Nigel, you must be careful near the canal,' I told him anxiously. 'You might fall in one day and it's very deep.'

'Yeah, yeah,' he said, in a sarcastic voice. 'I learned to swim at school – I'm pretty good now – so you needn't worry about me.'

The vision stayed with me, though, so later that evening I followed Mum into the kitchen and told her what I'd seen.

'Do you remember how I saw a president being shot in a vision and then it really happened? Well, I've just had a vision that Nigel falls in the canal and is unconscious. I'm scared it's going to happen, Mum. Will you keep an eye on him?'

Mum whirled around with a furious look on her face. 'How many times do you have to be told? You're a freak!' She grabbed me by the hair. 'I've tried and tried to beat this spirit nonsense out of you, but I can see I haven't tried hard enough yet.'

She dragged me to a chair and forced me to bend over it, then lifted up my skirt. Seconds later I yelled as she hit me hard across the backs of my legs with the big stick she still kept inside the utility room. She hit me again.

'What on earth are you doing? Stop it, Mum.' Nigel charged into the kitchen and wrestled the stick from Mum's grip.

'Stay out of this. You've got no idea what she just said.'

'Mum, she's too old. You can't beat her any more. I won't let you.'

He managed to get the stick away from her. I stood up and pulled my skirt down timidly not daring to meet Mum's eye.

'This is my house and I'll do what I like in it. You'll mind your own business if you want to stay here.' Mum blustered but I could tell that she was unnerved by Nigel's disarming her so easily.

'You beating my sister is my business,' Nigel said. 'If it happens again, I'll tell Dad. Do you understand? Come on, Nessa.' He grabbed my hand and led me out the back door. He marched in silence all the way down to the canal and hurled the stick into the water, where it floated off down stream.

'Thanks,' I whispered.

'Things are going to get better now. You'll see.' He put his arm round me, and it felt just like the old Nigel. It was a wonderful moment.

* * *

I still worried about the vision I had seen of Nigel lying face down in the canal, and my fears were confirmed about five days later when I got home from school to find the doctor's car there. Nigel was lying on the sofa, wrapped up in towels. Mum sat in her bathrobe smoking while the doctor examined him.

'What happened?' I asked.

Mum had no choice but to answer me civilly with the doctor present. 'Your brother had a fit while he was down by the canal fishing. He fell in the water, but fortunately I was nearby so I rushed down and pulled him out.'

'It was very lucky you were there,' the doctor said. 'No long-term harm done, but I think he had better stay away from the canal bank in future.'

I caught eyes with Mum. She was staring at me very curiously, her eyes boring a hole in me as if trying to figure out who or what I was.

I kept quiet about my premonitions from then on. Not long afterwards I saw an image of Auntie Pat falling headfirst down a flight of stairs and landing at the bottom with her neck twisted at an odd angle. There was a gin bottle beside her on the floor. Three days later, Mum told me that Auntie Pat had died after falling down some stairs. I didn't say anything, even though I was glad that Auntie Pat would not be coming here any longer. She had egged Mum on to some of her nastier moments and I wasn't sorry she was gone.

* * *

A few months after Nigel got back, I had a very clear premonition that Mum went to waken him in the morning and he couldn't be roused. He was stiff and cold and had died in the night. This was such a distressing vision that I ran crying out to the pigsty to ask the spirits about it. The Clown came to me.

'Yes,' he confirmed. 'Your brother will die young, but not yet. He will have a fit in his sleep. He won't know anything about it.'

'But when will it be? Can't I do something to stop it?'

'He will not live to see his twenty-fifth birthday. I'm afraid there is nothing you can do. You can never use your spiritual powers to affect the future, because it is set out already. You can't cheat fate, no matter how many precautions you take.'

I broke my heart that afternoon, sobbing by myself in the pigsty and praying to God to spare him, but I didn't tell anyone about Nigel dying young. I tucked the knowledge away deep inside me, hoping against hope that it wasn't true, and tried to enjoy the time we had. At the first opportunity I took him up to the farm to meet the Howards. He was the same age as David and Stephen, who were twins, and they hit it off straight away, often disappearing into the woods together for hours at a time. Nigel would come to watch me riding the horses, although he wasn't allowed to try it himself as it was judged too dangerous with his condition. He also started to come with Dad and me on our Saturday afternoon walks. Once Margery joined us and Nigel looked at her curiously, but I could tell he liked her easy, natural manner.

'You've got sparkly blue eyes,' he told her, 'just like Nessa's.'

'Thank you,' she smiled at him and then at me. 'That's a real compliment. Vanessa's eyes are very pretty.'

* * *

Life at home with Mum got infinitely better with Nigel around. There were no beatings, no nights spent in the pigsty, just a few slaps and pinches and mean comments when he wasn't in the room. She still had a need to punish me, though. I could see it burning in her eyes. Sometimes she rubbed her hands together as if itching to beat me black and blue. The next punishment she chose was cleverly calculated to cause me the maximum distress.

I got home from school to find Mum in the kitchen playing with a little chihuahua.

'This is Pancho,' she told me gleefully. 'Say hello.'

I bent down to stroke Pancho, who was a lovely glossy shade of caramel.

'Look. I've bought him his own basket and food bowl and blanket.' She pointed to some expensive-looking accessories over in the corner.

'Where's Janie?' I asked, looking round the kitchen. 'Have they met yet?'

'Janie's gone.' Mum was watching my face carefully, her lips twisted with malicious delight. 'She wasn't well so I took her to the vet and had her put down.'

'No!' I shouted. 'She was fine when I left her this morning. What have you done to her? Is this a trick?'

'No trick. I had her put down. Now we've got Pancho instead.'

I sat down heavily, feeling devastated. 'Janie was my dog. Dad bought her for me. You can't just kill her like that.'

'It's done. She's gone. Get over it.' Mum was enjoying herself greatly. I didn't want to give her the satisfaction of seeing me cry so I ran out to the pigsty to talk to the spirits.

'Is Janie really dead?' I asked them tearfully, but no one seemed to be able to give me a straight answer. She was a perfectly healthy dog of just six years old and should have had another ten years to live. I couldn't believe that a vet would really put down a healthy dog, and I hoped that she had been given away to be rehoused with another family – but I knew I would never find out the answer.

Nigel had been up at the farm all day so he hadn't seen Mum taking Janie away. He was sweet and sympathetic, but he hadn't known her well so he couldn't share the huge sense of loss I felt. As soon as Dad got home the following Friday I told him about it, but Mum had already spoken to him it seemed.

'I heard she had cancer,' he explained. 'The vet diagnosed it and said she was in pain, so your Mum did the best thing. Of course it would have been better if you could have been there, but you wouldn't have wanted her to suffer, would you?'

I remember looking at him and marvelling at his gullibility. Mum could put on a pretty dress and high heels and a slick of lipstick and give him that girly look of hers, with the cute little voice, and his entire capacity for logical thought flew out the window. He and Mum may have had troubled years in their marriage, as I had witnessed, but she still had the kind of guile that had allowed her to steal him from his fiancée in the weeks after they first met. She'd always kept that ability to wind him round her little finger whenever she wanted to.

* * *

I missed Janie very badly but the loss just made me more determined to get out of the house as soon as possible and be accepted into a convent. I was still sure that this was the future I wanted, even though Mum no longer attacked me in the way she used to once Nigel was home. Without his presence, the violence would probably have gone on much longer, because at the age of fifteen I was still only five feet two inches tall to Mum's five foot eleven, so there's no question she had the upper hand physically. She could have knocked me out cold with a well-placed punch any time she felt like it.

A religious existence, locked away from the world, still seemed like only kind of happiness I could hope for in life.

Chapter 31

I had choir practice on Wednesdays and Sundays, and afterwards I took to spending time in the graveyard that stood between Hadzor church and St Joseph's monastery. I liked the older parts, where slanting, lichen-covered grave-stones told tales of love, loyalty and family tragedy. An ancient yew tree spread its roots, buckling graves so that you could almost imagine a skeletal hand bursting through the earth. Its dark green needles carpeted the ground and its wide branches cast gloomy shadows. Squirrels scurried around, scraping up soil to bury their hordes of nuts and seeds with no respect for the graves' occupants.

There was one grave I was especially attached to. John Joseph Lupton, 1843–81, adored husband of Elizabeth 1845–1915, and much-loved father of seven children – Alice, Frederick, Charles, Jane, William, Anne and James. When I looked at the dates of the children's lives, I saw that only William had lived to adulthood. Alice had died as a baby. Frederick, Jane and Anne had all died in the same year, under the age of ten – was it scarlet fever or typhoid or one of those other infectious diseases that carried children off so readily in pre-antibiotic days? Charles had died aged fifteen and James aged seventeen. Yet their mother outlived them all, reaching the age of seventy after spending twenty-four years without her 'adored' husband. What a harsh life she had had with all that bereavement. I convinced myself that she finally died of grief after her only grandchild, William's son, was killed in 1915 in the Great War. I felt as if I knew the Luptons and cared about them.

I was never visited by a spirit from their family but there were lots of other spirits hanging around that churchyard, sitting on top of gravestones or strolling along the pathways. Some liked to show me the wounds or infections that had killed them, which could be disturbing. I saw teenage boys with half their faces blown off, men without limbs, women with purply-black growths on their faces, then they'd reappear whole again to show me what they had looked like before their fatal illnesses or injuries occurred.

Sometimes I strolled through the more modern part of the graveyard, watching as fresh graves were dug and left open to await the shiny new coffins accompanied by grieving relatives. I hated to see the tiny holes, just a foot wide and two or three feet long, that I knew were for babies.

* * *

One day as I sat quietly on a bench in the shade, a monk came along the path towards me. He was wearing the brown robes of St Joseph's and had very close-cropped silver hair.

'Hello. My name is Father John.' He smiled with a warm smile that crinkled the corners of his eyes. 'I've seen you here before. Do you prefer the dead to the living?'

'In most cases yes,' I replied, smiling back shyly. 'Actually, I'm in the church choir next door and I come in here after rehearsals if I have time.'

'It's very peaceful, isn't it?'

Of course it wasn't particularly peaceful for me with all the spirit activity but I had learned my lesson about blurting out such things to strangers.

Father John sat down beside me and asked my name, what school I went to, which lessons I enjoyed; then he asked what I planned to do when I left school.

I was nervous telling him in case he laughed or tried to put me off. 'Well, actually I was hoping to become a nun.'

If he was surprised, he didn't show it all. 'What a wonderful ambition. I suppose that if you are currently a member of Hadzor church you want to be an Anglican nun.'

'I thought all nuns were Catholic. I thought I would have to convert but I wasn't sure how to go about it.'

'The majority of nuns are Catholic but there are some Anglican orders. It sounds as though you need to find out more about the approaches of both religions and think through your options very carefully.'

'Where could I find out?'

'I'd be happy to talk to you about Catholicism, if you like, to give you an idea what you'd be getting into if you decided to convert.'

I was so unused to anyone being spontaneously kind to me that it made me feel guilty. 'I couldn't. I mean, I'm sure you've got much more important things to do with your time.'

'What could be more important than helping an intelligent young girl to find her calling? There's nothing I would like more, Vanessa.'

We agreed that we would meet regularly after choir practice, either in the graveyard or, if it was raining, in the office attached to the monastery. I didn't tell anyone about my new friendship at first, not even Nigel, because I would have been upset if they disparaged or mocked my plans. At the same time, I decided not to tell Father John about my ability to communicate with spirits because I wasn't sure whether the church approved of that sort of thing, and I didn't want to risk alienating him.

* * *

Over the next few weeks Father John taught me about the importance of the Virgin Mary, the significance of the rosary, and the meaning of transubstantiation – that the wine and wafer in Communion don't just symbolize the body and blood of Christ but that they *are* the body and blood of Christ. He taught me that every single word in prayer has a precise meaning, and that a vocation is a summons by God but that it need not lead to a cloistered life; God might have other plans for me but I had to watch and listen carefully to find out what they might be.

I learned my Catechism by heart and was utterly thrilled when Father John gave me a tiny crucifix on a chain for my fifteenth birthday. I wore it round my neck, tucking it carefully under my collar for fear that Mum would notice it. It would have given her immense pleasure to destroy something so special to me, but I managed to keep it hidden, thanks largely to the fact that she no longer attacked me physically since Nigel's intervention.

One day when Nigel and I were out walking in the fields, I decided to tell him about my plans. I explained about how Father John was preparing me to convert to Catholicism and that when I was eighteen I hoped to be accepted to take my vows in a convent. He was very disturbed by the idea at first.

'Nessa, you can't lock yourself away from the world like that. Don't you want to travel, have boyfriends, or have children? You would only be experiencing a tiny bit of what life has to offer. It seems such a waste.'

'But Father John says the rewards of a spiritual life spent in prayer and contemplation are immense. Being really close to God in that way must be amazing.'

'Mum thought she was close to God – and look what that led to!' Nigel said bitterly. 'I don't know how you can believe in all that.'

'But that wasn't really God, I know that now,' I answered. 'I've talked to Father John about it. He couldn't believe that Mum had said the things she did about God – he's nothing like the monster she made him out to be. I don't know if she really thought she was talking to him or not, but I believe it was just another way of terrifying us into doing what she wanted, or justifying the way she lashed out all the time. I mean, she's never been to church, has she?'

'No,' Nigel agreed.

'And beating up young children and deliberately hurting them is nothing to do with the principles of Christianity. It's all to do with loving other people, not trying to destroy them.' Since Father John and I had talked, it had become clear to me that Mum disregarded the most basic ideas of a Christian life. And I knew in my heart that the things she had done to me – and allowed others to do to me – were pure wickedness.

Nigel wasn't convinced. 'But you're telling me that by becoming a nun, you will have a special relationship with God. Isn't that almost the same thing as Mum claimed about her trips to the dining room?'

'No, no!' I desperately wanted him to see the difference. 'I'm praying to God as his humble servant, asking how I can best serve him. Mum pretended that God wanted her to be cruel to us, that he hated us. It's not the same thing at all.'

'No, I suppose not.' Nigel put his arm round my shoulders. 'I just don't want to lose you when I've only got you back so recently.'

'It's three years till I can take vows. You're stuck with me till then.'

Nigel grinned. 'By becoming a bride of Christ, you'll be breaking our engagement. Don't you remember how we used to say we'd get married one day?'

I laughed. That silly childishness all seemed a long time ago now. 'I'm not sure that would ever have been legal, even though we're not related by blood.'

'Probably not.' Nigel looked thoughtful. 'You know, it won't be long before I'm eighteen and I've decided that when I am, I'm going to try and find my real mother.'

'Really?' I couldn't imagine where to start, even though I'd always dreamed that I might find my mother one day.

'Yes. Do you think you'll try and find yours?'

'I don't know. Your mum always sounded nice, though, whereas mine sounds like a nightmare.'

'We've only got Mum's word for that. Which is not worth a lot.'

'True. I'm not sure. Maybe I will.'

'Think about it. If you can face it, then I think you should.'

Chapter 32

Once I'd turned fifteen, I'd had quite enough of school. I was never going to be university material and the teachers didn't seem interested in what I did with my life. Not one teacher had so much as asked what career I had in mind. My classmates were all boy-crazy and interested in fashion and pop music, and although I was quite fond of some of them, there was no one I would miss. All in all, I was looking forward to hanging up my blazer for the last time, even though I had no idea what I would do with myself.

Then Father John came to me with a very appealing offer.

'We're looking for someone to help out in the monastery office. I know you are planning to leave school soon and I wonder if you might be interested? It's not very well paid.'

'I'd love to!' I was immediately eager. 'But what would I have to do? I can't type or take shorthand.'

'It's just answering phones, managing the mailing list, taking money for cards and pens, nothing too taxing.'

'When can I start? Next week?'

'You are enthusiastic! Well, that's good. Yes, by all means, start as soon as you can.'

I was delighted to have found a job, and in a place that held so much meaning for me. I rushed home to tell everyone. Mum seemed happy for me to have a job, although she told me that I'd have to hand over most of my salary to pay for my keep.

'At least you'll be doing something useful for a change,' she told me.

Dad wasn't so happy, though. 'Why does it have to be there? It's hardly the start of a great career. You could do a lot better.'

I didn't listen to him. It sounded just what I wanted and the following week I started work. There were only two of us in the office – an older woman called Maggie, and me – but one of the monks would come and help us when we were particularly busy. It was routine work but I loved it. I had my own desk with a typewriter, a calendar, pens and a notepad, and I kept it scrupulously tidy. When members of the public came in to purchase memorabilia, I felt very proud to represent the monastery. I wrapped up purchases with especial care and smiled shyly as I handed over the change.

Father John often came to sit with me in the graveyard at lunchtime and one day he broached the subject of my conversion. I still felt passionately that I wanted to be a Catholic nun – it was as though I had discovered what my whole life was meant to be about – and I had been urging him to tell me how to initiate the process.

'Before we go any further, I think I should talk to your father. Is he sympathetic?'

'Not really,' I said. The few times I had talked about it with Dad, he hadn't been at all enthusiastic and had just tried to brush off my ambition. 'He's Church of England

and I don't think he likes the idea of me becoming a Catholic. But he hasn't objected to me working here so I hope he'll come round to it.'

'Would you ask him to come and see me some time so that we can have a chat?'

With hindsight, it was ridiculously naive of me to think Dad would give permission for me to convert, but I was in no way prepared for the strength of his opposition when I brought it up. He raised his hand and slapped me across the face for the first and only time in his life.

'How dare you!' he demanded, utterly incensed, his face scarlet with rage.

I clasped my hand to my cheek. It hadn't hurt – not like the slaps I got from Mum – but I was hugely shocked that my gentle, gentlemanly father would do such a thing. I felt as though the bottom had fallen out of my world.

'No daughter of mine will ever join the Catholic Church. And that's an end to it.'

'But Dad, I told you years ago that I wanted to be a nun. It's all I've ever wanted to do.'

'Absolutely not. I forbid it.'

'Please just come and talk to Father John. He thinks I have a calling. I'll be doing good for the community so does it matter which church I am working for?'

'Of course it matters. It makes all the difference in the world.' He buried his head in his hands. 'Where did I go wrong? You came to church with me for all those years and I thought you believed – but now you want to reject your religion wholesale?'

'They're not so different, I promise you. Please just meet Father John and listen to what he has to say. He's a decent man.'

'He's been corrupting my daughter and you call that decent? You're only fifteen years old, for goodness sake, and he's encouraging you to throw your life away. That's it! You are giving up that job at the monastery. We'll find you another, more suitable job in due course.'

I started to cry. 'Please don't do this. I love my job. It's my whole life.'

Dad ignored me. 'I suppose you'll have to work a week's notice, just to be fair, but I want you to tell them first thing tomorrow morning. I'll come in with you to make sure you do it.'

No amount of pleading would change his mind. The very next morning, Dad drove me to the monastery and led me into the office, holding my hand as if I was a naughty child. Maggie was the only person there so he explained to her that I was giving a week's notice. I stared at the ground, unable to speak. Dad had no idea how much he had taken away from me. I had never seen him so angry until now – all through the years of torment and abuse, he'd never been half as furious as he was when I'd told him what I truly wanted. It hurt so much that instead of supporting me, he'd destroyed everything in life that meant anything to me. Without my dreams of the future, I couldn't see anything else worth living for. I felt utterly bleak and defeated.

That lunchtime I went to the chemist's shop in the village and bought a bottle of aspirin, telling the assistant they were for my mother. Back at the monastery I took a glass of water into the tiny cubicle toilet and sat down on the seat. One by one I tipped the tablets out of the brown bottle, put them in my mouth and swallowed. They were quite big and got stuck in my throat so I refilled the glass at the washbasin and swilled them down.

When I'd taken the whole bottle, I sat and waited for them to take effect. I was in a deep black pit and the only light I could see was the light of Heaven, which I hoped was waiting for me. By slapping me, Dad had transgressed a boundary that I couldn't tolerate. I had taken that and more from Mum, but never from Dad. I felt totally alone and tired of living. The struggle just wasn't worth it any more.

Maggie knocked on the door. 'Are you all right in there?'

'Just coming.' I unsnibbed the lock and went back to my desk, where I sat poring over the mailing list. It was maybe about twenty minutes later that I began to feel woozy. Maggie didn't notice at first because she was talking on the phone. I laid my head down on the desk and nodded off.

* * *

I don't remember another thing until I awoke in a hospital bed with a tube coming out of my arm, leading up to a bag of clear fluid on a stand. Just beyond it, Dad was sitting watching me. I closed my eyes again. Why was I still here? I didn't want be alive.

'How are you feeling?' he asked.

I had a poisonous headache and felt very nauseous but I just said 'Fine.' It seemed simplest.

'The hospital are going to keep you in for seventy-two hours for observation but they think you'll be all right. You didn't take a lethal dose.'

Some kind of response seemed to be required from me but I couldn't think what it was so I just said 'Oh.'

'Why did you do it? What happened?' His voice sounded very old and tired.

I opened my eyes and looked at him now. 'I wanted to go to Nan Casey. I don't want to be here any more.'

'Oh, Vanessa. Is it my fault? Is it because I said you can't be a nun?'

'No.'

'Did the spirits you talk to tell you to do it?'

That question made me realize that I hadn't spoken to spirits for days. Where had they been when I was sitting on the toilet gulping back aspirin?

'No,' I said again. 'I'm sleepy, Dad. Do you mind if I have a rest?'

'Your mum's going on holiday with her sister next week. I'm going to take the week off work so we can spend some proper time together and have a talk about everything. Let's leave the explanations till then.'

I pretended to be asleep but as soon as he had left the room I began to focus on opening what the Clown called my 'third eye'.

'Where are you?' I asked. 'Where were you when I was trying to kill myself?'

'I was there,' the Clown told me. 'You just weren't listening.'

'I wanted to die. I still do.'

'You're not going to die for a long time yet,' he told me. 'You're going to have a baby, a little girl, and you'll call her Samantha. She'll be beautiful and loving her will help to make you whole. This is all I can tell you for now. First of all you have to make yourself healthy again.'

The Clown faded away, leaving me filled with a strange new emotion – a mixture of hope and bewilderment. A baby of my own! How could that be? I thought of holding a little one in my arms and feeding and cuddling and loving her – someone who was just mine and I was just hers – and I decided that would definitely be worth staying alive for.

Chapter 33

Mum came to see me once while I was in hospital, just before she was heading up to Anglesey with her sister. I guessed that Dad had talked her into it; I couldn't imagine she wanted to come of her own accord. She was wearing a pale grey sweater dress with a cherry-red necklace and matching cherry-red lipstick, and I remember thinking how inappropriate it seemed to look so perfectly groomed when visiting your daughter who has just attempted suicide. She pulled a chair over to my bedside and smoothed her dress under her as she sat, glancing round with distaste at a noisy group of visitors clustered round a nearby bed.

'So what was that all about?' she asked in a low voice, staring at me with glittering eyes. 'Were you attention seeking? Did you think a dramatic gesture would help you get your own way and you could go off and be a nun?'

I didn't answer. I simply didn't have the energy to deal with her.

She continued her attack. 'You wasted the time of the emergency services. All those ambulance men and doctors and nurses had to leave other, more deserving patients to

come and treat you. Seemingly the woman you work with
– what's her name, Maggie? – almost had a heart attack
when you passed out. And you've brought disgrace on
your family – your dad, Nigel and me. Do you still think it
was a clever thing to do?'

'No,' I whispered, honestly.

'Are you planning to try it again? Because if so, try to
make a better job of it. You'll need two bottles of aspirin,
not just one, and you should go somewhere quiet where
you won't be found for a few hours.'

Tears sprang to my eyes. I couldn't help it. I usually
tried not to cry around Mum because it gave her such
gratification, but I was feeling vulnerable and her cruelty
struck home.

'Still the cry-baby.' She smiled, pleased with herself. She
plucked a tissue from the box on my bedside table and
dropped it beside my hand. 'You'll probably do a lot more
crying next week. Your dad wants to have crisis talks with
you, so I'm glad I won't be around.' She smoothed her
skirt. 'Of course, you know that if you choose to tell him
anything negative about our relationship I'll just deny it.
He'll always believe me.'

So that was why she'd come – to warn me off. I decided
not to offer her any peace of mind so said nothing at all.

'Maybe the psychiatrists will lock you away for good
this time. Make sure you tell them all about the spirits you
talk to – that should do the trick.'

'The spirits have told me I'm going to have a baby,' I
volunteered. 'At least then I'll have someone to love who
will love me in return.'

'Don't be ridiculous,' she spat, obviously irked by the
idea. It was the one thing she'd never been able to do

herself. 'First of all, you're only a child; there's no way you're mature enough to look after a baby. Secondly, you'd have to get yourself a boyfriend and that doesn't seem very likely. Have you looked in a mirror lately?'

To other patients and visitors on the ward, we must have looked like mother and daughter having a heart-to-heart chat as we spoke quietly with our heads close to each other. I began to block her cruel words, tuning in to the spirit world, and she soon got bored.

Will she kiss me goodbye? I wondered. If not, what will anyone watching think? Of course she didn't. She scooped up her handbag, said 'Try to be good for Dad next week,' and clicked out of the ward on her little stiletto heels without a backward glance.

* * *

Dad picked me up the following day and drove me home. Nigel rushed out to greet me and gave me a huge hug. Under-eighteens weren't allowed on the ward, which is why he hadn't visited me in hospital. He never asked me why I'd taken the overdose – but then, he was the only person who knew the whole story and how much losing my job and my dream of being a nun meant to me.

For the first couple of days after I got back, I lay dozing on the sofa, watched a bit of television, ate some food and then went to bed. On the third day when Dad asked me to come out for a walk, signalling that Nigel wasn't to come along, I knew the first of our 'talks' was imminent.

'Lady Jane, I feel as though it's my fault you did what you did. If I hadn't been so adamant about you not becoming a nun …' He glanced at me for corroboration but I carried on walking, staring at the ground.

'I'm worried that you are attracted to monastic life for all the wrong reasons – to escape from the world and from other people rather than because of your love of the Lord. What I want to suggest is that if you get a job, make some friends and try to lead a normal life for the next three years, then you come to me at the age of eighteen saying you still want to be a nun maybe we can think about it again.'

'Thanks, Dad.' I squeezed his hand. I knew how much that concession had cost him.

'But I mean it. I want to see you having the life of a normal teenager. My friend Margery told me there is a youth club in the village hall on Saturday nights and I thought maybe Nigel and you might consider going along. Not necessarily this week, of course,' he added quickly. 'When you feel better.'

'All right, I'll give it a try,' I promised without enthusiasm.

* * *

During another talk, later in the week, Dad broached a rather more difficult subject. 'I know you and your mother haven't always seen eye to eye,' he said, 'but you should know that she loves you very much.'

I wished I could believe this but nothing about it rang true. I'd never seen or felt an ounce of love from the woman I called my mother. Our whole relationship had been one long struggle, and my only ambition had been to survive it. The idea that she might have loved me all along seemed ridiculous. The bleakness of my depression was lifting and I couldn't pretend to him that I agreed with him, even if it would make him feel better.

'Dad,' I said, 'she doesn't love me. She never has. I honestly don't think she ever wanted me. Maybe she would have liked a beautiful, obedient daughter who she could dress up in pretty clothes and show off but she didn't bargain on getting an ugly duckling who is antisocial and talks to spirits. I get on her nerves. I always have. I can't help it, but I do.'

Dad suddenly looked very old and sad. For a moment, I wanted to take the words back and let him carry on living with his illusions that all the awful things that had happened to me were just accidents, or misadventures, or self-inflicted.

He said quietly, 'Your mother has had a lot of disappointments in her life. She really wanted to have children of her own but we tried for five years before her health problems meant she had to have a hysterectomy. How do you think that felt? She said if she'd known how it was going to turn out she'd never have given up modelling, but after the operation she couldn't get back into it again.'

'It wasn't your fault, Dad.' I wanted to comfort him. 'These things happen.'

It wasn't my fault either, I added silently, hoping that he would say this himself – but he didn't.

'Yes, but it was me who talked her into adoption. She found it very difficult to bond with you two. I should never have done that to her. I suppose I thought women have a natural maternal spirit that takes over when you hand them a baby, but that was naive. Your Mum's always been very proud of her looks and she complained they were being ruined by exhaustion after getting up with you two in the night. No sooner would she get one of you settled than the other would wake up.' He shook his head. 'Then it was a huge blow when we found out about Nigel's epilepsy.'

'It must have been very frightening and very sad.'

'You don't know the half of it.' He sighed. 'But you're wrong to think it wasn't my fault. It was. I asked too much of your mother and I shouldn't have done it. Some things should never be asked in a relationship.' He seemed lost in thought for a minute. 'But everything settled down when we moved here to the cottage, didn't they? You two seemed to get on better.'

I couldn't believe my ears. 'Dad, you weren't here all week. You don't know what you're talking about. I …' It was on the tip of my tongue to tell him about sleeping in the pigsty and the beatings and standing in icy water and the frying pan – so many unthinkable acts of cruelty. But he looked lost and sad, with huge bags under his eyes, and I made a decision not to hurt him any more for now. He had aged a decade in the week since I took my overdose and I couldn't do it to him. It wasn't fair.

* * *

Towards the end of our week of talking things through, Dad asked me if I would like to visit his friend Margery. 'I know you miss your Nan and you've been telling me that you're still not close to your mum. I wondered if there are any things it would help to talk to a woman about, things you can't discuss with me? Margery's very nice and she was very upset when I told her what you had done.'

'OK,' I said curiously. I couldn't think of anything I would want to talk to her about but I had always liked her when we met outside the pub, though I hadn't seen her for a while. The walks with Dad had stopped as I got older and once Nigel came back, I didn't need to escape quite so badly. But I could tell Dad was keen on this meeting.

He took me up to Pear Tree Cottage that afternoon and when Margery answered the door, smiling nervously, Dad said he would wait in the pub until we had finished our girl talk.

'I hope your dad didn't force you into this,' she said, leading me through to a sitting room that was incredibly messy, with books and cardigans and bits of paper on every available surface. 'I just wanted to say hello to you and see how you're feeling and let you know that you should ask if there's ever anything I can help you with. I mean …' She swept some books on to the floor to make room for me to sit down. 'You probably think I'm a nosey old bat, but I wondered if you've thought about what you want to do with the next bit of your life?'

I couldn't understand why she seemed so agitated, even upset. 'Dad wants me to get out into the world a bit and make some friends so I'm going to do my best.'

'Excellent. I'm so glad. Are you going to try the Hadzor youth club? Your father said you were thinking about going there.'

'Why not?' I shrugged.

Margery perched on the arm of a chair. 'I'm sure it's not very sophisticated but it's a start. Tell you what,' she suggested, 'why not get a nice smart haircut and maybe some new clothes? There's a brilliant hairdresser in

Droitwich and I'm sure your dad would give you the money.'

'I've got some money of my own, saved up from the monastery.'

Margery nodded thoughtfully. 'Can I make a suggestion? Let your dad buy you some things. He's feeling very guilty about all this business and you know what men are like – they want to do something practical to make amends. I can suggest it to him if you like. Hang on – I've got something that might be useful.'

She pulled an American magazine called *Cosmopolitan* from under her chair and passed it across to me. 'Why not have a look and see if there are any hairstyles you like in there? Or clothes? You would suit the same kind of warm shades that I suit, like olive green or terracotta, or mid-blues to bring out your eyes.'

She came over to sit beside me and we flicked through the magazine together, commenting on styles we liked and groaning at those we hated and gradually she seemed to relax more with me. I felt a bit uncomfortable at first but she was making such an effort to be nice that it seemed churlish not to cooperate. I glanced surreptitiously round at the mess of the room; Mum would have had a blue fit if she'd seen it and that made me warm to Margery even more.

'I know you had to leave the monastery office,' she said. 'Do you think you'll get another job?'

'I suppose so. I haven't decided what, though.' I made up my mind to trust her. 'I'd like to have children one day.'

'I believe children can be a great blessing. My only advice would be to make sure you do it with the right man – someone kind, who will take care of you and stick by you.' She had a frog in her throat as she said this and I wondered again why she had never married. Maybe she'd had an unhappy love affair.

'Why didn't you have children?' I asked.

She gave me a strange, piercing look that I couldn't interpret and said, 'Oh, it just didn't happen that way.'

An hour or so later, we walked over to the pub to meet Dad and Margery warned him: 'I think you'd better get your wallet out, Derrick. Your daughter needs you to take her shopping.'

He gave a pretend groan but I could tell he was pleased. That afternoon, he drove me to Droitwich and hung around while I got a layered haircut like the one Margery and I had picked out from the magazine. He hovered uncomfortably in a trendy boutique while I chose a pair of trousers and two T-shirts and a little necklace with a ceramic flower on it. I used my own money to buy a pink lipstick in Boots the chemist. On the way home, I kept sneaking a look at myself in the mirror, pleased with my new hairstyle and the way the lipstick made my lips shine.

'You won't mention to your mother about seeing Margery, will you?' Dad asked. 'Women, you know. She might feel it wasn't Margery's place to talk to you.'

'I won't say anything. But thanks, Dad.'

Chapter 34

I began to recover from my suicide attempt and the bleakness that had engulfed me. Margery had given me a bit of hope, somehow, and I started to feel better.

On her return from holiday, Mum was predictably scathing about my new look, calling me 'mutton dressed as lamb' but, undeterred, I persuaded Nigel to come with me to the youth club on the following Saturday night.

I don't know what we had expected, but it was a tame affair. Girls sat on one side of the hall giggling and chatting, while the boys lined up to play in table tennis tournaments. On that first occasion Nigel and I stood together and no one attempted to talk to us, apart from the woman at the soft drinks stand who asked if I wanted a straw in my ginger beer.

Over the next few Saturdays, I got to know a few of the girls and began to enjoy myself. Mum tried to put a dampener on it, without fail telling me how ugly I looked as I set out, but I learned to ignore her. At the end of the evening, they used to dim the lights and put on some dance records and I nearly died of fright the first time a boy asked me to dance – what on earth should I do? – but he just shuffled from one foot to the other and by the end of the record I had worked out a few moves from watching the other dancers in the room. Nigel never took part in the dancing. After a few weeks he stopped coming at all; it wasn't his kind of thing.

* * *

One night, a group of boys I hadn't seen before came in carrying motorcycle helmets. It created quite a buzz amongst the girls and I was overjoyed when one of them made a beeline for me as soon as the lights were dimmed. Funnily enough, his name was Nigel. He had a harelip, but to me he was gorgeous and desirable, mainly because he had a motorbike. Usually I walked the mile and a half home but he offered me a lift and I accepted with great excitement.

He got on the bike first and showed me how to swing my leg over to sit on the seat behind him. Of course, you didn't wear helmets in those days. Shyly I put my arms round his waist and rested my feet on the footrests and we were off. I clung on for dear life but made the classic mistake at the first bend in the road when I tried to straighten up to counteract the way the bike was lowering to the ground.

'Don't do that,' he shouted. 'Lean into the bend like I'm doing.'

Next time I got it right.

All too quickly we turned into the bumpy lane that led up to the cottage and it was then I realized how noisy the engine was. I'd been hoping Nigel would stop for a chat in the garden and maybe ask me out on a date before he disappeared off into the night. Instead, I saw Mum's face at the sitting room window and seconds later she was charging out the front door in high dudgeon.

'How dare you make such a racket in a quiet area!' she snapped at Nigel. 'Get out of here before I call the police.'

Nigel looked at me uncertainly. 'I'll see you around, Vanessa,' he said.

'No, you won't,' Mum told him. 'You're common as muck and no daughter of mine will have anything to do with you. Get out of here.'

I tried to intervene but Nigel didn't want the hassle. He stamped on the bike's throttle and roared off.

Mum slapped me hard round the head. 'You little slut!' she hissed. 'I shouldn't have expected any better.'

'But we didn't do anything.'

'I don't care. What will the neighbours think? You've crossed the line and I want you out of here. Go and stay in your beloved pigsty tonight and I'll have your belongings packed and at the back door tomorrow.'

I was astounded. After everything that had happened between us, this was the final straw? It seemed unbelievable that something so innocent should incense her to the point where she would throw me out.

'You can't do that! Where will I go?'

'It's not my problem any more.' Mum stormed back into the house, slamming and locking the door behind her.

I knocked and shouted for a while but I knew that she wouldn't relent. Nigel would never waken because his medication made him sleep very soundly. I was outside for the night. At first I was filled with fury that she was making me go through this again, that she still wanted to

control me and make me suffer. Then I calmed down and
went to the pigsty to see what I could find.

It had been so long since I'd been there that I wasn't
sure what I'd left behind. Luckily I found a pile of sweaters
and a coat. It was not a cold night and I'd slept there so
often that it felt familiar and comforting. As soon as I had
settled down I began talking to spirits.

'Is she really going to throw me out?' I asked. 'What
will I do if she does?'

'Call your Dad at work on Monday,' one suggested. 'He
won't let her get away with this.'

I liked the suggestion the Clown made better. 'Go and
see Father John. He'll know what to do.'

I also considered going to see Margery because she'd been
so kind to me before, but then Mum might find out. I'd promised Dad I wouldn't say anything about meeting Margery.
Mum might be cross with him and I didn't want that.

* * *

When I woke the next morning there was a small brown
suitcase of clothes on the back doorstep. I looked in the
window to see Mum smoking at the kitchen table. I tried
the back door but it was locked. Mum made a shooing
motion with her hand, urging me to go away. I packed the
old coat and sweaters in my case then set out across the
fields to St Joseph's.

I was too embarrassed to go to the monastery office – I
hadn't seen any of them since my overdose, although I had
called Maggie to apologize – so I sat in the graveyard with
my bag by my side. Father John saw me from the window
and came out.

'How are you?' he asked, his eyes full of compassion.

I felt desperately ashamed. 'I'm so sorry for what I put you all through. I couldn't see any other way out.'

'You could have tried talking to me.'

'I know, I know. I'm sorry. I don't know what to say.'

'Vanessa, I know a little about your home life from our conversations, so I think I can understand to an extent. I want you to know that I will always help you in whatever way I can.'

I felt so guilty I couldn't meet his eyes. 'That's why I'm here today. Mum has thrown me out of the house and I don't know what to do.'

He looked at the suitcase on the ground. 'Yes, I wondered what that was doing here. You poor thing.'

'No, it's all for the best. It's time I found a job and some-where of my own to live.'

'But you're only sixteen. It's very young to fend for yourself.' He smiled. 'I have an idea though. A friend of mine has a hotel called The Raven in Droitwich. She's always looking for young girls to waitress and be chambermaids. You get room and board and a little money but she's quite strict about the time you get home at night and she keeps a close eye on her girls. Shall I give her a ring?'

I agreed straight away. What other choices did I have?

Chapter 35

The Raven was a smart, black-and-white-timbered
Tudor-style hotel in the heart of Droitwich. I was allo-
cated a small bedroom in the eaves to share with a tall,
pretty blonde girl called Caroline, and we soon became
firm friends. Apart from the new purchases Dad had given
me, my wardrobe was limited to corduroy trousers,
frumpy A-line skirts and sweaters hand-knitted by Mum,
but Caroline was happy to share her own, fashionable
clothes with me. Her jeans were too long, but I borrowed
floaty skirts, tight fitting T-shirts and colourful strings of
beads, and I felt like a million dollars. There were several
boys chasing after Caroline and she used to ask my advice
about them: should she date Harry because he was rich, or
Dean because he had a car, or William because he was the
best-looking? I felt very sophisticated and worldly-wise
discussing such issues, although I'm sure my advice wasn't
up to much.

As Father John had warned me, employees at The
Raven were subject to a strict curfew but Caroline got
special dispensation to borrow a spare key one night to
attend a family celebration. She made a copy of the key and

from then on, she and I could go out late so long as we crept in quietly and avoided the creakiest floorboards on the way up to our room.

The work wasn't fun, of course. Cleaning other people's toilets and making their beds, picking up their clothes and changing their towels was menial, arduous work, and the smells in some rooms took me back to my nights lying in urine-soaked sheets as a young girl. I was nostalgic for my days in the monastery office when I was so proud of the work I was doing, but at the same time I had a much better social life at The Raven.

Dad was even more disapproving than he'd been when I got my job at the monastery. 'When are you going to do something that uses your brains? You were always good at maths. Why don't you do a book-keeping course? Or even accountancy? I could help you to get work experience. Come back home and we'll see what's available.'

'But Mum threw me out!'

'She didn't mean it. You're our daughter and you can come back any time. Think about it, will you? You're far too young to leave home.'

I glanced at Mum. She raised her eyebrow just a fraction of an inch and I knew she was indicating that no, I wasn't welcome back home at all. I had no choice but to make the best of my new job at The Raven.

Caroline and I and a few of the other employees used to frequent a coffee bar down the road from the hotel where they had a jukebox with up-to-the-minute pop music and the crowd was young and lively. One afternoon when our shift had finished, we were sitting in there when a couple of boys came in and sat at the next table. Caroline knew one of them, Charlie, so I found myself talking to his friend, John.

'Are you a Beatles fan?' he asked. 'All the girls seem to be.'

I wasn't very well up on Beatles hits but I liked what I'd heard. 'I suppose so. How about you?'

'*Revolver* is the best album yet. I was reading an article about "Eleanor Rigby" today. Do you know it?' I nodded. 'It seems it was nearly called "Daisy Hawkins". Paul McCartney wrote that line about Daisy Hawkins picking up the rice in the church where the wedding has been and it was only later he decided to make her an old woman and called her Eleanor Rigby.'

I was trying to remember the lyrics of the song but could only think of the chorus about all the lonely people. 'It's kind of sad, isn't it?'

'Yes, but clever too.'

A catchy new song came on the jukebox, with lyrics about good vibrations.

'I like that. Who's that by?' I asked.

'The Beach Boys. It's number one right now,' he said, and I felt foolish for not knowing.

My pop knowledge didn't stretch to further conversation, so I asked him where he worked, and immediately kicked myself mentally for coming up with such a boring question.

He didn't seem to mind. He told me he was doing a mechanical engineering course at a local college, and was currently on a work placement with a car manufacturer. I found out he was eighteen, two years older than me and had just passed his driving test. He liked football and supported Aston Villa. On paper, it was hard to see what we had in common but when you scratched below the surface there were plenty of hints that he'd had an unhappy childhood. I later found out that he had a violent, aggressive father and a mother who was in love with someone else, a married man whom she kept hoping would leave his wife for her. We didn't go into much detail about our backgrounds but it was obvious we had both been victims of cruelty and emotional neglect.

'Will you be here again tomorrow?' he asked me when it was time for Caroline and me to go back to the hotel.

'Yes,' I nodded. 'I'll maybe see you then.'

'So?' Caroline demanded as we walked up the road. 'Do you like him? He's very good-looking.'

'Is he?' I wasn't an expert on such matters. He was taller than me, with brown, floppy hair and sad brown eyes. He had dirty fingernails and long, sensitive fingers. I wasn't attracted to him in any sexual sense but emotionally I felt a bond that made me look forward to seeing him again.

'Go for it,' Caroline advised. 'What have you got to lose?'

I wasn't quite sure how to 'go for it' but I turned up at the coffee bar the following afternoon. John was there and we chatted and before I left he'd invited me to the pictures on Saturday night. We saw Michael Caine as the philandering Alfie and both agreed he was brilliant in the role. Afterwards we went for a walk in the park and had a quick, clumsy kiss on the lips before John dropped me back at the hotel in time for curfew.

'See you next Saturday?' he asked, and I wondered how I would be able to wait that long. I felt so excited to be 'dating' someone that I wanted to see him again the next day. As it happened, we met up at the coffee bar two or three times during the week and soon slipped into a routine of going out every Saturday night. On Sundays, my day off, I got the bus back to Shernal Green for lunch and I took the first opportunity to tell Nigel that I had a boyfriend, when we were out for a walk in the fields.

'Lucky you!' he said gloomily. 'There's no chance of me meeting anyone round here.'

'Aren't there any nice secretaries at the office?' Nigel had recently started work at Dad's electro-plating company.

'They're all a bit dumb and twittery, you know?' He made a yak-yak motion with his hand, then reached into his pocket and pulled out a pack of cigarettes and a lighter.

'When did you start smoking?' I asked, surprised.

'A while ago. I used to smoke a bit at school, in a lane round the back of the dorm.'

'Does Mum know?'

He smiled grimly. 'She does now. She caught me nicking some of her fags last week when I'd run out and she gave me a right earful.'

'If that had been me, I'd be dead.'

'Yeah, you probably would have been.' Nigel laughed and shook his head. 'I can't believe it, you know. Little Nessa with a boyfriend. Is he being nice to you? Because if not, just let me know and I'll come and have a chat with him. Bloke to bloke.'

'He's being very nice,' I smiled. For the first time, I was glimpsing a life beyond my awful home and my mother. Perhaps there were people who would love me and perhaps I did have a chance to be happy. The main thing was that I had hope, something I'd never had before. It felt good.

* * *

It was December 1966 when John and I met. The following March, for my seventeenth birthday, he borrowed his dad's car, a red Austin A40 to take me out. We went to a pub called the Purdiswell in the countryside between Droitwich and Bromsgrove and although you were supposed to be twenty-one to drink there, he had a couple of pints of lager while I had ginger beer. He hadn't got me a birthday present or a card but I didn't mind. I felt very grown-up to be out in a pub with a boyfriend of my own.

After we'd finished our drinks, John suggested we drive out to a secluded spot he knew down a lane near some woods. There was a shy yet lascivious look in his eye and I felt nervous – but at the same time resolved to give him whatever he wanted, for lots of different reasons. I knew I wasn't beautiful, like Caroline or Mum, so to keep a boyfriend I would have to offer something else, something more than prettier girls would offer. Grandpa Pittam had always told me that letting him have sex with me would make him love me and although I knew that had been a black lie in his case, I still hoped it would work with John. I liked him. He seemed like a kindred spirit and I hoped so much that he was the one for me. If he was, then there was a good chance that he was supposed to be the father of the baby I longed for so much, and that she would arrive sooner rather than later. But if I said no to what he wanted, maybe he would break up with me and I knew I would be devastated about that.

All these things made me decide to let John go as far as he wanted. He began to kiss me, breathing heavily with excitement. I kissed him back. It was such a different sensation to what I had felt with Grandpa Pittam – that had been a revolting and unpleasant experience. John was softer and sweeter and I liked kissing him.

I would have liked to go on just kissing but after a while he ran his hand up my leg. I made no attempt to stop him. Then he put one hand on my breast and again, I didn't object. John was surprised and a bit nervous when he realized he wasn't going to meet any resistance from me.

'Do you want to ... do it?' he asked.

I nodded.

John stared at me for a moment, then suggested we got into the back seat where there was more room. Now that I'd agreed, he seemed in a hurry to get on with it in case I changed my mind. We scrambled over to the back seat and he began to kiss me again, this time more intensely, while he tried to unfasten my bra with one hand. At last he managed it and he cupped my breast in his hand, pulling and tweaking at it. After a few minutes of this, he moved downwards, pulling up my skirt again and feeling round for the top of my panties. Once he'd hooked them, he pulled them down my legs.

What am I doing? I asked myself. Is this sex? Is this really what everyone goes on about so much?

I knew that Grandpa Pittam had enjoyed what he'd done to me, but I had never understood how any woman could like what it all involved. Now, here I was with John and he wanted to do the same thing to me. Perhaps if

Grandpa had left me alone, I might be enjoying this now, I thought. I might be able to understand what it was all about.

As it was, I stopped liking what was happening to me. I hadn't minded the kissing, but once I realized that John was fumbling with his trousers and I knew what it was he had there and what was coming next, I turned cold and numb. I distanced myself mentally in the same way I had in the garage when I was bent over the rocking horse. I floated above my body and looked down on the car, where I could see a dark-haired boy struggling to get his semi-erect penis inside a mousy-brown-haired girl. I yelped with pain when he succeeded – it was extremely sore.

John kissed me sweetly, thinking I was a virgin and he'd just 'plucked my cherry'.

It was over very quickly, in less than a minute, and he handed me my pants to put back on. John seemed as pleased as punch, and I was glad he was so happy. It hadn't been as bad as it had been when I was younger. Perhaps I could even grow to like it.

'You're my special girl now,' he told me, grinning broadly. 'You and me are an item.'

He drove me back to the hotel resting his hand on my knee between gear changes, sneaking shy grins at me all the way. 'See you soon, girlfriend,' he said as he dropped me off. Upstairs, I got into the bath and soaked for ages, feeling very detached. What was I doing? I didn't love John. We only had a very basic level of communication and often sat in silence for ages before one of us could think up another topic of conversation. Still, it seemed I was officially his girlfriend now.

I wondered if I was falling in love with him. I certainly liked the feeling of being special to someone. He had chosen me and he liked me enough to have sex with me – and I liked him too. There was a softness, an insecurity about him that I found very touching. Was that what love felt like? I didn't know but I was looking forward to finding out.

Chapter 36

John and I increased the frequency of our dates to two or three nights a week. We always saw each other on Friday and Saturday nights and Sunday afternoons, and between times we'd leave little love notes under a brick near where he lived. We'd go to the cinema, to the Winter Garden disco, for meals or for walks. We'd have a snog at the pictures or in the park but he wasn't able to borrow the car again so we could have sex, and I was secretly relieved.

I didn't tell Caroline what I'd done that night; it didn't seem like any of her business. A month later, though, she guessed when I started throwing up in the toilet every morning, often having to clutch my hands to my mouth and run when I started retching unexpectedly. At her urging, I took a urine sample to a nearby clinic and they confirmed that I was pregnant.

I was filled with joy when I got the news. I had suspected that I was pregnant but now that I knew for sure, I was over the moon with delight. The Clown had been right. I knew that my little girl was growing inside me with every hour that passed.

'I'm going to have a baby!' I told Caroline, my face bright.

'I thought as much. Bloody hell, Vanessa. What will your mum say? You're going to have to get rid of it,' she said, with a disapproving tone.

'I'm not getting rid of it. I'm going to have it.'

'You seem very happy about it, I must say. Not many unmarried girls look like you when they find out they're expecting. Have you told John? Is he going to marry you?'

'Oh. I don't know.' Strange as it may sound, I hadn't considered this possibility for a moment. John and I were getting along perfectly well and I liked being with him but I'd never imagined being married to him. I'd known I might get pregnant if we carried on doing what we had that night in his car – although we hadn't had the opportunity since – but I'd always thought of the baby, and not of John. Of course, now Caroline raised them, there were practicalities to think about. John was the baby's father, and I would need financial help to raise it. But I didn't want to think about that now – all I knew was that I just wanted this baby more than I had ever wanted anything in my life.

'I'll tell him on Saturday,' I said. 'We're going to the pictures. I'll do it after that.'

'Rather you than me.' Caroline seemed quite cool. I'd transgressed some code of behaviour and she didn't approve – or maybe she was just cross that I hadn't confided in her at the time.

On the Friday that week, I was called to reception with the message that there was an important family phone call for me. We weren't usually allowed to take incoming calls but the manager made an exception just this once.

I took the receiver. 'Hello?'

'It's your mother here,' the familiar voice said. 'I'm calling with some bad news, to let you know that Grandma Pittam died yesterday. I don't suppose you'll care.'

I thought about the way that woman had scrubbed me in her corrugated tub and offered me to her husband for whatever disgusting purposes he had in mind, and I felt nothing at all. No grief, no triumph. 'I've got news for you as well,' I said. 'I'm pregnant.'

There was an audible gasp.

'Isn't it strange?' I continued. 'One life snuffed out just as a new one is beginning.'

'Have you told your father yet?'

'No, I haven't even told John, my boyfriend. I'm going to keep the baby, though, no matter what anyone says. I'm not giving it up.'

'Do you realize that this news is going to break your father's heart?'

'There's nothing you can say that will change my mind. I'm an adult now.'

'Oh yes, very mature. I can see that.' Mum's tone was heavy with sarcasm. 'You've got it all thought out, have you? Where you're going to live and who is going to support you? You're not just another slut who's got herself knocked up in her teens by being too stupid to know better? Surely not.'

'I'm going now, Mum. I'll bring John to meet you some time.'

Our conversation didn't rattle me at all. I felt calm and contented, positive that everything would work out somehow.

* * *

I told John while we were walking in the park after the movie. He recoiled as if someone had punched him hard in the stomach.

'But you can't be pregnant! We only did it once!'

'It seems once is enough.'

'What are you … I mean, what do you want to do?'

'I want to keep the baby after it's born.'

The panic in his expression made him seem very young and I felt sorry for him. I put my arm round him and kissed his cheek. Poor John. He hadn't banked on this happening that night in the car.

'Oh my God, Vanessa. How can we?'

'I'll manage. I don't know how yet but I'll work some-thing out.' I gave him a tight hug and could feel him shaking.

He pulled away. 'I'll drop out of my course and get a job, then we'll have enough money for a little flat somewhere.'

'I don't want you to stop your course. You've only got another year to go. Let's just wait and see.'

I could see that John was terrified, only a child himself, and I did get momentary cold feet. I knew I would love motherhood but how was he going to cope with the responsibility of being a parent? It was too late to worry about that.

We went to see his parents the next day. I didn't like his father, Fred, on sight, and not just because of the few anec-dotes John had told me about his violence. He had the same aura as Mum – an angry, pulsating red colour – and his eyes were those of a malicious bully. John's mother, Nelly, seemed a needy damaged person. She obviously disapproved of me but I couldn't blame her: she couldn't have wished this future on her son – making a girl preg-nant out of wedlock when he was only nineteen.

Nelly asked lots of questions about my family, Dad's electro-plating company and the cottage, and the answers seemed to mollify her somewhat as she realized the Caseys were substantially better off than her own family.

When John and I went back to Shernal Green to meet my parents the following weekend, Mum was on catty form. 'Where exactly do your parents live, John?' ... 'Is that a *council* house?' ... 'When you say you're studying mechanical engineering, does that mean you're going to be a *mechanic* one day? Fixing other people's *cars*?'

John answered her questions politely, as if oblivious to her patronizing tone. I felt proud of him then, and glad to have him as my boyfriend.

Dad hardly said a word throughout. He had greeted me with a kiss and a hug but he looked grey and shocked. This wasn't the future he'd wished for me either – perhaps now he was wishing he'd let me follow my dream of becoming a nun, I thought grimly. Nevertheless, I felt that he would stand by me and I wished I could have gone for a walk with him, just the two of us, so that I could tell him how happy I was and to put his mind at rest. But I couldn't have left John to Mum's tender mercies.

'Where are you going to live when you can't work any more, Vanessa? Don't think you're coming back here,' Mum said.

John interjected to explain a plan he had only told me about that morning. 'My mum is getting a flat in St John's in Worcester and she's going to find one that is big enough for the three of us to share. I'll carry on with my course but take a job in the evenings to make a bit of money and we'll get by.'

That sounded like a good solution, I thought. I would need someone to help me as I got bigger and I had a feeling that I wouldn't be able to depend on Mum to help me.

'What's happening to your father?' Mum asked, frowning.

John looked at the ground. 'Mum's leaving him.'

'Well, that's a good example to set,' Mum sneered. 'No wonder she's got a son with no moral values, who's happy to get a young girl up the duff.'

'Shut up! That's enough!' I snapped. She was furious – I'd never dared tell her to shut up before and I knew she would be dying to hit me but she obviously couldn't in present company. I stood up. 'We should probably be going now. I'll let you know the address when we move into our flat.'

Dad didn't offer to drive us back to Droitwich so we went out to the main road and stood waiting for the bus. I'd been hoping to see Nigel but there was no sign of him. At that moment I realized that I was putting my future in the hands of the timid young boy next to me and I shivered slightly, despite the warmth of the spring afternoon.

I'd been so positive and sure of what I was doing. Had I made a terrible mistake?

Chapter 37

We moved into a tiny two-bedroom flat in St John's in the middle of May 1967. John's mother was sporting a lurid black eye after a last, fierce run-in with his father. She sat in an armchair while John carried our boxes and suitcases up the three flights of stairs. I unpacked crockery in a kitchen the size of a small cupboard and tried to hang all Nelly's clothes on a rail that was shorter than my arm. There was a strong smell of damp and I could see where it was coming from: orange stains crept up the walls from the skirting board and a grey fungus was growing on the bathroom ceiling. The ancient, faded carpets stank of dust and stale tobacco, and the beds sagged so steeply in the middle that you could make out the exact shapes of the last people who had slept there.

I had already handed in my notice at The Raven and said goodbye to my friends there, promising to keep in touch. I threw myself into cleaning up the flat and making it as homely as I could, thinking that was where my new baby would spend her first months at least. I dragged the carpets down the stairs and out to the dingy back yard and I beat them and beat them, watching clouds of dust billowing out. I remembered reading somewhere that dust is mostly made up of shed flakes of human skin, so I turned my head away trying hard not to inhale it.

The landlord refused to pay for a few pots of paint and we couldn't afford any ourselves, but I bought some strong disinfectant and washed down the walls, woodwork and tiles, scraping off the fungus with a knife. I washed the windows and lightshades, the water quickly turning black with decades' worth of grime, and I aired the mattresses. The flat was still dingy afterwards but at least it was a little more hygienic.

While I did all this work, Nelly seemed struck down by lethargy. She had been hoping that once she left John's dad, her lover would also leave his wife and ask her to set up home with him, but it didn't seem as though that was imminent. She sat in her chair and talked to me endlessly about the soap-opera scenario of her marriage and her lover and never once asked how I was feeling. She seemed to take it for granted that I would do all the shopping, cooking and cleaning.

Meanwhile, John and I hardly saw each other. He had his course to attend during the day then he worked an evening shift for a metal castings company, so it was often eleven or midnight by the time he got home. If Nelly was seeing her lover in the evening, I stayed in on my own watching a little black and white rented television and talking to spirits and to the baby in my womb.

'Hello, little girl. I'm going to give you the best life any child ever had. I'm going to teach you all the things Nan Casey taught me – about pressing flowers and baking cakes and hopscotch and all about love.'

The Clown often urged me to conserve my energy and stop running around after John and Nelly. 'You will need your strength for yourself and for the little one,' he counselled.

But I really didn't have any choice in the matter.

* * *

I'd been feeling under the weather since we'd moved in to our flat. I felt very tired and heavy, and I often found it difficult to breathe in the stifling atmosphere of that flat. I was very upset in early July, during the fifth month of my pregnancy, when Nelly announced that she and her lover were going on holiday together for two weeks and then John told me he was heading off for a break with the lads somewhere near Stonehenge at the same time.

'Can't I come too?' I asked. I had thought I was part of the family now but it seemed not.

'It's all boys,' he replied. 'You wouldn't enjoy it.'

'Never mind,' Nelly soothed. 'You rest here and we'll be back before you know it.'

John seemed embarrassed and couldn't look me in the eye as he packed his case and kissed me goodbye but I didn't remonstrate with him. I didn't feel I had any right. Maybe it was fair enough that he had a holiday – after all, he worked hard to support us the rest of the time.

While they were away, I planned to catch up with my friends from The Raven and try to spend a day with Nigel, but I went down with a bad summer cold that settled in my chest. At the same time, I started to suffer from horrible lower back pain, which I attributed to the pregnancy and my rapidly changing shape. Although our little flat was roasting in the July heat, I seemed to feel cold the whole time. I wasn't sleeping at night because I couldn't get comfortable in the bed with the acute ache in my back and if I did nod off I woke myself again coughing. I became so weak that I didn't dare go out to buy food because I didn't think I'd be able to climb the three flights of stairs to get back again.

'Call a doctor,' the Clown urged me, but we didn't have a phone in the flat and I didn't know any of the neighbours well enough to bother them.

Besides, I thought, it's only a cold and back pain.

By the time Nelly and John got back, I was lying on the sofa unable to move. They told me that my skin was grey and my lips were blue. John rushed out to call a doctor, who examined me and told me that I had a serious kidney infection as well as bronchitis. He wrote a prescription for some antibiotics and sent John out to fetch them. Once he'd left, the doctor regarded me seriously.

'On top of your other health problems, it looks as though you have an incompetent cervix. It's opening slightly and you're at risk of losing the baby.' He frowned. 'You haven't had a pregnancy before, have you? Maybe a miscarriage or something?'

'No.' I flushed bright red at the suggestion.

'It's just that your cervix looks quite damaged. I recommend that you get as much bed rest as you can for the rest of the pregnancy, to try and keep that baby inside you to term. Where do your parents live?'

'Shernal Green. In the countryside outside Droitwich.'

'And how do you get on with them? I presume they know about your condition?'

'Yes. Why do you ask?'

The doctor looked around him at the stained wallpaper and filthy furniture. 'I don't think you should stay here any more,' he advised. 'It's not good for you and it's not good for the baby. You're very run-down and that's another factor that could compromise the pregnancy. Why don't you go home for a while and let your mum take care of you?'

If only you knew, I thought. 'I'll see what I can do,' I said.

More than anything I was determined not to lose this baby so I decided to see whether Mum and Dad would let me come home. I got John to phone Dad at his office that afternoon and tell him about my illness and he said he would be there within an hour.

As I lay waiting for him, I was thinking to myself that I knew exactly how my cervix had got damaged. Having Charles Pittam's penis inside me at the age of eight, ripping and thrusting at delicate tissues, had been responsible. It made me even more determined that I was going to keep this baby in my womb safe.

Dad was horrified when he saw the squalor in which I had been living and he helped me to pack my clothes into a little case and supported me as we walked downstairs to the car.

'This won't do, Lady Jane,' he said as we drove back to the cottage. 'We need to get you well and come up with a proper plan. John's just a kid and so are you. Neither of you is capable of looking after a baby.'

I was too weak to argue with him. All I wanted was to sleep, somewhere warm and clean and cosy.

Mum was not at all pleased to see me. 'Quick, get in the house,' she instructed. 'I don't want the neighbours to see your condition. You'll bring disgrace on us all.'

Dad let me lean on him as I staggered indoors and sat down heavily on the sofa, panting with exertion.

'You're not to go outside while you're here. Stay indoors out of sight,' Mum told me.

Only Nigel was pleased to see me. We sat for hours that summer playing card games – gin rummy was a favourite – as I gradually grew bigger and got my strength back. John came to visit me once every couple of weeks or so but he never stayed very long. We were never able to be on our own and the hostile presence of Mum hovering around making snide comments wasn't conducive to any kind of intimate conversation.

I followed the doctor's advice, spending most of the time resting, and somehow I managed to keep that baby despite my damaged cervix. I just willed it to stay inside with all the strength and determination I possessed.

* * *

Two months before the baby was due, Mum and Dad told me that they had booked me in to a mother and baby home in Accocks Green. They drove me there on a rainy Monday morning, along with a suitcase containing my clothes and the few items I had managed to make for the baby. The home was full of other unmarried girls 'in disgrace', who sat watching television in their dressing gowns all day, unwashed hair hanging round their shoulders and gloomy expressions on their faces.

'Aren't you looking forward to having your baby?' I asked one girl.

'Are you kidding? It's supposed to be like passing a melon. It splits you wide open then you need stitches and you can't walk properly for weeks. Why would I be look-ing forward to that?'

I stroked my huge belly and smiled. 'I don't care about the pain – it'll be over within hours. I just want to meet my little girl.'

'I've asked not to see mine at all. I've told them to take it away and not even tell me the sex. It'll be easier that way.'

'You're having your baby adopted?' I couldn't believe my ears. 'How can you face that when you've been carry-ing it inside you for nine months?'

'Better that than looking after it on my own for another eighteen years.'

The next girl I spoke to was also planning to have her baby adopted, and the next. I became suspicious and asked one of the nursing staff why so many girls were giving up their babies.

She gave me a curious look. 'Because they're not married. That's why you're all here – so you can avoid prying eyes spotting your condition in these last months of pregnancy. You can give birth, hand the baby over and go back to your normal life, more or less scot-free. You're being given a second chance to find a nice husband and do things right next time.'

'But I don't want my baby to be adopted.'

'Look, love, that's what this place is for. Think about it before you do anything foolish. It will be better for the baby to go to a nice, stable married couple somewhere rather than you struggling to bring it up on your own with the world frowning on you.'

I shook my head. There was no way I would ever do that! How could anyone be sure that my baby would end up with a 'nice, stable couple'? Look at what happened to me, and the adoptive mother I ended up with, for goodness sake. I could never risk that happening to another child, and certainly not to my precious girl. I was going to keep my baby and give her all the love and devotion that I never had.

I felt a terrible sense of betrayal. Dad had known what this place was for and he'd sent me here, even though he knew how much I longed for the baby.

I phoned him at work that afternoon.

'Hello, Lady Jane. How are you?'

'If you don't come and collect me from this place at once, I'll run away,' I said in a low and serious voice that contained all the fury I felt. 'This is not just a mother and baby home – this is a place for unmarried mothers who are having their babies adopted. You tried to trick me into giving up my baby!'

I'd never spoken to him like that before but I was furiously angry. Already I was having to fight tooth and nail to protect this child and she wasn't even out of the womb yet.

'All right,' he said quietly. 'I'll come for you later.'

Dad came to pick me up in the early evening. I was standing in reception with my bag packed, waiting. He lifted my belongings into the boot of the car, and as we drove off he said: 'Vanessa, you only have two choices and I want you to consider them very carefully. Either you give up this baby for adoption, or you and John will have to get married. I will not countenance a baby in my family being born out of wedlock.'

'But John hasn't asked me to marry him.'

'This is not about romance and proposing on bended knee. John will marry you if I talk to him man to man and explain his responsibilities. We'll have to get a special licence because you're under age but I will arrange that, and your mother and I will help out financially until you find your feet. Is that what you want?'

'I want to keep my baby,' I said stubbornly.

'Very well. Call John and ask him to come over to the house tomorrow.' He glanced at my swollen belly. 'From the looks of it, there's no time to be lost.'

Chapter 38

Over dinner the following evening, John sat very subdued as Dad outlined the reasons why he had to marry me.

'This baby is being born into a Christian household and it will be at a huge disadvantage in life if it is illegitimate. Do you really want to do that to your own flesh and blood? Vanessa's mother and I are very religious and it would bring scorn upon us in our own community. This is not how we do things in our neck of the woods.'

'Of course I'll marry Vanessa if she wants me to,' John mumbled, hopelessly outnumbered.

'Will you explain to your parents? We can't risk one of them turning up and objecting at the wedding.'

John looked petrified. 'I haven't seen Dad since I helped Mum to leave him. He'll kill me if I go back.'

'I suppose we could just keep it quiet and hope he doesn't find out.'

'I'll go and talk to him,' I heard myself volunteering. 'Surely he'll agree it's the best thing to do when he sees my condition. It's his grandchild after all.' I patted my belly. The baby was moving, her little foot kicking upwards into my diaphragm. I'd have walked over hot coals for that child, so confronting John's father didn't seem too daunting.

So by the end of the evening, I was engaged to be married. It wasn't exactly a young girl's dream of being proposed to – having her father threaten the man involved until he agreed to do it – but if it meant I could keep the baby, then I didn't care.

* * *

I went round the next evening to the Droitwich council house where Fred spent his leisure time drinking bottles of beer in front of the telly. I knocked on the door and waited but there was no reply, so I walked round and rapped on the window. I could see him sound asleep in his armchair so I knocked more loudly until he wakened with a start and looked up to see me waving at him.

Cursing, he staggered through to the hall and opened the front door. 'What the bloody hell do you want?'

'I just need to have a word, Fred. Do you mind if I come in?'

'Look at you. Size of a bloody house. You probably won't fit through the door.' He stepped back to let me in all the same.

I sat down on the sofa, which was so low that I worried I was going to have trouble getting up again. There was a hissing noise as Fred pulled open a can of beer.

'It's good to see you,' I lied. 'I just wanted to pop in to let you know that your grandchild is due in a few weeks now.'

'The little bastard,' he interrupted.

I ignored him. 'John has asked me to marry him and I've agreed. We'd like to get married before the baby's born and we wondered if you will come to the wedding.' I'd decided on this tactic, sure that the promise of some free booze would win him round – but I was wrong.

'My John's way too good for you. You've trapped him with your woman's wiles and wrecked his career prospects, and now you've got the cheek to ask if I'll come to your sodding wedding.' He snorted and took a gulp of his beer.

'Please. It's what John wants as well.'

'Why didn't he come and see me himself then?'

'He's so busy with his course and he's working in the evenings as well so he asked me to come. He's a credit to you – really he is.'

Various spirits were warning me: 'Watch out, Vanessa.' 'Take care.' 'Leave now – he's dangerous.' Fred's aura was getting stronger and more terrifying but I didn't want to go without his blessing.

'It would mean so much to us if you would come to the wedding,' I said.

Suddenly Fred flew from his seat and grabbed me by the throat, squeezing hard. I struggled and tried to prise his fingers off but he squeezed tighter until I couldn't breathe.

'Stupid little slut,' he hissed in my face. 'It's probably not even John's kid. You've probably been screwing all and sundry, a girl like you. If I kill you now, my son will be free of you and your sodding brat.'

I was terrified the baby was being harmed by the lack of oxygen or that the violence might trigger labour. I couldn't get Fred's fingers off my throat so I positioned my knee and brought it up hard into his groin. He yelled and let go of me immediately, doubled over with pain. I seized my chance and ran into the kitchen, hoping to escape through the back door but it was locked and there was no sign of the key. Roaring with rage, Fred rushed through and wrestled me to the floor.

'I know – I'll gas you and the kid,' he yelled. 'That'll get you out of the way.'

He opened the oven door, grabbed me by the hair and dragged me towards it. I knew that domestic gas wasn't supposed to be poisonous any more but I was still petrified that it would harm the baby so I struggled with all my might. Fred kicked me in the stomach and I curled myself into a ball, trying to protect my belly, while screaming as loudly as I could. Where on earth were the neighbours? Why didn't someone come to help?

'Shut up, bitch!' He kicked the base of my spine. I saw my chance and while his foot was raised I grabbed it, causing him to overbalance and fall heavily backwards, cracking his head on the kitchen units. I hauled myself up and ran through the sitting room, out the front door and down the street. I didn't stop running until I reached the main road, where shoppers milled round with their carrier bags.

I bent double, out of breath, desperately feeling my belly for signs that the baby was still moving and was overwhelmed with joy when she kicked my hand. This one was definitely a survivor.

* * *

Dad and I drove to the magistrates' court the next day and lodged an application for me to get a special licence and we were given a hearing date of 15 December. This was quite tight given the fact that the baby was due on Christmas Day but it was the best they could do. We then drove to the registry office and booked a ceremony for the afternoon of Saturday 16th.

Dad didn't say much as we went about this business. It wasn't what he had dreamed of for his only daughter's wedding. As a committed churchgoer, he would have loved to walk me down the aisle, but that was obviously out of the question now. After we'd booked the registry office, we drove to a restaurant attached to a local pub and booked a table for dinner straight after the ceremony. I was touched at this and gave Dad a quick hug. He kissed my forehead.

'I want the best for you, Lady Jane,' he said, his face sad. 'I only want to see you happy.'

'I will be, Dad, I promise.' I smiled to show him how positive I was but it didn't seem to lift his spirits at all.

* * *

The entire weekend of 15–17 December 1967 passed by in the blink of an eye, but changed my life profoundly. On the Friday afternoon at 2 p.m., Dad, John and I filed into Droitwich magistrates' court. The elderly magistrate looked sternly at my impossibly immense belly then directed his questions at me.

'Are you sure you understand what you are taking on, young woman? You want to marry this man and you're not under any duress?'

I agreed that I did and I wasn't.

'And you, sir,' he asked Dad. 'You agree that this is the best thing?'

'Obviously, in the circumstances,' Dad said, nodding his head towards me.

I stared at my lap, feeling like a leper. The magistrate stamped and signed the special licence and we were back outside again by 2.20 p.m.

The next morning was my wedding day but I don't think I had any of the usual emotions of a young bride. I was mainly concerned that I'd been getting twinges and worried that I was going to go into labour in the middle of the ceremony. The local doctor was called but he assured me they were false contractions, known as Braxton Hicks.

I got dressed in a huge emerald-green brocade smock – virtually the only garment I owned that I could still fit into. Nigel surprised me by bringing me a beautiful bouquet of white roses bound in silk ribbon as a wedding present from him. Mum was dressed to the nines in a pale blue Jackie Kennedy dress, matching jacket and pillbox hat – far be it for her to miss out on any opportunity to dress up. Dad and Nigel wore their suits and ties.

As we drove to the registry office, Mum couldn't resist a few little jibes. 'I hope he turns up and doesn't jilt you. It must be very depressing for him to be taking on such a burden.'

I ignored that so she continued, trying to get a reaction. 'Other brides are radiantly beautiful, whereas you just look fat and frumpy. If he turns up at all, I wouldn't be surprised if John runs a mile when he catches sight of you.'

'Leave her alone, Mum,' Nigel butted in. I gave him a little half-smile. I wasn't nervous at all. I knew John would turn up because the spirits had told me. I also knew that my delivery was near; it wouldn't be long before I could hold my baby in my arms for the first time.

John and Nelly were waiting on the steps outside the registry office. John gave me a quick kiss on the cheek and squeezed my hand. Mum and Nelly said hello, eyeing each other's outfits, and I could tell Mum was pleased that hers was much smarter.

We were called in to stand in front of the registrar, a kindly woman with a lacquered blonde helmet of hair. Seeing my condition, she asked that a chair be brought for me and a glass of water positioned on the desk where I could reach it. As she began reading out the service, I looked round at John, who was picking the skin by his nails, and I realized that I hardly knew him at all. A stranger and I were linking our futures to each other, just so that the child in my belly could never be called a bastard, the way I had been.

'Do you, Vanessa Annette Casey, take this man to be your lawful wedded husband?' the registrar asked, and I said, 'I do.'

John consented as well and I heard Nelly sobbing behind me but no one voiced any objections and soon we were being pronounced man and wife.

When we walked out of the registry office, it was perhaps telling that I was holding Dad's hand rather than my new husband's.

Chapter 39

The wedding day was not over yet. Far from it.

I didn't enjoy the meal in the restaurant. I hardly had any appetite in the last couple of months of pregnancy – my stomach appeared to have shrunk as the size of my womb increased. I'd also had a strange burning sensation in my gullet all day, like indigestion or maybe a gas pain. While the others tucked in to melon with a glace cherry on top, then chicken and chips followed by chocolate gateaux, washed down with Blue Nun white wine – the irony of which didn't escape me – I just sipped some water and moved the food around my plate.

It had been agreed that John and I would come back to stay in Shernal Green for a few months after the baby was born, just until we found our feet. Dad could drive him to college in the morning and he'd get a late bus home at the end of his shift at the metal casting works. With the money saved in rent, we hoped to save up a deposit to get a place of our own. This plan was one of the topics discussed over my wedding dinner, while Mum didn't miss a chance to boast to Nelly about her modelling career.

'I modelled hats for the *Daily Mirror*, you know. The photographer said I had the best profile he'd ever seen.'

I'd heard it all before. How old was that story now? I realized how it strange it was that I was now an adult, a married woman expecting a baby, with the experience of bringing her up awaiting me. For my mother, it was all over. And how much joy had it brought her? It certainly hadn't been a joyful experience for me. But I still had a chance to make things better. Her chances were all gone.

* * *

It was quite early when we drove home but I went straight upstairs to lie down, feeling unwell. An additional single bed had been carried into my room to give John somewhere to sleep. I was curled on my side on my bed, trying to quell the nausea I was feeling when John came in and sat beside me. He leant down to kiss me and I recoiled from the smell of the wine on his breath.

'What's the matter?' he slurred, and I realized he was drunk. 'You're my wife now. Surely I'm allowed my conjugal rights on my wedding night?'

With great effort I hauled myself up to a sitting position. 'I'm sorry, John, I'm feeling terrible this evening. I'm just not up to it.' I felt bad saying this. I'd almost invariably snubbed his attempts to have sex with me ever since that first time in the car.

'What's the bloody point of being married then, if you can't have sex when you want it?' I'd never heard him swear before.

'I thought it was about making our baby legitimate.'

'I never wanted to marry you,' he said. 'I could have done much better than you.'

If I hadn't been feeling so dreadful I might have handled the situation with more tact, but instead I said, 'Tough luck. You've got me now.'

'Only because you trapped me into it. I think it was your plan all along and if I'm right, then you're a bitch for doing it. I'm getting out of here.' He ran out of the room and down the stairs and moments later I heard the front door slamming.

Mum came up and popped her head round the door to find me sitting crying on the side of the bed. 'What's going on? Where has John gone?'

'He's run off,' I sobbed. 'On our wedding night. It's hardly a great start, is it?'

Mum folded her arms self-righteously. 'You've made your bed; now you can lie in it. It's up to you to make your marriage work and that means giving your husband what he wants so he doesn't run off like that. Your father's never raised his voice to me in twenty-six years of married life.' That familiar spiteful look flashed in her eyes. 'Of course, he loves me and John obviously doesn't love you. You trapped him into marriage, which is not a good start. You're going to have to shape up if you want to keep him, my girl.'

I barely slept a wink that night. John didn't come back and I wondered if our marriage might be over before it had started. I suppose in a sense it was true that I'd trapped him into becoming a father but it took two to make a baby. If he hadn't wanted a child he should have got himself a rubber johnny before he started messing around with me. Besides, I was fond of him in a way, fonder than I'd been of anyone else, and I hoped we could make our marriage work. Once we had a beautiful little baby, surely we would be happy.

The Clown came to see me. 'Be calm, child, and gather your strength. Your time is drawing near. Put all other thoughts from your head now and prepare for the physical challenge ahead.'

I was still getting painful twinges in my abdomen and a burning sensation in my gullet but it was only after the Clown's words that I realized I was actually going into labour.

I had a certain detached curiosity as the contractions got gradually stronger and then a huge one shook my abdomen, making me feel as though my spine was going to snap. I started timing the gaps between the big contractions and found they were roughly ten minutes apart. It was only five in the morning so I didn't like to wake Mum and Dad to ask for help. I whispered to the baby, trying to explain to her what was happening and telling her not to worry.

At half past seven I heard Dad getting up to go to the toilet and I shouted to him.

'What is it?' He put his head round the door.

'I need to go to hospital,' I said.

'Oh my goodness!' He disappeared and soon Mum came in to help me get dressed. 'There's an ambulance on the way. You be good, now. Don't embarrass us by yelling your head off.'

'Aren't you coming with me?' I asked, then gasped and bent double as a contraction took hold.

'Good grief, no. You'll be hanging round for ages. First babies never come quickly. Just give us a call when you're done.'

'Will you let John know? He's probably gone to Nelly's.'

'I will,' she said, almost kindly. 'Here, let's get you downstairs between contractions.'

Nigel came down to wish me luck and then I was driven off on my own to Ronkswood maternity hospital. I was examined on arrival and the doctor told me I had a while to wait. I was put to bed with a jug of water on the table beside me, the curtain was pulled around, and I was pretty much left alone all day. I realized this was how I wanted it though. My little girl and I had a journey to go on together and it felt right that it was just the two of us.

The contractions continued all day, still growing in intensity, and I learned to pace myself and rest between them so that I was ready for the next one. Sometimes I managed to snooze for a few minutes but mostly I whispered to my baby and talked to the spirits, who were coming in to offer encouragement.

The doctor came to examine me about seven in the evening and gave his opinion that the baby wouldn't be born till the following morning.

'Try to get some sleep,' he advised.

How on earth was I supposed to do that? I wondered. Only a man could say that to someone who was now being racked by agonizing contractions every five or six minutes.

I watched the clock and timed my contractions right through the night. At six-thirty in the morning I could feel something change internally. I felt shaky and hot and for the first time I felt an irresistible urge to push. I could feel the baby's head pressing hard against my pelvis and I wanted to help her all I could.

'Come on, little one,' I whispered. 'I'm here. Come to Mummy.'

A nurse looked in to check on me just after seven and gasped: 'Oh my God! The baby's on the way!' She rushed off and returned with a doctor.

'Why didn't you call for help?' he said crossly. 'You were about to give birth on your own.'

I couldn't speak because I was concentrating hard on moving exactly the right muscles that would help my baby into the world. Through the pain, I could somehow feel what I should be doing. All my life, I'd been developing ways of coping with pain by distancing myself from it and focusing on something else, and now my skills came into their own.

'It's crowning,' the doctor said, and I felt a sharp, tearing sensation and then the feeling of the baby slipping out of me.

'It's a girl,' said the nurse.

'Samantha Anne,' I whispered, and propped myself on my elbows to look at her. She was pink and wrinkly and her eyes were screwed tight shut so that there was a worried-looking crease in the middle of her forehead. She made a mewling noise like a little kitten. 'Can I hold her?'

They handed her to me and I examined the wisps of blonde hair, the ears the size of cockleshells and each one of her tiny fingers and toes. I kissed her eyelids and her lips and cheeks and the crown of her head, and I held her close to my heart with our faces next to each other, breathing each other's breath. In my head I promised to love and protect her for the rest of my life. I would cook and clean and look after her and buy her presents and do everything that was in my power to make her happy. It was an overwhelming sensation of pure, altruistic, primal love, more powerful than anything I could have imagined. I knew in that instant that I would lay down my life to protect her if need be. She and I were going to be a unit. Together, we would make each other whole.

Epilogue

As I followed the ambulance taking my mother to hospital, I felt a mixture of shock and fear. What would happen if she died? She had lived alone for years now, and she and I were the only members of our immediate family left.

Our relationship had mellowed a little over the years, but she still took every opportunity to thwart me and denigrate me. It seemed to give her great pleasure to hurt me, even after all this time. She was no longer able to beat me or use her superior strength, so she used her sharp, malicious tongue instead.

I had grown accustomed to it, even though it still stung when she called me names and told me how ugly and useless I was. Something kept me attached to her, though. After all, she was the only mother I'd ever had, and the little child in me still craved affection from her, even if my adult self felt a mixture of anger and pity towards her. If my mother had made my childhood a torment, she herself had been constantly miserable and tormented. It was more than likely that her father had subjected her to the kind of abuse he put me through – perhaps that was why she was not able to have children of her own. If what I suspected about her childhood and the difficulties in her marriage were true, then she had also suffered. The difference was that I had had a chance to experience happiness in my later life and she never had.

It was this pity for her total lack of understanding of the good to be found in human relationships and in love that kept me visiting her and looking after her when she became frail. Hers was a wasted, ruined life. She had tried to ruin mine, but she hadn't succeeded.

In the years since I had left my parents' home, my life had been transformed. There was my little daughter, Samantha, for a start. Being a mother was everything I'd dreamed it might be. I adored my perfect little baby and relished every moment of her childhood, even when she screamed all night and needed constant care and attention. I realized that I'd had love packed up tight inside me for years, with nowhere for it to go. Now I had someone who needed me completely, and I poured the love out unconditionally. I wanted her to have what I'd been deprived of. I could not have stood looking at her baby pictures and seeing Samantha gazing out, looking like I had done – worried, uncomfortable, scared and unwanted.

The birth of my daughter marked the end of my childhood. After that, I knew real happiness for the first time in my life. I was able to shut away the things that had happened to me and concentrate on the future, where life would surely be better. I had little to do with Mum – I was so busy and so bound up in my own life, a life that finally seemed worth living.

My marriage to John was, sadly, not to last. We tried hard to make it work but after four years, we realized that we could not overcome our problems. Our marriage had not been based on mutual love and trust and even though we did our best, it was the right thing to part. We divorced with a sense of sadness but with no regrets.

The spirits were right when they said that something wonderful was about to come into my life. I was twenty-two when I met a fantastic man named Bob. We fell in love and had two children together – Natalie, born in 1979, and Richard, born in 1980. He had three kids already, so my twenties and early thirties were dominated by being a mum to six children altogether.

* * *

One day in 1974, I had the phone call I had been dreading. My wonderful big brother, Nigel, had died in his sleep from an epileptic fit during the night, just as the spirits had predicted he would. Over the years, I had tried to forget what the spirits had said about his death and hoped against hope that they were wrong – but they had told the truth. Nigel's entire life had been marred by his severe epilepsy. He was never able to leave home, and although he continued to work at Dad's electro-plating company, he never had girlfriends or a social life. He was a wonderful uncle to Samantha, though – he adored her and visited once a week to play silly games and laugh with her. He was just twenty-four years old when he died and I was desolate. Life was never the same again without Nigel in it and I missed my brother dreadfully.

Losing Nigel made me think again about where I came from and who my true family were. In 1980, I decided to try and trace my birth mother, the woman who had given me up thirty years before. Without a birth or adoption certificate, I didn't know where to start. All I had was a piece of paper saying that Mum and Dad had changed my name to Vanessa Annette Casey when I was six months old. Then, one day, the name Susan Langman came to me. I had seen it on a certificate in Mum's room once and had asked her about it, but she just snatched the paper away and told me to keep my nose out of things that didn't concern me.

I went to the Birmingham Registry of Births, Marriages and Deaths and requested a birth certificate for Susan Langman, born on 3 March 1950. Sure enough, one was duly delivered. So that was my birth name. The mother's name shown on it was José Olmen Langman and she lived at an address just round the corner from our old home in Bentley Heath.

Several things struck me as odd about this. Would Mum and Dad really have been allowed to adopt from someone who lived so close to home? Did they know her? Wasn't it more usual for adoptions to be from some distance away so there was no possibility of the child and its real mother meeting? Besides that, I had always thought of José as a Spanish man's name. Lastly, there was no father identified, although presumably this was not uncommon for babies born out of wedlock.

I went to visit the address on the certificate but there was no answer. A next-door neighbour told me that José Langman had died several years before. When I asked if José had ever had any child who had been adopted, the neighbour was mystified. 'I never heard of any children,' she said, 'but I can give you her married name if you like.'

With José's married name, I tracked down her husband and managed to arrange a meeting. He was startled when

I showed him my birth certificate – it was certainly his wife who was named on it, but to his certain knowledge, she couldn't have been pregnant at the time indicated. 'José didn't have a baby in March 1950. We were engaged then, we'd been courting for two years and we got married in May 1950. I would certainly have noticed if she'd been pregnant.'

I came away convinced he'd told me the truth.

That evening I phoned Dad, but he was extremely unforthcoming when I asked about my real mother, telling me he didn't remember her name. I could hear my mother in the background, saying that I should stop poking around in things that didn't concern me. There was no point in dragging up the past.

I seemed to have reached a dead end.

* * *

Gradually the people who linked me to my childhood began to disappear. In 1993 Aunt Gilly, my rescuing angel who had listened to me when I most needed help and stopped Grandpa Pittam's abuse, died. Then, to my great grief, Dad was diagnosed with cancer in 1994. His battle with it was short but brave. I did everything I could to help him through it, visiting him at the hospital every day, sitting by his bedside to chat to him and cheer him up as best I could. He died in my arms. In my adult years, we'd become close friends, putting the past and our disagreements behind us. By mutual consent, we didn't discuss what had happened in my childhood – some things were too painful for either of us to admit to the other or to talk about openly. I was just happy that we had a chance to enjoy something of the normal father-and-daughter relationship that had been denied us for so long. When he died, I was devastated.

It was very hard to come to terms with Dad's death. I felt so alone without him, despite Bob and the children. It was as though my safety net had been snatched from beneath me. I missed our chats and his vast general knowledge and his good-natured view of the universe. More than that, I realized that I had to admit to myself how culpable he had been for the things that had happened to me, and to forgive him for it. He had been wilfully blind to my situation for many years and so, in a way, he had acquiesced to it. He was never able to talk to me about what I'd gone through or why. He couldn't explain why he'd left me alone with the person who most wanted to harm me.

I knew that he must have tried to protect himself from the truth about the woman he'd married – but it was hard to understand how he could have removed himself from her orbit and left me in it. I needed to make my peace with Dad, and I tried to do that after he'd died, wishing we had been able to talk openly and honestly while he was still here on earth. It was a comfort that he visited me in spirit many times to guide me – he always asked me to find forgiveness in my heart, saying 'Better to forgive than to hate'.

Dad also took with him the answers to the many questions I had wanted to ask him about where I came from and what lay behind the events in his marriage. It was then that I realized that if I wanted answers, I would have to find them myself.

* * *

In 1997 I travelled to Canada to visit Dad's big sister Audrey, who had emigrated there in the late 1940s after getting married to a Canadian airman. His brother, Graham, had followed a few years later, and both were still living out there.

It was a strange experience that answered some questions and revealed yet more unexplained mysteries.

Uncle Graham greeted me with a bear hug and the same amiable twinkle and warm smile as Dad's. During the course of our meeting, he said something that unsettled me.

We were talking about Gilly and Dad and how much we missed them, when I mentioned that Mum seemed to be doing well since Dad died: her health was still good and she enjoyed reading magazines to pass the time. Graham didn't comment, so I asked, 'Are you in touch with her?'

'In touch with her!' he exclaimed. 'I wouldn't piss on the woman if she caught fire. I was only aware of some of what she put you through but I heard tales from Audrey and Gilly that made me physically sick. The woman should have been locked up.'

I was shocked. 'I didn't realize you knew.'

'We all knew things weren't right and we feel guilty that we didn't do more, but it's hard to interfere in your brother's family without causing a huge rift. In retrospect we should have done.'

So the family had known after all. Did that make it better, or worse?

Then I visited Aunt Audrey, who was eighty-four and the spitting image of Nan Casey, with silver hair, glasses and a kindly face. Once again, several strange things emerged from our meeting.

Audrey hadn't seen me for well over forty years and she exclaimed loudly when she saw me, 'Oh my goodness! Just look at you!'

'What is it?' I asked, slightly alarmed by her tone.

She seemed genuinely stunned. 'I don't believe it. Who would have thought?'

'What?' I asked again, but she wouldn't explain.

As we chatted, I helped Audrey to prepare some tea and, as I arranged cups and saucers on a tray, she exclaimed again, 'Where on earth did you get that ring?'

I was wearing a pretty ring with an emerald surrounded by tiny diamonds. 'Mum gave it to me just after Dad died,' I explained.

'Did she say where it came from?'

'No. Just that it was a family ring.' It occurred to me that I'd never seen Mum wearing it. I vaguely remembered her saying that it was an unlucky ring.

'That was Margery's. Did you know that Derrick was engaged to a woman called Margery when he met your mum? Well, this was her engagement ring. Muriel bowled him over and he broke it off with Margery, so she gave the ring back.'

'Margery Wyatt?' I asked, startled, and Audrey nodded.

'I didn't know she had been engaged to Dad. I met her a few times at the Pear Tree Lodge when Dad and I stopped for a drink during our walks. She was very kind to me.'

'Did you indeed?' Audrey kept staring at me, as if trying to figure me out. 'Her father was the publican there. I'm surprised you met her, though.'

'Don't tell Mum, will you? Dad always said not to mention it.'

'I bet he did,' Audrey muttered. I assumed she meant that Mum would have been upset about Dad having a drink with his ex-fiancée.

I carried the tea tray through to the sitting room and the conversation turned to other matters, but I sensed that there were many things that weren't being said.

At five o'clock, there was a visitor: Audrey's daughter Deanne arrived. I'd never met my cousin before and as we laid eyes on each other, I gasped and she stopped dead in her tracks. I was looking at a woman just four months younger than me who was almost my mirror image: the blue eyes, the nose, the shape of the face, our height and build were all identical. When she smiled, I recognized my own smile. We had similar hairstyles and, in a bizarre coincidence, she was even wearing the same white anorak with yellow stripes on the sleeves that I had. Only her Canadian accent was different.

'Hello, cousin.' Deanne spoke first. 'You look familiar!'

'You too,' I said as we hugged. 'Isn't that peculiar?'

We looked round at Audrey, who said nothing.

When Deanne took her anorak off, I saw that she had the same curvy figure as me.

'How is it possible that we look so alike when we're not blood relatives?' I asked, but Audrey wouldn't be drawn on the subject. She seemed uncomfortable whenever family matters came up in conversation.

'Tell me more about Margery,' I asked over dinner. 'What did she do after Dad broke up with her? Did she find someone else?'

'No, she never married as far as I know. Derrick broke her heart, I'm afraid. She worked as a postmistress and lived on her own near her father's pub and wouldn't have anything to do with other men who might have been interested in her. She was a lovely, gentle soul.'

'Why did Dad choose Mum instead of her all those years ago?'

'Who knows? In my opinion he made a huge mistake, but you know how men are – their heads are easily turned by a pretty face, and your mother was a great beauty.'

'I thought Mum was a friend of yours.'

'Yes, she was. Still is, in a way. We write to each other every couple of months. But I wish I'd never introduced her to Derrick because she didn't make him happy. He'd have been better off …' Her voice trailed away and she was lost in thought for a minute.

I said stoutly, 'If she didn't make him happy, he should have left her. Life is too short to be miserable. My first marriage was a disaster so we both called it a day before we ruined our lives. Luckily for me, I made a fresh start and found Bob.'

'It wasn't done in those days, dear. It would have brought disgrace on the entire family. Men stayed in unhappy marriages and sometimes they made other arrangements that let them fulfil their needs. That's all I'm saying.'

Arrangements. I remembered hearing my parents talk of their deal – and my dad saying that my mother had agreed to whatever it was. 'Do you mean that Dad had other women?'

Suddenly I heard, clear as a bell in my head, Mum saying, 'He's with his other woman.' She said it as though it was a joke. Perhaps it had been deadly serious.

'We almost never saw him in the week,' I added. 'I always wondered where he was.'

'I've got no idea whether he did or not but your father was an honourable man and I'm sure he never meant to hurt anyone.'

'Mum isn't the easiest of people to get along with,' I said tentatively.

'I know that you had a tough time with her.' Audrey gave me a sympathetic look, peering over her glasses. 'Muriel should never have had children. She wasn't the type. She was far too selfish to be a parent. I could tell from when you and Nigel were babies that it was all going to go wrong.'

'How could you tell?'

She told me the story about Mum holding a pillow over Nigel's face to stop him crying, and about a letter she'd had from Mum when I was adopted in 1950 that said, 'I've got the girl child.'

'I don't think she wanted to adopt in the first place,' I said. 'Dad talked her into it. He told me he should never have done it.'

'No, you're right. None of it should have happened. It was all a tragic mistake.'

I could sense she knew more than she was letting on. After dinner, we took out the photo albums and pored over all the old photographs. Audrey identified people I'd never met and told me stories of holidays and birthdays and the occasions on which pictures had been taken.

'Is that Margery?' I asked, looking at a picture of a woman with shoulder-length brown hair, wearing a checked dress, standing talking to Dad beside a parked car. She certainly looked like a younger version of the woman I'd met with him.

'Yes, of course.'

I peered at the photo. Margery and Dad were smiling at each other in a very loving way. I'd never seen Dad look at Mum like that. 'But that's after Dad married. He's losing his hair and he looks much older than in the pictures taken when Mum and he were courting. They look as though they were very close.'

'Yes, I think they were. I'm glad he had a friend. Your mum was a challenging woman and obviously never very happy. In her letters she ranted on about how hard her life was, how much she'd given up, and how difficult you were. She's got no idea how mad she made herself look when she wrote to me about you being "a demon monster" or "the devil's child". I don't believe that children can be born evil ...'

'Did she really say all that to you?' I wasn't particularly surprised. 'What did you reply?'

'I said that you were only a child and that she shouldn't visit the sins of the father on you.' Audrey bit her lip as if worried she'd said too much. 'Anyway, it's all water under the bridge now.'

* * *

When I got back to the UK, some of what I'd learned preyed on my mind. In particular, I couldn't stop wondering about the strong resemblance between Deanne and me. It seemed too close to be coincidental.

Could I be Dad's natural daughter? It seemed the only possible explanation, and it would explain Mum's cruelty towards me. If it were true, it wouldn't have been easy bringing up her husband's love child and living with a constant reminder of his infidelity under her own roof. No wonder she resented me far more than she would a child who came from a completely anonymous background – like Nigel.

The pieces were beginning to fit together for me. I thought again about the letter Audrey told me Mum had sent in September 1950 saying 'I've got the girl child'.

But I couldn't see Dad as a philandering Jack-the-lad type. If he had had another woman, it was probably just one rather than hordes of them.

Margery's face kept floating before my mind's eye. Was it her all the time? Had Dad married the wrong woman, but come to an arrangement so that he could spend most week nights with the one he should have married in the first place? Could that be why we moved to Shernal Green, so he was closer to her?'

But then, what about the name on my birth certificate? It was not inconceivable that José Langman might have been paid to pose as my mother in order to disguise the identity of the real one – after all, checks were much less stringent in those days, and the Caseys could certainly afford to pay some poor girl a few hundred pounds to register the birth as her own child.

It was a huge leap but it was just possible that Margery was my real mother. I thought about how kind she had been to me that day when I was recovering from my suicide attempt, and how upsetting it must have been for her if I was really her daughter. How could she bear not to say something?

I decided that I had to see Margery again, and drove to Shernal Green one afternoon. Pear Tree Lodge had been converted into a big country hotel and there was no sign of life in Pear Tree Cottage, but just down the road there was a woman trimming her hedge so I got out of the car to have a chat with her.

'Do you know Margery Wyatt who used to live here?'

'Yes, indeed. Were you a friend of hers?'

'My dad used to know her and I thought I'd look her up.'

'I'm sorry, I'm afraid she died just a few months ago.'

My heart sank. 'Did you know her?'

'A little, but not well. She was a strange woman. Never married until late in life but she lived here on her own all that time. I couldn't quite fathom what made her tick. She wasn't a very open sort of person; it was as if she had her secrets and she wasn't going to share them.'

That all fitted but it didn't help me to confirm the truth. I'd hit another dead end. There was only one person who knew the answers. The only question was – would she be willing to tell me?

* * *

It was not long after this that I found my mother's unconscious body blocking the door to her little house, and followed the ambulance to the hospital. After undergoing emergency care, Mum was diagnosed as having suffered a minor stroke. When she was out of immediate danger, she was transferred to a rehabilitation unit in the heart of the Warwickshire countryside.

Mum was put in a ward with eleven other patients with varying degrees of disability. She was unable to walk, but when I visited I'd usually find her dressed and sitting in a chair by her bed, from which she couldn't quite see out the window. She quickly became very frustrated and angry about her situation, complaining about the way the staff treated her and the antisocial behaviour of other patients, but most of her vitriol was directed at me.

'Don't you think you should lose some weight? You're getting really fat,' she would say. 'You're such an ugly woman, aren't you?'

And she would issue orders. 'There's my washing. Make sure you get it done, and press it properly this time.'

When I arrived, her first question was always, 'What have you brought me?' I took magazines and chocolates, new clothes, perfume, cosmetics, face cream, whatever she requested and I let the nasty comments wash over me. I'd had a lifetime of them and I was used to it by now. It was her way of striking back at her illness and her inability to look after herself. If it made her feel better, I could tolerate it. I would just ignore her jibes and smile sunnily at her. That infuriated her more than anything.

One day I arrived to find her sitting at the window as usual. I stood in the doorway for a moment and observed her as she sat there. At the age of eighty-eight, Mum still had a faded beauty, with pronounced, angular features and bright blue-grey eyes. I had arranged for a woman to come to the rehab centre to do her hair and nails once a week, because she continued to take great pride in her appearance. Her skin was heavily wrinkled, of course, but her nose was neatly powdered and she wore a slick of soft pink lipstick. I bought most of her clothes – loose, comfortable garments to cover the thickening of her once-willowy figure – but she coordinated her outfits every morning and issued strict instructions to the nurses who helped her get dressed.

When she heard me in the doorway, she turned, demanding sharply, 'Where have you been? You never visit me. After everything I've done for you.'

'Mum, I was here yesterday,' I objected, but she ignored me.

'I prayed that you would come,' she said, folding her hands. 'Where's Dad? Why didn't you bring him?'

I hesitated. Did she mean my dad who had passed away ten years earlier, or her own father, Charles Pittam? That terrifying, sickening man had now been in the grave for over forty years.

'I wish Charles was here,' Mum said. 'Such a talented, clever man. He was so proud of me being a model, you know. He kept all my pictures. Such a wonderful father. A lovely man. I loved him so much …' She drifted off, lost in thought again.

I felt sick, thinking about what that 'lovely man' had done to me many long years ago. I wondered again if she had suffered the same as I had – it was the only way I could understand how she could have let any child undergo it, almost as though it were completely normal for an old man to rape a small girl.

I changed the subject and started reminiscing with her about Dad and then about Nigel – she got misty-eyed remembering the son I believe she had truly loved.

Then I decided I would ask her one more time for the answers that only she knew.

'Mum,' I said tentatively. 'There's something I wanted to ask you. You know that I met Audrey and Deanne when I went to Canada. Something Audrey told me has been weighing on my mind and I need to ask you about it. Is there any chance that I could be Dad's natural daughter?'

She was immediately on the alert. 'Your father's daughter?' she scoffed. 'I think your imagination's running riot again. Did your so-called spirits tell you this?'

'I really need to know where I came from, Mum, so that if there's anything hereditary my own three children are aware of it.'

'I told you before. Your father was a black man and your mother was an ugly old crone who got herself up the duff back in 1949.'

'But I look exactly the same as Deanne.'

'I haven't seen her since she grew up but Audrey's no oil painting so I'm not surprised she had an ugly daughter. Is she fat like you as well? Does she have trouble keeping a husband?' Mum had been fiercely disapproving when I divorced John and had never accepted Bob. I could understand this in a way – after all, she had been locked into an unhappy marriage.

I ignored her comments and said, 'Mum – did Dad carry on seeing Margery Wyatt after you were married?'

Her eyes turned cold and she stared out of the window again.

'There had to be some reason why he spent so much time away from home,' I persisted. 'And I heard you speak about your arrangement. You even mentioned "the other woman". Did Dad have a double life?'

Mum turned back to look at me and now she had a sneering, triumphant look on her face. 'Margery Wyatt? I don't know who you're talking about.'

'She was Dad's first fiancée.'

'If you say so. I've never heard of her.'

I could hear the gloating in her voice and my heart sank. I should have realized that if she guessed how important this was to me, she would take pleasure in denying me any information.

'Was she my mother?' I asked, hoping that I could somehow provoke her into speaking the truth. Would she finally tell me?

'You'll never know who your real mother is. I can't remember now. What does it matter? Nothing will ever make you any less of a miserable excuse for a woman.'

I saw the pleasure in her eyes and I knew that my last chance to discover the truth had gone. She knew how much it mattered to me now. She would do all she could to thwart me.

'And I was a perfectly good mother to you,' she added. 'You were the one who made everything so horrible.'

'Can I bring you anything next time, Mum?' I asked. I had to go. There was only so much that I could stand at any one time.

Her eyes flickered. 'Cold cream. You never bring me any cream and it's so drying on the skin sitting here all day long, day in, day out. That it should come to this!'

I bent slightly to kiss her on the cheek but she twisted her head away and stared towards the window.

'Goodbye, Mum,' I whispered and left her there.

* * *

Towards the end of 2007, Mum's health deteriorated rapidly after she succumbed to a chest infection. She became painfully thin, until I was scared to squeeze her bony hands any more in case they cracked under my touch. She also started to spend more and more time in the past, imagining herself back in the glory days of her twenties when she could get any man she wanted just by snapping her fingers and fluttering her lashes.

'He's madly in love with me,' she claimed, pointing at a junior doctor on his rounds. 'He wants to marry me, but I told him I haven't made up my mind yet.'

When I visited with Bob, her eyes would light up and she'd ignore me as she chatted to him with great animation about her glamorous life. She appeared to have no concept of how old she was. What did she think when she looked in a mirror and a heavily wrinkled, faded old woman looked back?

'You need to make your peace with her before it's too late,' Bob advised after one visit when she had seemed particularly frail. 'Just for yourself. She could go at any time, and you don't want to feel there's unfinished business.'

I knew he was right but felt stupidly nervous. I rehearsed what I might say over and over in my head, until I finally managed to get the words out one day when she appeared to be in a calm, benign mood.

'Mum, you and I haven't always had the greatest of relationships,' I began, searching her eyes for some indication that she knew what I meant – but they remained expressionless. 'I just want you to know that those things that happened when I was a child ...' I paused, not knowing how to put it into words. ' I just wanted you to know that I forgive you. And that I love you.'

There was a flicker of something, and then she finally said the words I'd wanted to hear all those years: 'I love you too.' But she said them in a casual, throwaway manner, just as she might have said 'I love chocolate' or 'I love that hat'. There was no depth, no sense that she had reached any understanding of our tortured, brutal history.

I wanted her to realize that this could be her last chance to try and put things right between us, so I said 'Mum, you will be going to Heaven soon.'

She turned and looked at me, her eyes empty.

'You go first,' she said stonily. 'You go first then come back and collect me. I don't want to go on my own.'

I was shocked. Why would she say such a thing? What mother would want their child to die before them? Even though I knew she wasn't in her right mind any more, I still felt like I had been kicked in the stomach. I left that evening feeling hurt and confused, with Mum's words ringing in my ears and with the awful sense that these would be the last words she would ever say to me.

My son Richard went to see Mum and spent four hours chatting and making his peace with her. She'd never been a loving or affectionate grandmother to him, but I was glad he'd had the chance to speak to her, to tell her that he forgave her and things were fine between them.

Somehow I still couldn't let go despite knowing there was nothing more she could give me. I visited her every day for those last few months, making the two-hour journey up the motorway and back. I was exhausted, but I could sense that I didn't have much time left with her.

Then one day I arrived at the nursing home to be told that Mum had slipped into a coma during the night. I kept a vigil by her bedside all day watching for signs that she might open her eyes, give me one last kind look before she went. The nursing home assured me that her vital signs were still strong, so the following afternoon I took a chance and slipped off to fulfil a long-standing commitment. I phoned the nursing home at four o'clock and they said Mum's condition was unchanged. About an hour later

I had the strangest experience. Suddenly I smelled Mum's lily-of-the-valley perfume and her old lady smell really strongly, as if in a cloud around me. There was no one near by, nowhere it could have come from. Instantly I knew something had happened and I called the nursing home again.

'I'm afraid she's passed away,' a nurse said. 'I'm so sorry.'

And with those simple words, my world changed. All those years of bullying, cruelty and violence were over. Just like that. She could never tell me I was fat or ugly or horrible ever again. I suppose I should have felt relief but instead a huge wave of sadness washed over me.

In the next few days the strength of my grief surprised me. It was a complicated kind of grief tied up with anger and longing and disbelief. Mum had been such a force of nature, it was hard to accept that she had been snuffed out like a candle flame.

The day before she was buried, I drove to the Chapel of Rest. I don't know why, but I wanted to see her actual body, partly to confirm to myself that it really was Muriel Casey who had died and not some other nursing home resident who had been confused with her. This was the same Chapel of Rest I had seen both my brother Nigel and my father in when they died. It was hard enough then, I didn't know if I could bear it again. I made myself get out of the car and walk up the path. As I pushed the door open, I felt my mouth go dry. The woman lying there had Muriel's features all right but it didn't look like her. The character I'd known as Mum simply wasn't there. What was left of her was just a deathly mask, an empty shell. I couldn't bear to look for more than a few seconds before I had to run out of the room, gasping for air. That was it. She was gone. Forever.

Around thirty to forty people came to the funeral on a grey, drizzly March morning. Most of them were strangers to me, but Uncle Roy was there and the daughter of Mum's sister Hetty. None of the Canadian relatives came over. I don't remember much about the day because I broke down and sobbed hysterically, as if my heart was breaking.

My head was filled with regrets: that she never said sorry for what she had done to me over all those years; that she never relented and told me the truth about my real parents. But over the weeks after her death, I realized that her refusal to say anything was an answer in itself. In my heart, I felt that Margery had been my mother, and Dad my own father, but I would never know for sure.

Then a strange sense of peace came over me. Perhaps I didn't need to know as much as I thought I did. What difference would it make now, anyway? Margery was dead, Dad was dead, Mum was dead – none of them could be a parent to me now. Towards the end I had been the parent anyway and Mum had been the child. I've got no regrets about all the time I spent caring for her, despite our history. I do sometimes slip into thinking that if only Dad had left Mum and I had been brought up by him and Margery, everything would have been completely different for me. But that kind of speculation gets me nowhere.

It was time to let the past go, as I had before when I released myself from the pain of my childhood and looked forward to the future and the good life I could make for my own children.

I thought of Mum during the years she spent in a nursing home – bitterness had etched lines on her face, two frown lines between her brows, grooves running down from the corners of her mouth, multiple little smokers' furrows on her top lip – and I realized that I felt sorry for her.

What kind of life had she led, if my theories were true? A husband who gave her a beautiful house and all the money she wanted for clothes and shoes, but who went elsewhere week on week for warmth and affection. An adopted son with severe epilepsy that killed him at the age of twenty-four, and a daughter who may have been the bastard child of her husband's lover.

The only person Mum ever seemed to have loved was her father, Charles Pittam, a sick and twisted man. More than ever, I was convinced she used to be 'Daddy's special girl'. If I'm right, then the only love Muriel ever knew was flawed, damaged and unhealthy. The only love she was able to feel was for a paedophile.

* * *

I look at my own life now and I admit it's been a long, hard journey but I am lucky enough to have learned about love along the way and am so grateful for it. As a child I was loved by Nan and Grandad Casey, by Dad and Nigel, and that is what helped me to survive. They say that the abused often become abusers but I have been able to break this pattern and bring up my children with limitless, unconditional love. From the first moment that I held Samantha in my arms, I knew that I would walk over burning coals for her. I felt the same when Natalie and Richard came along. I know, and they know too, that whatever happens in the future I will always be there for them if they need me and will do whatever I can to make their lives happy.

But, most of all, I am a survivor. I came through the torments of my childhood and I am still here.

Learning to give love is an even bigger gift than being able to receive it and for poor Muriel, it's a lesson she never learned. I loved her, but I realize now that she never knew what it felt like to love. She missed out on the most important thing in life. In the end, despite everything she put me through, she was the one who was truly punished.